Young Africa

Realising the Rights of Children and Youth

ALEX DE WAAL AND NICOLAS ARGENTI (EDS.)

Justice Africa

Africa World Press, Inc.

P.O. Box 1892
Trenton, NJ 08607

P.O. Box 48
Asmara, ERITREA

Africa World Press, Inc.

First Printing 2002

Cover Design: Debbie Hird
Book Design: Roger Dormann

Book Design: Roger Dormann
Cover Design: Debbie Hird

Cataloging-in-Publication Data available from Library of Congress

ISBN 0-86543-841-2 (hardcover)
ISBN 0-86543-842-0 (pbk.)

Table of Contents

Acknowledgements

The genesis of this book was a series of papers prepared for the Pan African Forum on the Future of Children in Africa, held in Cairo in May 2001. This was convened by the Organisation of African Unity, hosted by the Government of Egypt and supported by UNICEF. The purpose of the Forum was to formulate and adopt the 'African Common Position' on the rights of the child in Africa in preparation for the upcoming United Nations General Assembly Special Session on Children. The papers tabled benefited from the discussion at the forum, including presentations by among others, Mrs Suzanne Mubarak, First Lady of Egypt and a substantial contributor in her own right. H.E. Dr. Salim Ahmed Salim, Secretary General of the OAU provided indispensable personal attention and leadership. Carole Bellamy, Executive Director of UNICEF, and Dr Sadiq Rasheed, Deputy Executive Director of UNICEF, and other senior UNICEF staff and a countless number of support staff in all the country offices of Africa tirelessly pursued the African agenda for children substantively as well as logistically. The young people who participated in the Forum were instrumental in making us honest and deserve a special thanks. Urban Jonsson provided outstanding institutional and intellectual leadership, most specifically insisting that the obligations enshrined in the Convention on the Rights of the Child necessitate a rights-based approach to development and programming, and that HIV/AIDS be given a high priority. Rima Saleh deserves special mention for her leadership and passion which led to the mobilisation of all the country offices and governments in West and Central Africa. Her generosity to assist was contagious. The support and encouragement of Ibrahima Fall was instrumental in mobilising the North African region. Among others who contributed, special mention must be extended to Abdul Mohammed, who made it possible for UNICEF and OAU to co-own the project and contributed substantially to the overall thesis including insisting on expanding the remit to cover young people as well as children as conventionally addressed by UNICEF. Numerous other UNICEF staff members also made valuable contributions, including Nick Alipui, Boudewijn Mohr, L. N. Balaji, Fatima Bahri, Mark Stirling, Marcus Betts, Nankali Maksoud, Nejwa Abdelkafur, Judy Otieno and others. Credit must go to the UNICEF staff in Cairo who made possible the convening and smooth running of the Pan African Forum. At the OAU, Professor C. A. L. Johnson was instrumental in ensuring that the partnership between UNICEF and OAU would result in a substantive outcome for children, and with the support of key members of his staff, especially Sadiqa Rahim ensured the African Common Position truly reflected the consensus of the Forum. Chidi Odinkalu's comments and insights on chapter 10 were very useful. Dr Teddy Brett at the London School of Economics assisted through recruiting and supervising research students.

This book has been supported by a grant from UNICEF. However, the writers and editors have retained editorial independence throughout and nothing in this book should be taken to represent a position of UNICEF.

Preface

URBAN JONSSON
UNICEF Regional Director for Eastern and Southern Africa

Africa is overwhelmingly a continent of young persons and children. The average age of Africans alive today is less than twenty years, and for the countries recording the fastest population growth, a majority of the population is under eighteen. This fact defines the reality of Africa as it exists today. In turn, we can measure the performance of policies and programmes in Africa, whether by governments, international organisations or NGOs, against the standard of what they provide for Africa's children and youth.

The condition of Africa's children and youth today is appalling and it is an indictment on the world that matters have been allowed to degenerate to the current levels. The gains of previous decades are being rolled back by deepening impoverishment, continuing armed conflict and above all by the HIV/AIDS pandemic. We are not only confronted with a moral imperative, we are faced with a legal obligation to put this situation right.

Today, the United Nations Convention on the Rights of the Child, and the African Charter on the Rights and Welfare of the Child, are in force, and we have moved decisively into a new era: the era of the rights of the child. By ratifying these international conventions, governments have assumed legal obligations that mark a fundamental shift in the way we approach children and youth. In September 1990, when 71 of Heads of State and Government gathered for the World Summit for Children, the focus was on making promises and setting goals. Twelve years on, the framework for our action has radically changed with the coming into force of these international conventions. In addition to targets and commitments, we are dealing with legal obligations. As well as looking after the interests and welfare of children, we have undertaken a duty to realise their fundamental rights. Reflecting this, the UNICEF Mission Statement, approved in February 1996, recognises the CRC and the Convention on the Elimination of All Forms of Discrimination Against Women as foundations for its work.

Among the rights enshrined in the CRC are the rights to life and education. African countries are poor and their governments have weak capacities. Their prospects have been further undermined by an adverse international economic order, structural adjustment programmes, war and HIV/AIDS. But resource constraint does not absolve parties to the CRC from undertaking every effort to realise the rights of the child. Article 4 underlines that 'States Parties shall undertake such measures to the maximum extent of their available resources and, where needed, within the framework of international cooperation.' The nature of this obligation is clarified by the so-called 'Limburg Principles', adopted by the UN Economic and Social Council in 1986, which state with reference to the UN Covenant on Social, Economic and Cultural Rights:

> 'The obligation "to achieve progressively the full realisation of the rights" requires states parties to move as expeditiously as possible towards the realisation of the rights. Under no circumstances shall this be interpreted as implying for states the right to defer indefinitely efforts to ensure full realisation. On the contrary, all states parties have the obligation to begin immediately to take steps to fulfill their obligations under the covenant.'

These principles apply with equal force to the CRC. Indeed, the CRC has more far-reaching implications in that, for the first time for a UN Convention, it specifies a wider range of duty bearers including international aid partners and civil society organisations. Taking expeditious action to realise the rights of children is an obligation on all of us.

The CRC enshrines obligations of three types: to respect, protect and fulfil. Duty-bearers—primarily states but also, as I have emphasised, a range of other actors too—are required to refrain from interfering directly or indirectly with children's enjoyment of their rights. They are obliged to protect children's rights, taking measures that prevent third parties from interfering with children's and young people's enjoyment of their rights. The obligation to fulfil requires States to adopt appropriate legislative, administrative, budgetary, judicial, promotional and other measures to facilitate the full realisation of children's right. In addition, this obligation requires States and other duty bearers to directly provide assistance or services for the realisation of these rights.

Moreover, we must recognise that human rights are indivisible, interrelated and interdependent. The realisation or violation of one right affects the quality of enjoyment of other rights. Hence we are obliged to seek to realise *all* the rights of children and youth and not relegate any rights to a lower rank in a supposed hierarchy or prioritisation.

In short, as this book so eloquently testifies, the last decade has seen nothing less than a revolution in the way in which we approach the challenge of responding to children and youth in Africa. That is the revolution in the rights of the child.

The African Common Position, adopted at the Pan African Forum on Children in Africa in Cairo in May 2001, was a landmark in Africa's determination to realise the rights of children. The Forum was the culmination of an exercise in preparation for the Global Movement for Children which culminates in the convening of the United Nations General Assembly Special Session for Children. The African Common Position is Africa's agenda for the coming decades. It is a standard against which the performance of all African countries will be measured. We hope that success in meeting the goals laid down in the African Common Position will be an exit from Africa's predicament, through investing in children and realising the rights of Africa's young people .

This book is one of the products of the Pan African Forum. It reflects a continental consultation and reflection in which policymakers, civil society organisations, and children and young people have directly participated. It identifies the key challenges facing Africa's children and those whose duty it is to realise their rights. It paints a bleak picture but also an honest one, in which children across the continent are denied every one of their rights, and young people are marginalised and frustrated. Taking the rights of children and youth seriously is a means of overcoming this dire situation. In fact, let me go further and assert that realising child rights is *the* primary road out of Africa's current plight. I hope that a decade hence, we will be able to reflect with more pride and optimism on what we, and Africa's young people, have achieved.

Foreword

K.Y. Amoako

Executive Secretary, Economic Commission for Africa

If Africa is to claim the 21st century, then today's African children and youth must inherit a continent in far better shape than it is today. Moreover, African and international leaders must make our young people into partners in a common enterprise of overcoming poverty and deprivation. Our future is based on our human resources, that is, our children and youth.

Over recent years, a new international development consensus has emerged, that places people at the centre of development efforts, and which sets long-term targets for poverty reduction and human resource development. For example, the International Development Goals set at the United Nations Millennium Summit have 2015 as their target date. In this volume, Dr Ali Abdel Gadir argues that we should be thinking even further ahead, and the 'duration of development' in Africa will be a generation or more. Certainly, it will require a monumental effort for African countries to achieve the very high rates of growth required—about seven percent per annum, twice current levels—to meet the goal of halving poverty in the coming thirteen years. On any scenario, today's children will have grown into adults, and today's youth into elders, before Africa can achieve its goal of eradicating poverty. This fact alone impels us to focus our efforts on children and young people.

Africa is not only the world's poorest continent, but it is slipping further behind. This can be seen most starkly in our performance on basic human indicators. Sub-Saharan African countries spend perhaps \$11 per person per year on health, whereas the most developed countries spend \$1,907, a figure 173 times greater. Across the globe, in rich and middle-income countries, life expectancy is increasing. But, despite national and international commitments, including the near-universal ratification of the Convention on the Rights of the Child, African life expectancy is not increasing. Much of this reversal is due to the HIV/AIDS pandemic, which is a survival issue for the continent, and which is well highlighted in this book. But even before AIDS begun to have a major impact on mortality, and even in countries with very low rates of HIV, we have been failing to register significant cuts in child mortality. In chapter 2, Anne Bakilana reminds us that one in six children born in sub-Saharan Africa today will not live to see their fifth birthday. Equal opportunity must start with being alive.

Recently, I had the privilege to serve on the Commission on Macroeconomics and Health, which presented its report to the director of the World Health Organisation, Gro Harlem Brundtland, in December 2001. The Commission calculated what would be required for the world to meet the 2015 International Development Goals for health and life expectancy. Our global figure amounted to an extra $66 billion annually by 2015, of which $38 billion would have to come from international aid budgets. Although this is a huge figure in comparison to current aid disbursements, which totalled about $53 billion worldwide in 2000, and a fivefold increase on current international health assistance, it is perfectly achievable given the political will. It is equivalent to no more than 82 cents per person per week for residents in the developed world. And our calculations are that the resulting improvements in life expectancy and productivity would yield a phenomenal $360 billion in increased global GDP.

There is a moral imperative at work here: the life chances of African children born today are unacceptably low. Millions of African children are deprived of their basic rights. I join Mary Robinson, the UN High Commissioner for Human Rights, in labelling extreme poverty as the most extensive abuse of human rights in the world today. But let us also look at realising children's rights to life and health as an investment. The entire world will benefit from the fulfilment of our children's potential.

A similar logic works for education. Sub-Saharan Africa's investment in education is just $49 per student per year, compared to

$4,636 in OECD countries. Currently, an estimated 45 million children in sub-Saharan Africa aged 6-11 do not attend school. And on present trends, within a decade, Africa will have the dubious distinction of having most of the world's out-of-school children. UNICEF has produced estimates for the cost of universal primary education in Africa, which amount to about $2 billion per year. But this figure excludes the requirements for building new infrastructure, and does not deal at all with secondary and tertiary education.

To date, there has been no commission on macroeconomics and education that can calculate the economic returns to universal primary education, improved secondary education and a revitalisation of Africa's universities and research institutes. But, even without detailed research, we have no doubt that the returns will be very substantial indeed. The globalising world economy depends more than ever on a skilled workforce and the production of knowledge. In response to this, there are a number of initiatives aimed at making Africa more internet-connected and ICT-proficient. But all these initiatives can only fulfil their potential if our children achieve a high level of basic education.

And much the same argument can be made for peace and good governance. None of our agendas can succeed in the absence of peace. The costs of war, not only in terms of expenditure on arms and armies, but also in the destruction of capital and the loss of irreplaceable human life, are completely unsupportable. Recent research is measuring ever more accurately the cost of conflict, concluding that it has held back Africa's growth by a decade's worth or more. We must redirect our human resources from this destructive enterprise into productive activities and civil politics, and engage our young people in production rather than destruction. In this respect, noting Okwir Rabwoni's suggestion in chapter 7 of reducing the voting age to sixteen, I recall that Nelson Mandela made a similar suggestion, in the conference that drew up South Africa's first democratic constitution, so as to incorporate the youth, who had been at the forefront of the struggle for freedom, into democratic politics.

In the same vein, we must recognise that unleashing the energies of our young people will be the key to achieving the rates of economic growth that will be necessary for Africa to overcome poverty. Africa's youth are economically active. They are enterprising, creative and quick to learn. And, given our fast rates of population growth, they are the majority of both producers and consumers. Young people are flooding onto the labour market at a rate much faster than formal employment opportunities can be provided. Most are therefore entering the small-scale private sector, starting small and micro-businesses. So let us explore how we can tap their potential. We should enable young men and women to participate in policymaking—for example through engagement with drawing up Poverty Reduction Strategy Papers. We should also make it a priority to ensure that they have access to the skills and resources that can enable them to thrive in the private sector. We should teach young people how to run small businesses and identify market opportunities, and provide simple and quick lines of credit.

Young Africa challenges us all. African governments are challenged to fulfil their responsibility to their children and young people. The Millennium Development Goals provide us with the framework for realising this obligation. The main tools are in our own hands: they are policies and programmes backed by political commitment. In this context, young Africa also challenges the international community to enter into an enhanced partnership with African governments, in which both parties are mutually accountable to achieving these goals. Then we can at last fulfil our responsibilities to our children and youth. When our children are assured of survival and health, provided with a good education, protected from war and violence, and when youth participate in the democracy and development of their countries, then Africa will be set to claim the 21st century.

1

Realising Child Rights in Africa
Children, Young People and Leadership

Alex de Waal

Introduction

The state of Africa's children and youth is unacceptable. Already facing the world's worst survival chances, death rates for African children are increasing. Already the least literate of the world's children, school enrolment rates are falling. The world's poorest today, they face a long struggle if the next generation is to rise out of poverty. Far too many are victims of conflict. Every one of Africa's wars includes child soldiers. Both national governments and the international community have performed poorly in meeting their commitments to children in Africa. The continent's youth are frustrated and increasingly angry; they are not being enabled adequately to build a future for themselves and their continent. More than a decade after the Convention on the Rights of the Child came into force, this is not an impressive scorecard. Yet, grand promises are still being made. At a succession of international conferences, African and other governments have committed themselves to a range of ambitious goals for poverty reduction, overcoming diseases, and providing education.

This chapter develops a framework, to examine how we are to make these promises into a reality. It develops a four-pronged approach. First, the *rights framework* emphasizes that there is a fundamental obligation, laid down in law, for states to realise the rights of children. This is a more far-reaching agenda than simply stipulating child rights into law and taking steps to provide improved services for children. It entails an holistic approach to planning and development that is founded on effective participation and good governance.

Second, approaching children's rights and welfare in Africa as a *global public good* compels us to develop a rigorous analysis of the economics of child survival, education, protection and participation. Research in this area indicates that the economic returns of health and education are dramatically more substantial than previously considered—and conversely that the adverse effects of poor health and illiteracy are much worse than has been recognized (Taylor et al. 1997, Commission on Macro-economics and Health 2001). If we switch from seeing spending on services for children not as consumption but investment, we can make a far stronger case for the necessary public-policy measures. And note too that the benefits of investing in Africa's children will be realised not just by Africa, but by the entire world community.

Thirdly, we must focus on the demands of *mobilizing a campaign*. How are we to make the case, not only morally and intellectually, but also politically, that children must be a priority? There is increasing interest, both academic and policy-related, in how human rights norms become domesticated (Risse and Sikkink, 1999) and how global civil society can mobilize to promote human rights and public goods (Edwards and Gaventa, 2001). The theme of practical citizens' action to promote child rights runs throughout this book. It is a challenge to leadership at all levels: to inspire and mobilize a diverse range of groups and constituencies, forging a social movement capable of enacting real change.

These comprise three distinct but convergent approaches to the challenge of making a real change in the lives of Africa's children and youth. The fourth component is *engagement with youth*. Currently, most national and international policymaking for children is concerned with infants and primary school children, while teenagers are neglected. This book makes the case for treating young people inclusively with children. One reason for this is that any effective campaign for children must be led by young people themselves.

This chapter concludes with a brief examination of how this four-pronged approach transforms international partnership for Africa's future. At the centre of this is an appeal for promoting the participation of youth in democratic national politics and international partnership: involve young people, and they will become Africa's biggest asset.

The Rights Framework

We are now in the era of the Convention on the Rights of the Child (CRC). The Convention has come into force, becoming the world's most widely-ratified international convention. In a dramatic step for global political culture, respecting the rights of children has become a fundamental obligation for states. By extension, the obligation also falls in differing ways on communities, civil society, the private sector and the international community.

But how deep is the consensus that underpins the CRC? It is notable that the United States has not acceded to the Convention. It has failed to do so, not because it is unfriendly to children, but because of the particular human rights tradition in the U.S., which treats rights as the legally-enforceable obligations of a state towards its citizens. Within this framework there is a strong and coherent argument that, first, children do not have rights because as legal minors, they cannot go to court to enforce those rights, and second, social and economic rights (to education, health care etc) should not be regarded as rights because they cannot be enforced in the same way. This critique rests on a distinction between basic civil and political rights that can be respected chiefly by restraining government action, and social and economic rights that require more substantial resources and public action to be realised.

While this book cannot seek to resolve this fundamental debate, we must take it seriously. Our basic position is that all rights are 'work in progress', and that as societies develop alongside humankind's moral sensibilities, the arena of 'rights' expands. In reality, all rights—including such core liberal rights as the right to a fair trial—require resources and state action. The question is, what is socially acceptable for a particular society at a particular time. Hopefully, Americans' acceptance of the need for national and international action to promote the welfare of children will increase, to the extent that their rights become accepted as such.

More directly relevant to Africa is the likelihood that some states acceded to the Convention without their leaders' genuinely acknowledging the commitments they were making, or simply in bad faith, without a real intention to deliver on the commitments. Some presidents may have regarded ratifying the CRC as little more than signing up to the World Declaration and Plan of Action at the September 1990 World Summit on Children, which are indeed no more than an unenforceable set of promises. But state ratification of a convention is a serious step. The provisions of the convention should no longer be regarded as pious promises: they have become state commitments that should be enforced.

The African Charter on the Rights and Welfare of the Child (ACRWC) was adopted by the Organisation of African Unity (OAU) in July 1990 and came into force in December 2000. It is broadly similar to the CRC. It is an interesting commentary on the politics of international conventions that African states rushed to sign and ratify the CRC—Ghana was the first country in the world to do so, and more than half of the early signatories were African—but it took more than ten years for just fifteen African states to accede to the African Charter, even though its provisions are little different. Is this because signing an international convention is regarded by many as a largely symbolic act, a means of acquiring status in international fora? And African governments care more for their status in front of the wider international community than with respect to their African peers? It is possible that some felt that signing the CRC was little more than a promise to give milk to babies if they felt like doing so, and some attended the WSC because it was a chance for a favourable photo-op. But a state does not accede to an international treaty in good or bad faith: it simply accedes. Social and political mechanisms for ensuring that governments comply with ethical and rights norms are discussed further below.

In this regard, we can again regard ratification in a positive light. It is a step towards the domestication of a norm. Over time, a government's pro forma commitment to an international standard can translate into actual respect for that norm (Risse and Sikkink 1999). The standard becomes the basis for debate with national and international civil society, and citizens' action towards realising the substance of the commitment. And government officers themselves become committed to achieving the goals.

Rights are therefore entangled with *goals* and *strategies.* A state's legal obligation under the CRC is a deeper commitment than adopting a goal or a target—the latter are essentially instruments. Realising the rights of the child implies the achievement of a range of other goals. Targets are useful in governments' planning and monitoring strategies aimed at the progressive realisation of rights. Goal-oriented strategies and rights-oriented approaches are therefore complementary. There are arguments in favour of ambitious 'stretch goals'—they generate enthusiasm and energy. There are arguments for setting modest and more easily achievable goals, but these hold the danger that after they have been achieved there may be a slackening of effort. The most important consideration, however, is that goals and targets must always remain as instruments in pursuit of higher objectives: in particular they must never be elevated to have equal standing with rights, which have universal applicability. Strategies include mechanisms for designing and implementing public policy, at both national and international levels (of which more, in the discussion on global public goods, below). Strategies are also means whereby citizens and civil society become engaged in realising child rights (further discussed under 'creating a social movement', below).

Child rights are not compatible with war. Peace is a prerequisite for realising the CRC. The most egregious abuses against Africa's children are perpetrated during war. The continent's young people have been manipulated and abused by militarists for too long. The agenda for children is also the agenda for peace.

The achievement of child rights is embedded in the realisation of a range of other rights, including democratic rights and the rule of law. This requires good governance: a multifaceted improvement of political representation and institutional capacity, alongside economic development and poverty reduction. In turn, these require strategies for international partnership and social mobilization. These are the concerns of the following sections. Aspects of the fuller and more effective participation of youth and children are explored in the final section.

Realising Child Rights as a Global Public Good

Spending on children is beneficial. This is not in dispute. The challenge is to try to understand exactly why and how much. For this purpose, the framework of 'global public goods' is useful. A global public good is something that is not owned by any individual or institution, but brings benefit to all people across the world (Kaul et al. 1999). Thus a clean environment, the eradication of a disease, or an increase in scientific knowledge—or for that matter the development of a new style of music—are all public goods with a global reach.

Why should we regard respecting and fulfilling the rights of children in Africa as a global public good? First, because private market-driven actions alone cannot deliver health, education, peace and human rights. Realising these rights demands *public action*. As African governments at present do not have the resources and capacities to deliver this good, it also demands partnerships—with civil society, with the private sector and with the international community.

Second, the benefits are not private: they accrue to a *whole society* and to *succeeding generations.* Children and young people who are socialised into democratic and tolerant behaviour are the foundation of an orderly and peaceable society. Development targets can be better achieved by engaging poor people in the devlopment process affecting their lives, and a human rights approach to development empowers people to make their own decisions (DFID 2000: 7). Children who are healthy, well-educated and optimistic about the future will themselves bring up the next generation to be more healthy, better educated and to be better world citizens. In this respect, realising the rights of children is an inter-generational public good (Sandler 1999).

On the other hand, disillusioned young people with no sense of a stake in the future are likely to realise the worst nightmares of the continent. Child victims of abuse are likely to perpetuate the cycle when they become adults. Uneducated young people are less likely to escape from poverty, and more likely to succumb to disease and participate in violence.

Third, the rights of African children are of *worldwide concern and benefit.* In a globalized world, no country can be considered remote and isolated from any other. The whole world has reason to be concerned about the poorest and most unstable corner of the globe. This is evident in the flows of refugees, the incubation of terrorism, and the emergence of new strains of disease. Africa's problems affect the world; solutions to those problems benefit the world.

While the immediate beneficiaries of investment in African children are those children themselves, and the secondary beneficiaries are their families and communities, the realisation of African children's rights will benefit all. To be precise, the realisation of the rights of poor and vulnerable African children is a 'continental merit good,' and a 'continental inter-generational public good,' but with global benefits. This we argue is enough to class it as a global public good.

The global public goods framework allows us to reconceptualize international cooperation for children. Instead of 'aid programmes' aimed delivering specific benefits to a targeted population, international development cooperation is a joint effort to provide the common good of healthier, better educated, better protected global citizens for the next generation (Martin 1999). The implications in terms of new forms of international partnership are the concern of the last section of this chapter.

A succession of studies, many of them sponsored by UNICEF, has made a strong case for investment in human capital development (Cornia et al. 1987, Stewart 1995, Mehrotra and Jolly 1997) and Amartya Sen has argued that development itself can be defined as increasing the capabilities and choices of individuals (Sen 1999). Much of this case rests on the positive examples of countries that have invested in human capital and achieved social development and economic growth. A well-educated populace and workforce is increasingly seen as the essential precondition for effective participation in the global economy. Others have calculated the economic costs of war (Collier 1999, Ali 2000, Ali in this volume) and found that it has cost Africa about a generation's worth of development. The Commission for Macroeconomics and Health (2001) has put figures to this argument, estimating that approximately $63 billion is required annually to provide adequate health care to all poor countries, and that this will save eight million deaths annually with economic returns of at least $186 billion (p. 12).

The WHO-sponsored Commission on Macroeconomics and Health also highlights another important global public good: specialist research and advocacy. Multilateral organizations such as WHO, UNICEF and the Economic Commission for Africa represent, among other things, global or regional expert communities that can pioneer new research, synthesize existing knowledge, and embark upon international advocacy. In the past, UNICEF has had a strong record in this field. The experience of the CMH on public health and the ECA in researching and advocating new forms of international partnership challenges UNICEF to spearhead a similar initiative on behalf of realising the rights of Africa's children.

One core argument of this book is that any approach to human capital development must be child-focused. Young people under eighteen represent half of Africa's population. Health and education are overwhelmingly concerned with children and young people. Most importantly, young people represent the future. In short, children and youth represent the possibility of either an exit from Africa's current predicament, or an intensification of that predicament. The scale of Africa's social crisis is such that Africa's children and young people need to be considered a global policy priority. The special demands of Africa's young people need to be adequately reflected in international instruments, policies and programmes.

Creating a Social Movement

The Convention on the Rights of the Child departs from traditional human rights thinking not only in the breadth of rights it awards, but in the range of actors it calls upon to participate in realising these rights. This recognizes a social and political reality: rights are realised through a combination of government action and citizens' mobilization. Solemn declarations and economic models are important, but political change is the essential component of successful social progress. In the case of a group with little direct power—children and young people—it is necessary to mobilize a broader social movement on their behalf. This is the third dimension of our analysis.

What does it mean to organize a social movement, whether local, national or international, in favour of child rights? Despite the commitment of UNICEF, the Save the Children Alliance and other national and international organisations to a 'global movement for children', and widespread writing by rights activists, there has been rather little theoretical thinking on what such a movement might entail.

The human rights approach to development and programming (UNICEF 2001) is an important step towards forging wider and more active participation in the struggle for child rights. This is concerned with reshaping development practice in such a way that it is no longer an external agency 'acting upon' individuals and communities, but a process of change and emancipation driven by the priorities of the people concerned, with their full engagement in defining the targets and setting the strategy. This is a significant step. But it is in the nature of social movements that they resist any control and direction by external bureaucratic forces, however enlightened they may be. Social movements for emancipation take control themselves.

Chapter 10 outlines some of the components of an effective movement for children, how it should combine the mobilization of the main constituency—children and young people—with professional advocacy and research and coalitions with policymakers. It summarizes how it is necessary to define the issues of concern in a certain way, breaking them down into manageable pieces and pursuing them in a flexible but strategic manner. It also highlights the best conditions for effective social mobilization to occur, namely open and democratic societies. It notes that in more authoritarian or unstable countries, local groups may rely more heavily on international alliances to press their case, a strategy which has dangers because domestic constituencies may lose their leadership role.

The narrow goal of a social movement may be to enact a change in government policy, perhaps ensuring that a right is enshrined in law. The broader goal is to change the moral climate, creating a new social consensus that a wrong, previously common, is now completely unacceptable. This is the process whereby slavery was abolished, women's rights were won, civil liberties were enforced, famine was conquered in India, anti-personnel landmines were banned, and the costs of treatment for AIDS were brought down. In some cases, these movements have seen themselves as struggling for 'rights', and their successes have been marked when a new set of rights has passed into law. But in many other cases, although the activists may have called for 'rights', the outcome has been more in the way of a robust public policy—for example workable famine prevention policies or a free health service. In these cases enforcement occurs through democratic political process and not through the courts. For example, post-independence Indian governments fear the wrath of journalists and voters (Sen, 1990, de Waal, 1997a) and ultimately the force of numbers of the hungry rather than the verdict of a court. 'As one labourer aptly put it, "they would let us die if they thought we would not make a noise about it".' (Dreze 1990: 93). This is best seen as a 'political contract' between rulers and citizens: a commitment to provide a public good, enforced through democratic processes including popular protest.

Ultimately, a movement for children may succeed in getting all the provisions of the CRC passed into domestic law, and thoroughly enforced through the courts. But this is a long way off even in developed social democratic countries. A more tangible aim is to establish a 'political contract' whereby the full array of children's rights are accepted by the state, and enforced by a wide range of democratic actions. Electoral sanctioning is the ultimate weapon: voting out a government that has failed to deliver. Short of that, an informed and effective legislature, can ensure that government is transparent and the executive is accountable. Judicial activists can be a vanguard force in social action litigation for child rights, as has occurred in South Asia (Gooneskere, 1998) and is emerging in parts of southern Africa. Special institutions such as a child rights commissioner can be a focal point for information and activism. A vibrant, independent and well-informed media can set the terms of public debate. In some countries there are young journalists who are taking the lead in bringing the concerns of youth and children to the public arena. Research into children's needs and outlook, where possible including young people as active participants, can be an important tool in gaining understanding and setting policies. An active NGO sector that engages in advocacy and service provision is a complement to an effective state service sector.

At an international level, the reporting requirements built into the CRC can be utilized to bring pressure to bear on countries that are failing to comply. The CRC allows for civil society participation in this reporting mechanism. At present, sanctions do not go beyond 'naming and shaming', but to date not even this modest penalty has been adequately utilized. The rationale has been that it is preferable to keep all countries on board, maintaining a commitment—however modest—to child rights, in the hope that this will provide opportunities for improving children's lot. But there may be room for a division of labour here, with some organizations focussing on constructive engagement with abusive or lagging governments, while others engage in public condemnation.

The driving factor in the establishment and enforcement of a child rights 'political contract' has often been the extent to which domestic organizations and movements are able to establish networks and alliances with international partners, jointly setting an agenda that governments follow. This has been the case, for example, in Mozambique (Lent and Trivedy, 2001) and Sudan (Mahjoub, 2002). Several of the chapters that follow focus on the challenges and opportunities of social mobilization; whether it is instigated by children and young people, or on their behalf.

The greatest challenge for any social movement is to combine the vigour and spontaneity that comes from an authentic mass movement, with professionalism and sustainability that demands institutions. Too often, the vigour of a mass movement has dissipated as its leadership has become professionalized or co-opted into policy debates. A special role for young people and children themselves is essential to any effective movement for children. In Africa today, it is highly significant that the specialist institutions for children—including UNICEF—are disconnected from the most vibrant movements of young people.

Recognizing Young People

One of the central themes of this book is that we must expand our focus from the traditional concern with young children to embrace 'youth' as well. Taking this step has immense consequences for the entire approach to children, both by policymakers and by young Africans themselves. In particular it transforms our approach to participation rights and to the demands of mobilizing a campaign to realise child rights: young people will need to lead any such campaign. In the second half of the book, many of the limitations of the concept of 'childhood' will become apparent.

Africa is a continent of the young. Any serious study of society, politics and economics in Africa must recognize the importance of young people. They are simply very numerous, outnumbering their elders. But they are marginalized in national and traditional political structures alike, which are dominated by the elderly, a fact that contributes to political tension. The scandal of child soldiers in Africa's conflicts cannot be understood without recognizing that the vast majority of soldiers in Africa are young people who can be readily mobilized by leaders. The HIV/AIDS pandemic—Africa's number one threat to survival—cannot be overcome without a focus on youth.

The CRC and common international practice defines a child as anyone below age eighteen. This is in fact a somewhat arbitrary and Euro-centric cut-off point for 'childhood'. In Africa—and elsewhere—older children and young adults (spanning both sides of the age of eighteen Rubicon) represent a unified social and cultural category. They are not simply 'future potential', receptacles for learning, but they are active and contemporary social, political and economic actors in themselves.

Africa's young people are tremendously important. And we don't know much about them. Despite their numbers and despite the historical contribution of young people and youth movements to Africa's political history, young people have not been a priority for research or public policy. Even the term 'youth' gives rise to confusion and conflicting images—some see youth as a threat to the established order while others focus on young people as the hope for the future.

Who are Africa's 'youth'?

Governmental and non-governmental organisations alike have long faced difficulties in dealing with youth, partly because the child-adult dichotomy divides their focus either onto younger children or onto adults, and partly because of the problematic indeterminacy of the category 'youth'. UNICEF's is a typical example of the problem; its mandate cut-off point of 18 years seems to fall in the middle of the category 'youth'.

When does childhood end? The cut-off at age 18 is a political definition. The idea of a single (gender-equal) age of legal maturity reflects the western juridical tradition, and concepts of citizenship built around the universal franchise and eligibility for conscription into the army. Eighteen years is the outcome of a convergence between a reducing age of majority and an increasing school leaving age in western societies. (In Europe and North America a hundred years ago, the school leaving age would have been 14 or 15 and the age of maturity 21, leaving a transitional age in between, during which most boys would have taken apprenticeships and most girls would have worked in domestic service, or married.) In non-western (e.g. African) societies, a chronological age cut-off is an arbitrary concept: girls would usually be married shortly after achieving sexual maturity, and consolidate their adult status when they became mothers, while boys would achieve 'adult' status by degrees, through initiation, eligibility to fight, marriage, acquisition of land, and elevation to the position of elder. In law, responsibilities accrued at different ages: the 'age of reason' in which an individual could be responsible for criminal acts, the age of sexual maturity, and the time at which a mature individual becomes a 'full' member of the community. Note that in gerontocratic kinship-based socio-political systems, only those men who achieved full status (through relative wealth and social standing), and a very small number of older women, would have the status of community members with a full set of rights and responsibilities. Adult women, male paupers and outsiders would retain the juridical status of minors, however old they were. With colonialism, mission education, social and economic development, and the ratification of international conventions by African governments, the concept of a single juridical age of maturity has gradually been introduced, though not fully accepted, across Africa. In reality there is no clear distinction between older children and younger adults.

Like 'childhood', the concept 'youth' is a Western concept and a political construct. In traditional African societies there were sequences for the maturing individual: for men, child-single man/warrior/labourer-married self-supporting adult-elder, for women, girl-wife-mother (Aryee, 1997). In western societies, and the small subset of African societies dominated by colonial norms, the sequence would be: school-employment, with perhaps an intermediate stage for higher education or training (which would delay marriage). But with the decline of possibilities for self-employment in agriculture or in formal employment, the sequence has become school–'youth'–unknown (c.f. Seekings, 1993). 'Youth' is therefore a problematic, intermediary and ambivalent category, chiefly defined by what it is not: youths are not dependent children, but neither are they independent, socially responsible adults. It is typical of our ambivalence towards older children and young people that we should objectify them by means of a term that, while seeming to connote concern, in fact elicits anxiety. 'Youths' are not typically conceived of as productive and constructive social actors, nor, as they often are in reality, as victims, but rather as potential sources of political disruption, delinquency and criminality.

'Youth' also has political colours specific to Africa. Pre-colonial movements for religious and political renewal were often led by young people (Last 1992). The independence generation of African political activists defined themselves as 'youth' in opposition to their elders who were supposedly content either to be loyal colonial servants or placid rural chiefs and smallholders. Some political parties were explicitly organized around youth, for example the Somali Youth League that achieved that country's independence in 1960. Independence was not only a revolt against colonial rule, it was a revolt of educated and ambitious young men against their fathers, and thus an overturning of traditional gerontocratic socio-political orders. In left-leaning African politics, 'youth' or '*jeunesse*' has continued to have these radical connotations. The ANC appealed to South African youth to spearhead their revolution in the 1980s, leftwing guerrilla leaders elsewhere have done the same. Many are the parties that have acceded to power on the back of young people's energy, idealism and self-sacrifice, and many are those that have soon afterward distanced themselves from youths as volatile and untrustworthy 'trouble-makers' once these had become disillusioned with their new leaders.

Politically, 'youth' is not gender neutral. The category refers primarily to males, because females are less socially (publicly) and politically visible. Note that even those who espouse gender equality less often practice it, and even in revolutionary countries women are pressured to marry younger than men and thus abandon their 'youth' status. Moreover, a married woman—especially one who has children—is rarely a 'youth', but a married father can still retain that status.

The upper age limit of 'youth' in Africa is therefore very elastic. Leaders of youth organizations can be in their late twenties or thirties. The special 'youth' MPs elected to the Ugandan parliament may be just as old. But we must acknowledge that youth is not adulthood: the lower age limit of 'youth' is in the early teens. Many of those who count as youth count legally as minors. In reality, age eighteen falls right in the middle of a transitional age that starts with the onset of sexual maturity and political awareness (early teens) and concludes at an indeterminate age of independent adulthood ('normally' the mid-twenties).

Faced with these complexities, it is tempting to conclude that this elusive and politically-constructed category 'youth' is best left alone. But the centrality of youth to the current social and political plight and dynamics of Africa compel us to take it seriously. Those whose responsibility lies with children have an obligation to deal with youth, if only because many youths fall under the age of maturity and are therefore legally children.

Young People and Children

Traditionally, child-focused organizations—such as UNICEF—tend to regard parents (especially mothers) as the key intermediaries for reaching children and helping to promote the welfare and rights of the child. The pivotal role of mothers cannot be disputed. But young people—a substantial proportion of them children themselves—are also crucial intermediaries.

First, young people have children. Most African women bear their first child before the age of twenty, and about 15-20% of all births are to teenage mothers. Equally significantly, many of these mothers can be defined socially as 'youth'—they are not partners in a stable, economically independent marital household. There is plentiful evidence of the adverse implications on children of being born to mothers who are young, single and unemployed, or who are engaged in unstable partnerships. Currently, most programmatic interventions target these young women solely or primarily in their capacity as mothers, without also seeing them as young people, embedded in the social networks and sharing the cultural and social attributes of young people.

Second, young people relate directly to children. They are role models for children. Young people are older siblings, neighbours, part-time carers, school-mates and friends to children. The social and cultural environment of non-infant children is strongly influenced by youth subculture, and this influence becomes stronger as children get older. Children's attitudes to health, education and social norms as well as their incipient political development are all powerfully influenced by older children and young people. We cannot expect Africa's children to make progress in these areas unless there is positive influence from young people.

Incorporating young people into public policy-making also has important implications for operationalizing the CRC in Africa, and in particular enabling children to participate. While children are defined as legal minors, the right to participation is a problematic concept. Children are not entitled to the full range of civil and political rights enjoyed by adults (e.g. they cannot vote or be elected to office, their freedoms of association and expression are circumscribed). Participation rights are confined to the right to have one's views taken into account in court (a step up from the legal doctrine of the court acting 'in the best interests of the child', which denies the child his or her right to be heard), and poorly-defined rights to be consulted in wider social and political affairs. However, on reaching 18, individuals are entitled to the full range of civil and political rights.

Treating middle teenagers (aged 15-17) solely as children is problematic. Most of these young people are social and political beings, impatient to express themselves, organize and engage in the social and political affairs of their communities and nations. They often long to escape from their families and are already engaged with extra-familial networks. Given the chance, many join political parties and become among their most active and dedicated members. Some volunteer for armed rebel movements, which in some cases can become a means for personal as well as political emancipation. Most are sexually active, both with other 'children' and (especially for girls) with adults. If these young people are treated solely as children, they are in fact infantilized, and their needs are not met, their rights are not realised and their active contribution to society and to social change is not recognised.

However, if middle teenagers are given a dual identity, both as children and a category of youth that includes legal adults, then their needs, aspirations and rights can be met more effectively. Young people aged over 18 have legally enforceable participation rights (civil and political rights). Enabling middle teenagers to participate in youth organizations, albeit with a junior status in certain areas, would enable the more effective realisation of their participation rights. We need to ask, how can we best facilitate the effective participation of young people, combining civil and political liberties with a degree of protection?

Young People and Social Change

Young people are the principal actors in Africa's social and political creativity today. As chapter 6 argues, under the onslaught of a range of adversities—HIV/AIDS, unemployment, political repression, conflict, and the collapse of education systems—young people are actively fashioning new social orders. Most of these emergent social networks, organizations and belief systems are poorly understood.

Among the best-studied youth-based social movements in Africa are the Pentecostal churches and militant Islamic movements. These two formidable contemporary social movements are both marked by a powerful youth orientation, and by the message that personal moral salvation can redeem or transform a corrupt public moral order. Yet, even these religious movements' appeal to, and impact upon, young people is inadequately understood. We need to ask, what are the impacts—present and future—of these religious movements on governmental policy-making in Africa? How are we to engage with these religious organizations?

Organized students have long been one of the main motors for social and political change in Africa. Student unions and similar associations have been at the forefront of radical political change in a number of African countries. While university student unions have been the most politically prominent, student unions are also active in schools, and political activism sparked by university students commonly spreads to secondary schools as well. It is also noticeable how the friendships formed at secondary school can be extremely influential in later-life political networks, and the values and patterns established at this age can strongly influence the political trajectory of a cohort of politicians. Engagement with student unions at both school and university could prove to be an important learning experience for both students and national governments, with the potential for positively influencing the evolution of political culture over the long term.

Alongside organized religion and student organisations, there are a multiplicity of less visible youth organizations and movements. These are perhaps the most interesting. In many places, and especially outside relatively privileged urban centres, young people are finding creative means of articulating their aspirations—and their alternatives to established social and political orders—using cultural idioms and establishing modes of association that may be invisible or obscure to national policy-makers. These are crying out for recognition. How are they set up? Who joins and what influence do the organisations have on their members and on the wider society? How do they relate to the more formalized civil society and NGO sector? What opportunities do they have to offer their members that overt, formalised political and social organizations lack?

The prevalence of youth-initiated and renewal-oriented movements is both a sign of a socio-political vigour, and a danger signal for a possible breakdown in cultural transmission. On the one hand, this vibrancy illustrates the refusal of Africa's young people to accept the deplorable social and political circumstances in which they find themselves, and a determination to find new ways to give meaning to their lives in an environment in which almost all avenues for self-advancement are closed. Assumptions regarding the innate 'rebelliousness' of children and young people as nothing but a phase or cycle without further implications are therefore inapplicable to the contemporary situation in Africa—young people in Africa address crucial social issues with real political implications. On the other hand, the breakdown in the transmission of social values and traditions that young people's resistance implies may leave some groups of young people as a blank slate, susceptible to forms of extremist mobilization. The tendency of militant fundamentalist groups to find fertile ground in refugee camps (e.g. the Taliban in Pakistan, Burundi Hutu extremism in camps in Tanzania) reflects this. Internally displaced and deracinated populations are in a similar position. Movements for renewal can easily become nihilistic-millenarian armies. By listening to young people in an open and supportive context, by seeking to learn from their associations and their expectations and ideologies, we can identify the potential sites for such militant movements—and the causes that give rise to them.

The majority of youth associations and organizations represent a middle ground between 'moderation' and 'radicalism': they offer potential for solving problems (such as unemployment, drug abuse, high-risk sexual behaviour), but simultaneously potential for exacerbating exactly these same problems through inappropriate 'solutions' or the introduction of new problems. And many of them are too weak, too poorly organized and financed, and too transitory to offer anything of substance to their members other than a fleeting sense of belonging and solidarity. There is a pressing need to study, understand and engage with these organizations.

Youth and Conflict

In European, American and Asian history, mass mobilization of conscripts for war has always generated pressure for democratic political change. Those called upon to fight for their country, enduring hardship and danger, have generally been a force for social emancipation. In Africa, this does not seem to be the case. One reason for this is the sheer numerical availability of young people and their estrangement from the formal social and political order. Young people are not a scarce resource, and as a result, political and military leaders tend to regard them as expendable (often with tragic psycho-social side-effects).

Africa's armies are composed of youth. Government mobilization of young people takes a number of forms. Conscription for the army is one case: though such is the scarcity of alternative employment that most army recruits are volunteers. Party youth wings are another important phenomenon. These range from institutions with a real educational component to licensed thugs whose chief duty is to intimidate the opposition. The Rwandan Interahamwe represent an extreme case. The so-called 'war veterans' in Zimbabwe are another variant. Most African countries—including 'democratic' ones—have paramilitary youth wings, sometimes referred to by the euphemism of 'party militants'. Often, their leaders turn a blind eye to delinquency, drug taking, rape and other anti-social and criminal behaviour, or even encourage them. We can expect HIV positivity rates among these groups to be very high.

We know very little indeed about the demographic and social profile of Africa's armies and paramilitary groups. This information is vital for effective disarmament, demobilization and reintegration programmes, and also for the project of building truly civilian political parties. We know even less about soldiers' health status, although there are extremely disturbing indications of ultra-high rates of HIV infection among these groups.

Child soldiers have become the subject of much programming,

advocacy and research in recent years. This is welcome. The focus has been on the illegitimacy of recruiting *children* (initially under 15, more recently under 18) as combatants, and the need for their demobilization and rehabilitation. The next stage in a campaign against child soldiers is to broaden the agenda to include young people and militarism. While it is not possible to make a legal or human rights case against adult (over age 18) soldiers, it is both necessary and possible to address the structural conditions that make it so easy to militarise Africa's youth.

This approach will also enable us to address the problem that significant numbers of middle teenage soldiers are not only well-informed volunteers, but that they have gained many advantages from serving as soldiers. For example, for some Eritrean girls from traditional villages, joining the EPLF was a means for personal emancipation. Demobilization would have merely condemned them to a life of illiteracy, early marriage and domestic servitude. If such teenage volunteers can be treated not as misguided child soldiers, but as young adults demanding and requiring progressive social change, we can remove them from the military without demobilizing their social and political energy. To treat them merely as deluded or wayward children would be to depoliticize their project and to fail to address their grievances. Much better to give them a real opening in democratic civil politics.

In most African countries, there is little meaningful interaction between governments and young people excepting recruitment for the army and paramilitary forces. Government attitudes are that 'youth' are a problem: the source of social ills such as crime, delinquency, HIV/AIDS etc, or that they represent a danger of political upheaval—as opposed to reform. The combination of youth's demographic preponderance, political and economic marginalization, and readiness to engage in innovative forms of social and political mobilization, makes for an explosive mix. Positive governmental policies towards young people, in all sectors, need to be developed. Rarely do poverty reduction strategies, health programmes, 'child' protection initiatives, and conflict prevention mechanisms pay adequate attention to young people.

Youth and Health

Young people's health is an important concern not only as an end-in-itself, but also for those concerned with children per se. HIV/AIDS is the major item for consideration in this section, but we should not overlook other communicable diseases, including especially sexually-transmitted infections, drug, alcohol and tobacco abuse and their health implications, accidents associated with dangerous occupations, violent crime, etc.

HIV/AIDS is the number one threat to Africa's young people. The median age of infection for women in Africa early twenties, implying that a substantial minority of girls are HIV positive before they turn 18. Young women are both biologically and socially vulnerable to HIV. It is only by focussing on young people that it will be possible to halt the HIV/AIDS pandemic. There are many components to this. It is clear, however, that effective intervention will require far more research and analysis than is available at present.

A focus on HIV/AIDS and young women is imperative. Measures to reduce the rates of HIV incidence among young women and girls will be the single most effective means of blunting the AIDS pandemic. There is much that can be done with young women themselves, both directly (providing access to sex education, life skills, condoms, microbicides, etc.) and indirectly (increasing girl's educational and socio-economic opportunities, thereby increasing their power and decreasing their reliance on selling or trading sex). There are many things that must be done to address the wider social environment in which women and girls are vulnerable to HIV/AIDS.

Dealing with HIV/AIDS in schools is an important component of overcoming the pandemic. Schools are a locus for sexual activity, between teachers and pupils and among pupils themselves. They are a key site for HIV/AIDS educational activities, partly because most young people can be found in school at one time or another. And schools are models for society: modes of social interaction and hierarchy that exist in school are replicated in society. If students learn exploitative relationships, command models of authority, and gender inequalities at school, then it is unlikely that they will promote the necessary social change in society later in their lives.

Any concern with children under 18 entails a concern with the age of sexual maturity, and the age at which millions of African girls become HIV positive. Schools are one of the key sites for HIV/AIDS prevention. This response is best mounted in the context of a programme to deal with youth as a whole: the age 18 cut-off is not meaningful in this context; indeed, it hampers continued intervention. Likewise, the wholesale adoption by African governments of western models of childhood and 'youth' into their policy-making devalues local-level cultural and political forms that offer transitional social models that potentially empower young people, enabling them to contribute positively to social change.

Young People, Governance and the Convention on the Rights of the Child

A number of issues arise from recognising young people that African governments must address in line with their commitment to the CRC. How could governments best engage with the force for positive change represented by Africa's multifarious informal youth movements? How could the potential for a positive social contribution of young 'party militants' be maximised, and their criminal or radical potential minimized? How could the political motivations that child soldiers might harbour be translated into peaceful activism? What might be the best way to engage fruitfully with student unions and youth political movements?

This is an emergent agenda for young people and governance that represents a radical change in existing practices. The participation rights of young people need to be taken seriously, so that they are more adequately represented in legislatures and other mechanisms for ensuring that citizens' voices are heard and taken into account. Institutions that represent the young, and that deal with the young, need their capacities enhanced. Young people, aged over 16 for example, could be granted the vote. This would be a very powerful symbol of the emancipation of youth, and, more importantly, a means of channelling their political energies into strengthening democracy. Mechanisms for delivering services to the young, ranging from schools and clinics (especially sexual health services) to banks and micro-credit institutions, need strengthening with greater and more effective participation by their young clients and stakeholders. Civil society organizations, youth organizations, schools and universities, government departments, and regional organizations should all become concerned with young people, both as citizens in their own right and if they are to deal effectively with older children. Indeed, the evidence provided in this book shows that there is a need to introduce a new category of childhood, taken in its widest possible sense, to include young adults in order to do justice to Africa social, cultural and political realities. Addressing all of these issues promises to yield benefits not only for children and young people, but also to increase the stability of the governments that are able sincerely to engage their young citizens in the national project.

New Partnerships

It is notable that the CRC is unique among international conventions in that it not only specifies the obligations of the national government, but also lays down international responsibilities for acting in solidarity to promote child rights. These solidarity obligations may be vaguer and less easily enforceable, but they exist. Clearly, multilateral organizations such as the IMF have not acceded to the CRC. But most international donors have done so, and the development of mechanisms of accountability for these development partnerships is an important exercise.

The CRC also reflects realities when it recognizes the role of civil society in realising the rights it contains. It implicitly calls for two sets of partnerships, one between governments and their own people, and the second with the international community. The first—a commitment to participation and good governance—is desirable for its own sake, as well as being a precondition for effective international development partnership. The CRC thus anticipates and echoes new concepts of partnership that are emerging for international development cooperation in Africa. This is seen in the concept of 'enhanced partnership', developed by the Economic Commission for Africa's 'Compact for African Recovery' (ECA, 2001), and central to the New Partnership for Africa's Development (NEPAD) initiated by President Thabo Mbeki of South Africa (Government of South Africa, 2001).

"Enhanced partnership" is first and foremost a strategy for improving governance in Africa, by deepening democratization and creating a capable state that provides an enabling environment for development. This book makes one distinctive new contribution to this governance agenda: engage children and youth. Children have participation rights. These rights are not an abstraction: they require serious policies including new structures for democratic politics. This means giving children a voice in policies that affect them—for example, in how schools are run. For older children, for example above 16, this means granting them political rights—including, we argue, the right to vote.

In addition, 'enhanced partnership' envisages a new relationship between African countries and the international community. It moves away from the existing practice in which donors impose conditionalities on recipients, but there are few controls on the quality and coherence of donor assistance, which may for example have high transaction costs and low predictability (Helleiner, 2000). Instead it is based on African ownership of goals and processes for development. It envisages guaranteed long-term resource provision in line with joint commitments to common goals, with joint processes of evaluation. The message from this book is that these common goals must focus on children and young people.

It is unlikely that the ideal of 'enhanced partnership' will be achieved rapidly. But it charts a new paradigm for development cooperation, in line with the main strands of thinking developed in this chapter. The human rights approach to development, combined with the theory of social mobilization, allows us to envision an African government's commitment to good governance as a form of 'political contract' enforceable by its citizens. The analysis of realising child rights as a global public good enables us to recast development partnership as cooperation in a shared enterprise bringing common benefit. And it entails making young Africans real partners in this enterprise.

Conclusion

When the CRC was adopted, the implications of taking child rights seriously were poorly understood. Twelve years on, it is evident that the provisions of the Convention are as relevant and urgent as ever. Globally, there has been much progress towards realising child rights, while in Africa the progress has been disappointing, to say the least. But we have moved on: we have learned much and a broad movement may be taking shape that can give substance to the promises made more than a decade ago. The approach outlined in this introductory chapter and implicit throughout this book provides a framework for approaching the entirety of child rights and policies and programmes for children and young people. The convergence of the four approaches provides not only the substance for a comprehensive realisation of the rights of children and young people, but also a framework for a plan of action for achieving the conditions under which these rights can be realised.

Finally, enthusing all of the above, we must not dull our sense of moral outrage. The condition of Africa's children and young people is simply scandalous, and all citizens should be furious that the leaders of the continent—and, no less, of the world—have allowed such an unacceptable state of affairs to greet the dawn of the 21st century. The fate of Africa's children has never been beyond our control, and no diplomatic pieties should obscure the fact that it is an unmitigated moral outrage that so many African children die young, that so many cannot expect to attend a decent school or indeed any school at all, and that so many are abused in war or infected with HIV. Twelve years after the adoption of the CRC and the massive attendance at the WSC, world leaders should hang their heads in shame at what they could have done, and have thus far so conspicuously failed to do. The next twelve years must be better.

2

Child Survival and Development in Africa in the 21st Century

ANNE BAKILANA AND ALEX DE WAAL

The ratification of the Convention on the Rights of the Child by almost the entire community of nations in the early 1990s, enshrined every child's right to life. The CRC underlined that all societies have a legal duty to ensure the survival and development of every child. However, if we review Africa's progress in reducing infant and child mortality and increasing life expectancy, the results of the last ten years have been, to say the least, disappointing. While the decades leading up to the adoption of the CRC and the convening of the World Summit for Children marked the most rapid progress in improving life chances ever, the succeeding years have seen stagnation and even reversal of gains made. This is not to belittle the efforts made, including the acceleration of health campaigns, improving nutrition and food security, increasing access to prenatal and postnatal care, and other related activities. But few of the targets for 2000 have been met. In a word, the right of the child to survival has not been realized.

Table 1 provides an overview of these rather dismal figures. For Sub-Saharan Africa, the annual percentage improvement in child mortality between 1990 and 2000 was a meagre 0.4%.

By 1990, the causes of high childhood mortality were sufficiently well established to plot out the route to achieving the WSC goals for child survival. Specialist analyses—backing up actual country experiences such as those of South East Asia, Sri Lanka and Costa Rica—had already established and charted directions for policy makers as to exactly what was needed to lower infant and childhood mortality. What has gone wrong?

The report of the WHO's Commission on Macroeconomics and Health (2001) reviews the world's spending on health care, highlighting the immense discrepancies between expenditure in rich and poor countries. While high-income countries averaged $1,907 per capita total spending on health in 1997 ($1,356 public, the balance private, mostly through health insurance schemes), the least developed countries averaged a mere $11 ($6 public, $5 private, mostly out-of-pocket) (CMH 2001: 56). The difference is almost two hundred-fold. The CMH estimates that $40 per capita is required for the most basic health coverage, sufficient to reduce mortality levels. Scaling up to this level would entail a total global outlay of about $66 billion, but the economic returns in terms of increased productivity and greater life expectancy would be about six times that.

The CMH's goal is laudable and—despite some severe capacity constraints in many countries—achievable. An investment in global health on the scale implied would have far-reaching positive consequences. But the analysis begs an important question: how was it possible for developing countries to achieve the rapid progress that they did before 1990, without this scale of intervention? A major part of the answer lies in the unparalleled impact of the HIV/AIDS pandemic, which has hugely complicated the health challenges of the immediate future.

Progress in Child Survival before and since 1990

In important respects, the period 1945-1990 witnessed more significant improvements than have been marked subsequently. It is ironic that the WSC and CRC crowned these partial achievements, rather than setting the scene for the fulfillment of the promise of health for all. The decades up to 1990 were marked by a number of global and regional health initiatives. These included the late-1940s International Tuberculosis Campaign, the worldwide smallpox eradication campaign, the 1977 Universal Child Immunisation Initiative, the Alma Ata Declaration in 1978 'Health for All by 2000,' and the 1987 Bamako Initiative among others. This period witnessed rapidly rising life expectancy across Africa, primarily due to improvements in child survival (Hill, 1991). A number of factors are implicated in this success (National Research Council 1991), including the development of antibiotics and anti-malarial drugs, the implementation of population-wide immunisation campaigns, and the widespread use of insecticides against mosquitoes, as well as certain aspects of socio-economic development such as increased levels of education. In Kenya, under-five mortality declined from 262/1,000 live births in 1947 to about 100 by 1985.[1]

These health gains were more rapid and marked than for any other period in history: they represent an immense achievement. However, by 1990, the prevailing mortality levels were still comparatively high, especially in the countries which had started off with the worst child mortality rates. North African child death rates were the lowest, West African rates generally the highest. And despite the general upward trend, some countries suffered stagnating or even increasing death rates, mostly due to civil wars. For example, Mozambique's child mortality levels rose from about 260/1,000 in the 1930s to almost 300 in the mid-1970s. Angola similarly witnessed stagnation and upward trends during much of this period, while Uganda saw an erratic pattern in child survival influenced by civil wars, economic collapse and, more recently, the HIV/AIDS epidemic. There were, however, one or two worrying augurs. For example, child mortality rose in Zambia in the 1980s, before the onset of the AIDS epidemic, probably related to the decline in health service provision (Simms et al 1998).

Despite these clear overall declines in childhood mortality, the level of Africa's childhood mortality in 1990 remained high. Africa's health provision was still not sufficient to improve survival prospects to levels enjoyed by children in other parts of the world (Mosley 1991, UNICEF 2000). This was the situation immediately preceding the health crisis of the 1990s, which threatens to intensify in the 2000s.

The years since 1990 have not seen a slackening in international initiatives aimed at improving child survival. The 1987 Bamako Initiative, has been an important framework for encouraging community participation in management and financing of local health care, in improving quality of service and in guaranteeing access for those who could not afford to pay. The WSC and CRC themselves have been followed up by a number of specific initiatives aimed at specifically addressing child survival and women's health, most notably the 1992 Dakar Consensus. In addition, there have been targets at eradicating specific diseases spearheaded by the World Health Organisation and partners, such as the Roll Back Malaria initiative of 1998, which aims to halve malaria deaths by 2010. Every year about 400 million people suffer from malaria, and more than one million die from the disease; a large proportion of them children. The Polio Eradication initiative was initiated in 1988, aiming to eradicate polio by 2000 (later revised to 2005). Furthermore, the Measles Eradication initiative is intended to eradicate one of the top ten killers of children world-wide: the disease kills more than 800,000 children every year, mostly in Africa. Measles kills more children than any other vaccine-preventable disease. The most recent initiative in eradicating preventable diseases is the Global Alliance for Vaccines and Immunisation, which is intended to ensure that every child is protected against vaccine-preventable diseases.

One of the notable advances of the last decade has been the

improvement of data on child morbidity and mortality. Africa still lags well behind other continents in the quality of its demographic and epidemiological data, but matters are improving.

But the raw figures speak for themselves: in Sub-Saharan Africa child mortality has scarcely improved and immunization rates are stuck at around 50%. Was the pre-1990 progress precarious and easily reversed? Have there been major new adverse developments in the last decade? Again, if we have to point to one overriding factor, it is the HIV/AIDS pandemic.

Major Determinants of Child Mortality in Africa

The downward trends in childhood mortality described above are explained by changes in the determinants of childhood mortality. Background factors include socio-economic determinants such as maternal education, place of residence, etc. Though termed 'background', these exert an immensely powerful influence on child survival chances. Proximate factors include maternal age at birth of children, the length of birth intervals, duration and intensity of breastfeeding, sufficient and hygienically prepared nutrition following weaning, hygienic living conditions in which to raise children, as well as access to adequate sanitation and potable water, etc. This section examines these factors.

Maternal Education. One of the most important determinants of child survival is maternal education, which has in fact emerged as the most powerful of all socio-economic factors (Adetunji 1994, Caldwell 1981, Gupta 1990, Cleland et al. 1992). Educated women understand far better how to protect their children's health, both in terms of everyday child care and sanitation and also in terms of seeking health care. Educated women also have greater aspirations for their children, and tend to have lower fertility and longer birth intervals. It is important to note that the maternal education factor is significant only when the mother completes primary education or beyond. Women who complete less than primary school before dropping out do not register significantly increased survival chances for their children.

Parental Survival. The death of a parent—especially the mother—is adverse for the prospects of child survival. This factor has become particularly prominent due to the HIV/AIDS pandemic. The African custom of caring for orphaned children through the extended family has, in the past, mitigated the negative consequences of parental death. However, the scale of adult mortality related to the HIV/AIDS pandemic is stretching this coping strategy to its limit and beyond (Guest 2001).

Place of Residence. Urban and rural differentials in child mortality in Africa are high, a reflection of the unequal balance of the availability of key public social services including health care facilities, clean water and sanitation. However, sprawling urban settlements can be a danger to health, suffering overcrowding and lack of services. Urban women are more likely to be better informed about the advantages of immunizing their children and more accessible to family planning messages that might ensure the health of their children through better child spacing.

Environmental Factors. The source of water supply, type of toilet facilities and general living conditions are important determinants of children's health. Mortality in households without a toilet has been found to be three times higher than mortality in households with a toilet, while provision of piped water has been shown to reduced child death rates (Sastry 1994).

Health Care and Immunisation. Countries that have invested in good quality primary health care have reaped huge benefits in terms of child survival. In rural Senegal, for example, improved access to new and efficient health services is responsible for decreasing child mortality from 350 to 81/1000 within 25 years (Ewbank and Gribble 1993). Immunization against the major child killer diseases is also crucial. Of all the measures that were taken in the mid-1980s to early 1990s, immunization had the most effect in advancing child survival in Africa, (Brockerhoff, 1995). Immunization against measles alone is believed to have increased babies' survival by more than one third.

Immunization is a prime example of a targeted 'vertical' programme, focusing on a single intervention that can have a significant outcome. The eradication of smallpox is the *cause celebre* of those who advocate such an approach. The drawback of these kinds of programmes is that, if the disease in question is not eliminated entirely, vaccination levels need to be maintained over a long period of time to prevent a resurgence of the disease. Vertical programmes do not always prioritize sustainability or health capacity building. Unfortunately, vaccination levels have stagnated or dropped in many countries in the last few years.

Contingent/Transitory Factors. Much of Africa remains highly vulnerable to transitory food insecurity (famines) that has often caused very sharp increases in child mortality. In the mid-1980s for example, Ethiopia suffered more than 500,000 excess deaths related to famine, and Sudan suffered an estimated 200-250,000 excess mortalities. More than half of these excess deaths occurred among children between the ages of 12 months and five years. Subsequently, there have been major episodes of famine-related excess mortality. However, since the 1980s, transitory increases in death rates have largely been associated with civil conflict and forced displacement rather than drought. While droughts have remained frequent, sharply increased mortality rates associated with them have declined.

The reasons for this appear to be related to two major changes in response. One is the increase in food security planning in drought-prone countries. More significant, however, was the appreciation in the late-1980s that excess child mortality in drought-related famine was primarily a factor of 'health crises': namely increased incidence of normal communicable diseases such as malaria, measles and various water-borne infections brought about chiefly by distress migration (de Waal, 1989). Measures to increase child immunization and to reduce the transmission of water-borne diseases significantly reduced the mortality impact of subsequent droughts, particularly in northern Sudan, the Sahel and Southern Africa. More significant still have been efforts to reduce the extent of distress migration during drought. In fact, one of the unannounced successes of famine response policies in the post-1985 period was the adoption of such measures that have blunted the impact of drought-induced health crises, thereby substantially reducing famine mortality across Africa.

Responses to floods have also improved. The major flooding that affected Mozambique in early 2000 caused major economic disruption but remarkably little loss of life. This is accounted for by an effective national emergency preparedness plan coupled with a subregional response (Christie and Hanlon 2001).

These gains have, unfortunately, been offset by a continued high rate of civil conflict and associated mass distress migration. While the period 1990-92 saw the ending of wars in Mozambique, Namibia, Ethiopia and Eritrea, it also saw the outbreak of conflicts in Liberia, Sierra Leone and Rwanda. Meanwhile, wars have continued in Somalia, Sudan and Angola. There is no truly effective way of responding to the health and nutrition crises unleashed by these wars.

Bio-demographic Factors. Factors such as mothers' age at the birth of a child, the spacing of children and total fertility all influence child survival (Mosley 1991). Very young mothers are more likely to end with premature or low birthweight babies and they are often poor users of health care services. Children born to teenagers have 35 percent higher risk of dying before age one compared to children born to mothers in their 20s. Short birth intervals are associated with early weaning of older infants, with associated risks of infection.

Gender. There is one important factor notable by its absence in the analysis of infant and child mortality: gender. In some parts of the world, notably South Asia, girl children have markedly poorer survival chances than boys. Under optimal conditions, for example in northern Europe, girls have marginally but consistently better survival rates than boys. In Africa, this is also the case: Africa has no gender bias in its survival rates. This is equally true during normal times and times of famine. It is more so in Sub-Saharan Africa than in North Africa, indicating that there may be a small gender bias in the latter countries, but the difference is marginal.

The World Summit on Children and After

At the World Summit for Children in 1990, a number of targets for better child survival were identified, including:

> Reduction of infant mortality by one third or to 50 per 1,000 live births; and under five mortality by one third or to 70 per 1,000 live births, whichever is less.
> Eradication of polio by 2000, elimination of neonatal tetanus by 1995, reduction of measles deaths by 95 percent and reduction by 90 percent of measles cases compared to pre-immunisation levels by 1995.
> Maintaining a 90 percent immunization coverage of children aged under one year by 2000 against diphtheria, pertussis, tetanus, measles, polio, tuberculosis and reducing incidences of tetanus for women of child-bearing age.
> Halving maternal mortality rates.
> Halving severe and moderate malnutrition among children under five years old.
> Ensuring universal access to safe drinking water and to sanitary means of excreta disposal.

In addition, at the 1992 International Conference for Assistance to African Children held in Dakar, African governments reiterated the following pledges:

> To raise the coverage for measles immunisation to 90 percent;
> To raise coverage for other vaccine preventable diseases to 80 percent;
> To achieve 80 percent usage of oral re-hydration therapy;
> To eliminate iodine deficiency disorders;
> To eliminate vitamin A deficiency; and
> To encourage exclusive breastfeeding for 4-6 months and sustained breastfeeding for up to 24 months.

These targets have not been reached. Table 1 below shows levels of under-five mortality in 1990 and in 2000, the average annual change in under-five mortality in that decade, and whether the countries reached the target. The table also shows the ranking of countries in Africa from a list of all countries of the world in 2000, as well as the coverage of immunization for four key diseases, and other indicators. Table 2 shows under-five mortality figures for a number of countries that held the lowest under-five mortality levels in the world in 2000.

From Table 1, it is clear that under-five mortality for most countries in Africa remains unacceptably high. Of the 20 countries worldwide with the highest under-five mortality rates, 19 of them are found in Africa. For most of Africa, child mortality remains above 100/1,000. Only ten have rates below the minimum target of 70/1,000 set at the WSC. These are mostly in North Africa—countries that started off at the top of the list and also made the most rapid improvements. Angola, Malawi, Mozambique, Niger and Zambia all have child mortality rates above 200/1,000.

Much but not all of the stagnation can be attributed to HIV/AIDS. The most striking reverses in earlier gains have occurred in high-HIV countries in Southern and Eastern Africa. Kenya, formerly a success story, now provides a clear example of a negative trend. Similar reverses are evident in Botswana, South Africa and Zimbabwe. But some countries with very low levels of HIV prevalence, such as Niger, Chad and Mauritania, also display very high child mortality levels and very slow improvement. Meanwhile the level of child mortality in Sierra Leone—over 300/1,000, the highest in the world in 2000—is shockingly high.

The problem of low birthweight for infants is still a major obstacle for improvements in survival prospects. Only a handful of African countries have less than the specified target of less than ten percent of babies with low birth weight (the Comoros, Ghana, Libya and Senegal). Most countries have around 12-15% of children born with low birthweight.

Table 1 also shows that malnutrition remains rampant in Africa. The percent of children who can be classified as moderately or severely stunted is high as are the figures for the percent of children that are severely and moderately malnourished. Malnutrition rates range up to 50% for countries such as Eritrea, Ethiopia and Niger.

African women have progressively shortened the duration of breast-feeding over the years (Lesthaeghe 1989). One of the targets of the Dakar meeting was to encourage exclusive breastfeeding for 4-6 months and sustained breastfeeding for up to 24 months. Only 34% of infants 0-3 months old are exclusively breast-fed and only a handful of countries are close to the target.

Africa has faltered in its progress towards targets for immunization against the major child killer diseases. On the aim of eradicating measles, only eight of the countries listed here reached the Dakar target of 90% immunization. Many remain below 50%. The immense increase in immunization coverage, up from about 20% of children in the early 1980s to 50% by the early 1990s, has undoubtedly had a major positive impact. But it has not progressed towards a stage of eliminating these preventable diseases as major public health problems.

Maternal mortality ratios (MMRs) in 2000 are still high, at 1,100 deaths per 100,000 births in Mozambique and Central African Republic and 1,000 in Eritrea. A third of countries listed here have

MMRs of greater than 500, only four countries have MMRs below 100. These figures are a reflection of women's health in the region, reflecting a poor diet and lack of access to health-care and advice during and after pregnancy. The proportion of women whose births were attended by health personnel is very low for a number of countries.

Implications

Africa is simply not progressing at the rate required for its children to face the prospect of substantially increased life chances in the next decade. Africa is behind the rest of the world, and is falling further behind. Moreover, this is occurring at a time when we know with great precision why children die, and what can be done to prevent them dying. And the world has the resources to deliver on this basic goal.

The implications of the current trends are disturbing. With few exceptions, the incremental improvements in child survival, nutrition and health marked in Africa in the last decade are not sufficient to allow us to state with confidence that Africa is on target to meet the WSC targets even within another decade. The major factor in this is of course HIV/AIDS, but even in countries where the HIV/AIDS pandemic has not struck hard, the prognosis is not encouraging. In short, Africa is not on target to meet the WSC goals on child survival and thereby fulfil the most basic right guaranteed in the CRC.

The Impact of HIV/AIDS

The devastating impact of the HIV/AIDS pandemic is a theme that runs throughout this book. The pandemic has a direct impact on the health of children through vertical mother-to-child transmission (MTCT), and a major impact through orphanhood. About four million African children have died from AIDS, mostly contracted through MTCT.

The AIDS pandemic also has important indirect impacts through undermining economic growth and emasculating important institutions such as schools and the health sector. It may even contribute to political instability and armed conflict. Each of these factors in turn impacts upon child survival. Child death rates have risen sharply in the worst-affected countries. In Botswana, according to UNAIDS estimates, an estimated 64% of child deaths are AIDS-related. This section will examine two components of this: MTCT and children orphaned by AIDS.

Mother-to-Child Transmission

Mother-to-child transmission is a major contributor to HIV prevalence (Pisani 2001). An HIV positive child is approximately three times more likely to die in the first two years of life than a child free from the virus. These HIV positive children tend to die from the same diseases as other children; they are just die more easily, whether from increased susceptibility to infection or reduced resistance when they become infected, or both.

Transmission occurs either in utero, at birth or during breast-feeding. The probabilities of transmission are approximately, intra-uterine, 5-10%; intra-partum, 10-20% and breast-feeding, 15-30% (Brass and Jolly 1995, Gregson and Anderson 1994). Mortality shows a bimodal pattern. Children infected through breast-feeding survive longer than those infected at birth. About 20% of HIV positive infants develop AIDS within 15 months and die four months later. Overall, about 80% of AIDS infected children die before age five.

Reducing the risk of transmission during pregnancy and birth is medically straightforward. For example, a short course of AZT given late in pregnancy can reduce the risk of transmission by about half. The challenge is to make this treatment available, and to ensure uptake. In addition to the political problems of some governments being unwilling or unable to implement these measures, there are wider social obstacles to implementing such treatment on a large scale.

Many pregnant women are reluctant to be tested for HIV, for several reasons. First, there is generally little public information about the MTCT, so that women are not aware of the risks of transmitting HIV to their children, and how these can be minimised. Moreover, a woman learning of these facts late in pregnancy is much less likely to absorb and act upon them than one who was aware beforehand, and may even have considered these facts before her pregnancy. Second, women fear the implications of finding out that they are HIV positive. They fear the reactions of their husbands/partners—there are cases of women suffering abandonment or worse when they have told their partners of their HIV-positive status. They may be unable to cope with it personally, especially at the time of giving birth to a child. As a result, uptake rates for offers of voluntary testing are uneven, and significant numbers of women do not come back for their test results even after agreeing to be tested. Many women prefer not to know their sero-status, even if it means increasing the risk to their child.

Eliminating the risk of transmission during breast-feeding is also technically simple: do not breast-feed. However, this is also a more complex issue. There are the factors outlined above: a woman must know she is HIV positive before taking the necessary steps. In addition, breast-feeding is common across Africa and universal in many places. It is highly valued. A woman who does not breast-feed her infant is not only foregoing a personally and culturally important experience, but may be advertising the fact that she is HIV positive. In addition, breast-feeding was promoted over the use of infant formulae for a good reason: the latter present a risk to the health of the infant, especially where clean water cannot be guaranteed, while breast milk is the best start in life for a baby. Breast milk substitutes may also be expensive. This problem calls for two alternatives. One is a programme of free or subsidised infant formulae combined with clean water supplies, to back up any programmes of voluntary counseling and testing of pregnant women.

The other is an important but often-neglected third alternative: the use of cows' milk augmented by sugar and micro-nutrients. This is a traditional, commonly-used baby food for orphans and other infants unable to consume breast milk, that has been unjustly overlooked by the infant formulae producers. Another factor needing consideration is that secondary factors such as nipple lesions and mastitis massively increase the risk of MTCT during breast-feeding. An implication of this is targeting breast-milk substitutes at these high-risk women. These considerations point to a general need for education and advocacy on MTCT. The targetted interventions will be most effective in the context of wider public awareness.

Children Orphaned by AIDS

The scale of the HIV/AIDS pandemic is such that the lifetime probability of a teenager today in Botswana dying of AIDS is about 65%. In South Africa it is perhaps 40%. This implies that a huge number of African children will see one or both parents die of AIDS. This in turn will have major adverse implications for child survival.

Already there are currently more than 13 million children orphaned by AIDS in Sub-Saharan Africa. This figure will continue to rise rapidly through the coming decade. Orphanhood levels have risen from about 2% before the AIDS epidemic to more than 7% today in some Africa countries and may rise to 20-30%. In 1999, Zimbabwe alone had an estimated 500,000 children orphaned by AIDS, and by 2005 this number may reach 1.2 million. More than a quarter of Zambian children under 15 are orphaned (Guest 2001). Figures in other Southern African countries are comparable. Note that the number of children orphaned by AIDS will further increase as MTCT is reduced, which will entail more children outliving their HIV positive mothers.

At present, an accurate assessment of AIDS orphanhood is remarkably difficult to come by. There are a number of issues that need to be considered. There are problems of definition: should orphans include children who have lost both parents, or just the mother or just the father? Are there differences between children orphaned by AIDS and other orphans (and children living apart from one or both living parents)? There are problems of data: while a number countries have carried out national profiles of orphans, only Botswana has attempted a comprehensive national enumeration.

Overwhelmingly, the evidence points to increased distress for children orphaned by AIDS. Children do not start to suffer only when they become orphaned. Their health, development and emotional well-being are at risk long before either parent dies. It is difficult for parents living with HIV to provide adequately for the physical and emotional needs of children given the debilitating nature of their illness. The social stigma surrounding HIV/AIDS can lead to feelings of guilt, shame, remorse and anger further complicating the parent-child relationship (Miller and Murray 1999). Children may have worries, unattended by others, as they watch their parents become ill and die. HIV illness could lead to unbalanced family relationships as needs go unattended or unnoticed.

AIDS in the family causes poverty. Studies in urban households of Côte d'Ivoire show that when a family member has AIDS, average income falls by 52 to 67%, while expenditures on health care quadruple (UNAIDS, 1999a). Orphans run increased risks of being malnourished, with a significant though transient decrease in family food consumption on the illness and death of an adult family member (World Bank 1999b: 222-3). It is likely that more are compelled to enter the workforce (UNICEF 2001a). Although AIDS orphanhood is not the sole, nor even the main reason for children's non-attendance at school, it is an important contributor. Hence, even before they suffer orphanhood, these children are deprived.

The role of wider family networks in caring for children orphaned by AIDS is important. But it is clear that these networks are under serious stress Orphanhood is a well-known phenomenon in Africa, and was much commoner among previous generations than recently due to historically higher death rates. There are strong traditions of extended family networks caring for orphans. What is not known is how resilient these traditional coping mechanisms are, under the strains of social and economic change and the burden of the sheer numbers of children orphaned by AIDS. The strain on social and kinship support systems may simply be too much. Evidence from Zambia indicates that HIV/AIDS serves to break down kinship systems, a fact highlighted by the rapid growth in the number of street children (Foundation for Democracy in Africa, 2000).

The emergency of child-headed households, children forced to take on parental obligations, or households with only old people and young children, is increasing. The number of child headed households is undoubtedly growing (Foster et al. 1998, Smart 1999). Girl children commonly take on parental responsibilities for younger siblings, even though they are not ready to do so, a phenomenon referred to as 'parentification' (Stein et al. 1999). The guardian sibling is often forced to drop out of school and try to earn an income. In other cases, AIDS leaves affected children in the care of elderly grandparents (Beers 1988; Marcus 1999). However, the flexibility of the African kinship system means that there are often adults of working age to be called upon.

Challenges and the Way Forward

While this chapter has largely focused on health-specific factors, it is important to put these in the context of poverty. Most of the factors outlined here are poverty-related. Even if African governments were to double their expenditure on health care, this would still meet less than a third of the $40 per capita spending identified as a minimum by the Commission on Macroeconomics and Health. Blame for this enduring poverty can be widely distributed among African governments, the Bretton Woods institutions, and western governments' aid, trade and debt policies.

The main factor in child survival in Africa is health care provision, taken in the broadest sense to include basic social services and poverty reduction. In this regard, Africa needs more resources and better policies. The resources required for basic health care are available. To provide for 400 million Africans in low-income countries, this implies an additional cost of $10-16 bn per annum—a three to four-fold multiple of all current donor support to health programmes in all developing countries (based on CMH 2001). Providing these funds would therefore represent a major commitment on behalf of donors, but these are the levels of resource mobilization that need to be contemplated if we are to provide acceptable life chances for Africa's children.

Resources can also be mobilized from within Africa. There are notable examples of African countries that are relatively wealthy in terms of average income per head, but which have failed to improve child survival rates. Gabon and South Africa are cases in point. Even where financial resources are strapped, there are opportunities for more effective utilisation of human resources and institutional capacities.

Better policies and capacities are needed. Health programmes need to be integrated more closely and coherently into government planning—they should not merely be a concern for ministries of health: all government departments should be concerned with these issues. In the health sector itself, a variety of programmatic approaches are required. 'Horizontal' programmes aimed at building up the basic health infrastructure at all levels need to be complemented by 'vertical' interventions, notably immunization programmes aimed at combating the key killers. Thus Africa needs simultaneously to build up its basic health infrastructure and take advantage of targeted initiatives, especially those aimed at vaccine-preventable childhood diseases, malaria and HIV/AIDS.

1. Unless otherwise indicated, 'child mortality' refers to under 5 mortality rates by one thousand live births.

Table 1: Under Five Mortality and Indicators of Child Health in Africa.

Countries		Under-5 Mortality per 1000 births, 1990	Under-5 Mortality per 1000 births, 2000	Annual % Change, 1990-2000	Target by 2000	% Infants with low Birth Weight, 1995-1999	BCG	DPT	Polio	Measles	TT2	Access to clean water urban population 1999	Access to clean water rural population 1999	Access to sanitation urban population 1999	Access to sanitation rural population 1999	Maternal Mortality Ratios per 1000000	Births attended by Health Personnel	Moderate &severe Malnutrition	Moderate & severe wasting	Exclusive Breastfeeding 0-3moths
North Africa							% of one year olds fully immunised									1980-1999				
Algeria	87	48	41	1.8	25	9x	97	83	83	78	52	98	88	90	47	220	77x	13	9	48
Chad	14	198	198	0.0	>33	-	57	33	34	49	27	31	26	81	13	830	15	39	14	2
Libya	123	42	22	7.2	T	7x	100	97	95	92	-	72	68	97	96	75	94	5	3	-
Mali	5	254	235	0.9	>33	16	84	52	52	57	62	74	61	93	58	580	24	40	23	13
Mauritania	16	183	183	0.0	>33	11x	76	19	19	56	13	34	40	44	19	550	40x	23	7	60
Morocco	72	85	53	5.2	T	9x	90	94	94	93	36	100	58	100	42	230	40	9x	2x	31
Tunisia	101	52	30	6.1	T	8x	99	100	100	93	80	-	-	-	-	70	81	4	1	12x
North East																				
Djibouti	27	175	149	1.8	>33	11x	26	23	24	23	14	100	100	99	50	-	79x	18	13	-
Egypt	73	104	52	7.7	T	10x	99	94	95	97	66	96	94	98	91	170	61	12	6	60

Countries		Under-5 Mortality per 1000 births, 1990	Under-5 Mortality per 1000 births, 2000	Annual % Change, 1990-2000	Target by 2000	% Infants with low Birth Weight, 1995-1999	BCG	DPT	Polio	Measles	TT2	Access to clean water urban population 1999	Access to clean water rural population 1999	Access to sanitation urban population 1999	Access to sanitation rural population 1999	Maternal Mortality Ratios per 1000000	Births attended by Health Personnel	Moderate &severe Malnutrition	Moderate & severe wasting	Exclusive Breastfeeding 0-3moths
Gabon	28	164	143	1.5	>33	-	60	31	31	30	25	73	55	25	4	600	80x	-	-	32
Gambia	60	127	75	5.9	7	-	97	87	88	88	96	80	53	41	35	-	44x	26	-	-
Ghana	48	127	101	2.5	>33	8	88	72	72	73	52	87	49	62	64	210	44	25	10	36
Guinea	17	240	181	3.1	>33	13	76	46	43	52	48	72	36	94	41	670	35	-	12x	13
Guinea Bissau	12	246	200	2.3	>33	20x	-	-	-	-	-	29	55	88	34	-	25	23	-	-
Liberia	5	235	235	0.0	>33	-	43	23	25	35	14	-	-	-	-	-	58x	-	-	-
Niger	3	320	275	1.7	>33	15x	36	21	21	25	19	70	56	79	5	590	18	50	21	1
Nigeria	15	190	187	0.2	>33	16x	27	21	22	26	29	81	39	85	45	700	33	31	16	22
Sao Tome & Principe	58	90	76	1.9	24	7x	80	73	72	59	31	-	-	-	-	-	86x	16	5	-
Senegal	37	147	118	2.4	>33	4	90	60	57	60	45	92	65	94	48	560	47	22	7	16
Sierra Leone	1	323	316	0.2	>33	11x	55	22	72	29	25	23	31	23	31	-	-	29x	9x	-

Countries		Under-5 Mortality per 1000 births, 1990	Under-5 Mortality per 1000 births, 2000	Annual % Change, 1990-2000	Target by 2000	% Infants with low Birth Weight, 1995-1999	BCG	DPT	Polio	Measles	TT2	Access to clean water urban population 1999	Access to clean water rural population 1999	Access to sanitation urban population 1999	Access to sanitation rural population 1999	Maternal Mortality Ratios per 1000000	Births attended by Health Personnel	Moderate &severe Malnutrition	Moderate & severe wasting	Exclusive Breastfeeding 0-3moths
Eritrea	46	160	105	4.7	>33	13x	64	56	56	55	28	63	42	66	1	1000	21x	44	16	66
Ethiopia	19	193	176	1.0	>33	16x	80	64	64	53	35	77	13	58	6	-	10	47	11	84
Somalia	7	215	211	0.2	>33	16x	39	18	18	26	16	-	-	-	-	-1*	2x	26	12	1
Sudan	43	123	109	1.3	>33	15x	100	88	87	88	62	86	69	87	48	550	86x	34x	13x	14x
West Africa																				
Benin	24	185	156	1.9	>33	-	100	90	90	92	90	74	55	46	6	500	60	29	14	15
Burkina Faso	13	210	199	0.6	>33	21x	72	37	42	46	30	84	-	88	16	-	27	36	18	5
Cameroon	26	139	154	-1.1	>33	13x	66	48	48	46	44	82	42	99	85	430	55	22	6	16
Cape Verde	62	73	73	0.0	>33	9x	75	69	70	61	52	64	89	95	32	55	54	14x	6x	57
Cote D'Ivoire	22	155	171	-1.1	>33	12x	84	61	61	66	44	90	65	-	-	600	47	24x	8x	4
Equatorial Guinea	23	206	160	2.8	>33	-	99	81	81	82	70	45	42	60	46	-	5x	-	-	-

Countries		Under-5 Mortality per 1000 births, 1990	Under-5 Mortality per 1000 births, 2000	Annual % Change, 1990-2000	Target by 2000	% Infants with low Birth Weight, 1995-1999	BCG	DPT	Polio	Measles	TT2	Access to clean water urban population 1999	Access to clean water rural population 1999	Access to sanitation urban population 1999	Access to sanitation rural population 1999	Maternal Mortality Ratios per 1000000	Births attended by Health Personnel	Moderate &severe Malnutrition	Moderate & severe wasting	Exclusive Breastfeeding 0-3moths
Mauritius	119	25	23	0.9	32	13	87	85	86	80	75	100	100	100	99	50	97x	16	15	16x
Mozambique	10	235	203	1.6	>33	12	100	81	81	90	53	86	43	69	26	1100	44	26	8	38
Rwanda	18	161	180	-1.2	>33	17x	94	85	85	78	83	60	40	12	8	-	26x	27	11	90x
Seychelles	139	21	17	2.3	19	10x	100	99	99	99	99	-	-	-	-	-	99x	6x	2x	-
Tanzania	30	150	141	0.7	>33	14	93	82	81	78	77	80	42	98	86	530	35	27	6	41
Uganda	32	165	131	2.6	>33	13	83	54	55	53	49	72	46	96	72	510	38	26	5	70
Zambia	11	192	202	-0.6	>33	13x	87	92	92	72	55	88	48	99	64	650	47	24	4	11
Southern Africa																				
Angola	2	283	295	-0.5	>33	19x	65	29	29	49	16	34	40	70	30	-	-	42	6	12
Botswana	69	50	59	-1.8	>33	11	98	85	82	74	56	100	-	-	-	330	87	17	11	39
Lesotho	31	148	134	1.1	>33	11x	68	64	60	55	-	98	88	93	92	-	50x	16	5	54

Countries		Under-5 Mortality per 1000 births, 1990	Under-5 Mortality per 1000 births, 2000	Annual % Change, 1990-2000	Target by 2000	% Infants with low Birth Weight, 1995-1999	BCG	DPT	Polio	Measles	TT2	Access to clean water urban population 1999	Access to clean water rural population 1999	Access to sanitation urban population 1999	Access to sanitation rural population 1999	Maternal Mortality Ratios per 1000000	Births attended by Health Personnel	Moderate &severe Malnutrition	Moderate & severe wasting	Exclusive Breastfeeding 0-3moths
Togo	28	152	143	0.7	>33	20x	63	48	48	47	48	85	38	69	17	480	51	25	12	15
Central Africa																				
Central African Republic	21	177	172	0.3	>33	15x	55	28	34	40	25	80	46	43	23	1100	46x	27	7	23
Congo	44	110	108	0.2	>33	16x	39	29	29	23	33	71	17	14	-	-	-	17x	4x	43x
Congo Democratic Rep	9	207	207	0.0	>33	15x	22	15	16	15	-	89	26	53	6	-	-	34	10	32
Eastern Africa																				
Burundi	19	180	176	0.2	>33	-	71	63	59	47	9	96	-	79	-	-	24x	37x	9x	89x
Comoros	54	120	86	3.7	21	8x	84	75	75	67	22	98	95	98	98	500	52	26	8	5
Kenya	37	97	118	-2.2	>33	16x	96	79	81	79	51	87	31	96	81	590	44	22	6	17
Madagascar	24	168	156	0.8	>33	5	66	48	48	46	35	85	31	70	30	490	47	40	7	61
Malawi	7	230	211	1.0	>33	20x	92	94	93	90	97	95	44	96	70	620	55x	30	7	11

Countries		Under-5 Mortality per 1000 births, 1990	Under-5 Mortality per 1000 births, 2000	Annual % Change, 1990-2000	Target by 2000	% Infants with low Birth Weight, 1995-1999	BCG	DPT	Polio	Measles	TT2	Access to clean water urban population 1999	Access to clean water rural population 1999	Access to sanitation urban population 1999	Access to sanitation rural population 1999	Maternal Mortality Ratios per 1000000	Births attended by Health Personnel	Moderate &severe Malnutrition	Moderate & severe wasting	Exclusive Breastfeeding 0-3moths
Industrialised Countries		37	9	4.2	3	6		93	94	89	89	100	100	100	-		99	-	-	-
Developing Countries		102	90	1.4	50	17		72	74	70	70	91	70	81	34		52	29	10	44
Least Developed Countries		182	164	1.2	85	18		58	59	58	58	80	54	73	33		28	40	12	
42																				
World		92	82	1.3	49	16		75	76	72	72	93	71	84	36		56	28	10	44

Source: The State of the World's Children, 2000. UNICEF

Countries		Under-5 Mortality per 1000 births, 1990	Under-5 Mortality per 1000 births, 2000	Annual % Change, 1990-2000	Target by 2000	% Infants with low Birth Weight, 1995-1999	BCG	DPT	Polio	Measles	TT2	Access to clean water urban population 1999	Access to clean water rural population 1999	Access to sanitation urban population 1999	Access to sanitation rural population 1999	Maternal Mortality Ratios per 1000000	Births attended by Health Personnel	Moderate &severe Malnutrition	Moderate & severe wasting	Exclusive Breastfeeding 0-3moths
Namibia	65	84	70	2.0	22	16x	80	72	72	65	81	100	67	96	17	230	68x	26x	9x	22x
South Africa	66	60	69	-1.6	>33	-	97	76	72	82	26	92	80	99	73	-	84	9	3	10
Swaziland	51	115	90	2.5	25	10x	94	96	96	72	96	-	-	-	-	230	56x	10x	1x	37
Zimbabwe	51	80	90	-1.3	>33	10	88	81	81	79	58	100	77	99	51	400	84	15	6	16x
Regions																				
Sub-Saharan Africa		180	173	0.4	93	15		50	50	51	51	82	40	60	41		37	31	10	34
Middle E. & N. Africa		79	63	2.4	24	11		91	91	91	91	96	79	94	65		69	17	8	42
South Asia		128	104	2.4	40	31		67	67	56	56	92	85	76	21		29	49	17	46
East Asia & Pacific		57	45	2.8	15	8		81	87	82	82	93	66	75	35		66	19	6	57
Latin Am. & Caribbean		53	39	3.6	10	9		88	91	91	91	91	63	86	47		83	9	2	37
CEE/CIS & Baltic		42	35	2.0	16	7		92	93	92	92	95	80	-	-		94	7	6	-

Table 2: Ranked Estimated Under five mortality Rates for Developed Countries 1999.

Country	U5 Mortality Rate per 1000 births*
Cuba, United States	8
Belgium, Canada, Italy, Spain, United Kingdom	6
Denmark, Finland, France, Germany, Iceland, Switzerland	5
Japan, Norway, Sweden	4

3

Africa's Children and Africa's Development: A Duration of Development Framework

ALI ABDEL GADIR ALI

Introduction

The view of Africa as a continent doomed to poverty and conflict is captured by lead story, 'Hopeless Continent', in the 13-19 May 2000 issue of *The Economist.* The motivation this seems to have been the complications, at the time, brought about by the abduction of UN troops by Mr. Sankoh and his fighting faction in the context of the Sierra Leone civil war. The leading article—entitled 'Hopeless Africa'—draws a comparison between the start of the 19th century when 'Freetown was remote and malarial, but also a place of hope' and the start of the 21st century where it 'symbolizes failure and despair'.

Inside, *The Economist* ran an article entitled 'Africa: The Heart of the Matter'. Following a succinct arraying of the evidence on Africa's poverty and underdevelopment the article dismisses two rival theories that endeavour to explain the continent's incapacity to effect meaningful development. These are the racial theory that takes these failures as 'just the way Africa is' and the 'externalist theory' that holds slavery, colonialism and the cold war as responsible. Instead, *The Economist* presents a variant of an environment-geography theory where nature has been unkind to Africa purely due to its location, augmented by a variant institutional theory based on tribalism and the failure of state formation. The closing paragraph argues that more 'than anything, Africa's people need to regain their self-confidence. Only then can Africa engage as an equal with the rest of the world, devising its own economic programmes and development policies. Its people also need the confidence to trust each other. Only then can they make deals to end wars and build political institutions; institutions that they believe in'.

The Economist suggests the following as major tasks that need to be confronted by Africans: 'reducing African poverty', 'changing African leadership', 'regaining African self-confidence', 'building African institutions', and devising 'African development programmes and policies'. These, we suggest are not much different from the challenges for the future identified by UNICEF (2000) for the UN (2000). These challenges are seen as 'poverty', 'armed conflicts and other types of violence', 'discrimination', 'HIV/AIDS', the 'creation of an enabling environment' and 'enhancing participation'.

In its report to the UN General Assembly UNICEF argues that future 'actions must embrace the principle of a 'first call for children' and promote the allocation of resources to their maximum extent for the realization of children rights, starting with the rights to survive and develop' (UN 2000: 12). Reviewing the achievements and challenges, UNICEF concludes that 'major progress within a generation is possible. The world has the knowledge, the financial resources and the technology. The essential component for marshalling these resources is political will. Inspired leadership is the key to changing the world for children and making major progress in human development within one generation' (UN 2000: 17). This, we suggest, is an important proposition embodying a very well defined 'time dimension'. In the context of Sub-Saharan Africa (SSA), however, we suggest that such a proposition is overly optimistic. A major difficulty with the proposition, which may be due to the global mandate of UNICEF, is the neglect of the 'initial conditions' of African children as they enter the 21st century. Although the world-wide goals may be met, SSA's goals may not be.

In this paper we propose a framework based on UNICEF's view and *The Economist's* concerns. The framework identifies poverty, conflict and institutions as the pillars on which a new development paradigm for the continent needs to be built. The three are closely related, but we look at them in separate sections for ease of exposition. The major message of the framework is that African development, broadly defined, requires a very long time horizon and that even a 30-33 years horizon could be too short to achieve 'major progress'. The time duration of development is an important aspect that has so far been neglected in the literature (see, for example, Tinbergen 1994).

Poverty, conflicts and institutions will remain long-run challenges. There is a huge literature on Africa's economic performance, which aims to identify the factors responsible for such performance over the period since the mid-1970s (see, among others, Collier and Gunning (1999-a, b) and O'Connell and Ndulu (2000)). In addition to a number of policy variables, this strand of empirical literature has identified historical, geographic, environmental, and political conditions as important explanatory variables. Some of the greatest methodological difficulties with this literature, however, have been pointed out by, among others, Pritchett (2000) and Sala-i-Martin (1997). Regaining self confidence by Africans, we suggest, requires more than a search for causality in the context of economic models, however rigorous these models may be.

The following section deals with poverty in the continent. In addition to standard results at the aggregative level a set of new results dealing with children in poverty is presented. The most important aspect of these results is that the continent is dismally poor to the extent that International Development Goals (IDG), agreed to in international conferences to reduce poverty in a medium term horizon (by 2015), are almost impossible to achieve. The HIV/AIDS epidemic and its severe economic impacts compounds the existing difficulties. The third section deals with children and conflicts where we present a set of estimates of the cost of conflicts in terms of forgone development. The costs are very high indeed and they must have impacted African children in a huge negative way. The fourth section looks at the institutional structure of the continent. This is an essential context in which initiatives for children get implemented. Alternative estimates of the time required to achieve 'high quality' institutions that can uphold the rights of children are shown to be very long. In the last section we offer a few concluding remarks.

Children and Poverty

Motivation: A Story from a Gambian Village

In *The Financial Times* (13-14 March 1999) a World Bank manager recounted his experience of spending a week in the Gambian village of Demfaye Njagga. The visit was arranged in the context of a World Bank's 'executive in development program', perhaps also in the context of the World Bank adopting as a mission statement to 'fight poverty with passion and professionalism'. The personal experience was told with a welcome measure of sensitivity to the plight of the Gambian villagers and their children.

The World Bank's manager reported that the villagers consistently told him that their problems revolved around 'lack of water; insufficient access to health care; inadequate food during the rainy season; environmental decline; and poor communications'. That this is a familiar list of problems in a poor African village should not come as a surprise to any one. It is a list of basic needs, lack of which should signal poverty and deprivation. Despite its familiarity, the World Bank's manager was struck by problems that the villagers 'did not mention'. The first problem is lack of information: 'not a single person knew the world price of groundnuts, the key variable to them'. The second problem is the lack of role models. 'School children wanted to be president, ministers, soldiers, police or teachers (boys), and nurses or teachers (girls). Not a single child wanted to use his or her education to become a private-sector farmer or a business person. Yet Gambia's economic future, as elsewhere, hinges on the development of a vibrant private sector'!

The reaction of the World Bank's manager to the preferences of the Gambian school children, and the Gambian villagers' list of familiar problems, is an example of how Africa continues to be treated by its so-called 'development partners'. The implication of this reaction for the so-called 'ownership issue' is particularly noteworthy. Thus, from an ownership perspective the manager would have liked it infinitely if the villagers mentioned 'lack of information on the world price of groundnuts' as a problem or had the children told him that they would like to become 'private sector farmers or business persons'. As such, therefore, one possible interpretation of the irritation of the World Bank manager is that the poor Gambian villagers didn't know what was good for them: monitoring the 'world price of groundnuts: the relevant variable for their economy' and the centrality of the private sector for their future development.

While the manager expressed bewilderment as to what can be done to help Gambian villagers out of poverty, he decided on a personal two pronged strategy. The first is 'to see how information and literate materials and access to a wider range of role models might be made available to those not yet connected to the global information economy'. The second is 'using techniques learned from business schools, I am already trying to reduce the bureaucratic impediments to my staff's getting on with their work; after the village visit I am impatient with the bureaucracy of the Bank, though I recognize that some of it is inevitable'.

The above, then, is the gist of the story a World Bank's manager wanted to share with the readers of *The Financial Times*! Judged by his irritation with the missing economic reform components and by his personal strategy to fight poverty, it is open to question of how long it would take the World Bank to fight poverty in Africa with or without passion, with or without professionalism! This, we suggest, is an important 'duration of development' question.

Measuring Poverty

Before we proceed to reviewing the evidence on African poverty, we offer a few remarks on the measurement of poverty. These will be selective in nature due to the vast technical literature that has developed.

(a) The dominant approach to the measurement of poverty is the money metric approach. This requires a relevant measure for the standard of living, such as (for developing countries) per capita consumption expenditure. In advanced countries it is income. From this we can determine the threshold of deprivation below which a person can be identified as poor—the poverty line.

(b) The relevant method for determining poverty lines for developing countries is the cost of basic needs. This method involves identifying a typical diet for the poor that is necessary for leading a healthy life, costing it and adding the cost of other requirements needed by individuals to live in a social context (e.g. clothing, shelter and medicine) to arrive at the poverty line.

(c) While the international debate has been conducted in terms of a fixed poverty line (e.g. one dollar per day) applied to all countries, there is increasing realization that poverty lines vary among countries. This is tantamount to saying that, in general, the poverty line will be expected to be a function of the standard of living.

(d) An immediate measure of poverty is the ratio of the poor thus identified to the total population in society. This is the 'head-count ratio,' the most widely used, and easily understood, measure of poverty. Thus, for example, the International Development Goal on poverty is to reduce the head-count ratio to half its current level by the year 2015. The head-count ratio measures the spread, or incidence, of poverty in a given society. Another useful poverty measure is the poverty-gap ratio, which takes into account the extent to which consumption by the poor falls below the poverty line. It measures the depth of poverty in a society.

(e) To be able to identify the poor we need information on the distribution of consumption expenditure or income, in the society. This information is usually obtained from household budget, or expenditure, surveys. Such surveys, like population censuses, are very expensive to conduct rigorously and as a result such information is usually lacking in Africa.

(f) In general, any poverty measure could be expressed as depending on mean consumption in society and on a measure of the underlying inequality in the distribution of consumption. As per capita consumption increases, other things remaining the same, poverty declines. Similarly, as inequality in the distribution of consumption declines, other things remaining the same, poverty declines. If one believes that the inequality in the distribution of consumption depends also on mean consumption in society, then one can get a simple, yet powerful, relationship between poverty and economic growth. This relationship says that changes in poverty over time can always be calculated as a product of the elasticity of poverty with respect to mean consumption, after allowing for changes in the distribution of income[1], and the rate of change in mean consumption. The elasticity involved is called the 'growth elasticity of poverty'.

We should also note that much use is made of aggregate correlates of poverty. These include, for example, life expectancy at birth (as a proxy for health status in a society) and school enrolment ratios (as a proxy for educational achievements). An example is to be found in the Human Development Index of the UNDP (see UNDP 2000).

In generating our results we use a poverty line that changes with income. A poverty line equation was estimated from an available set of national poverty lines where the poverty line and the per capita consumption are expressed in real 1985 purchasing power parity dollars as in the Summers and Heston (1991) data set. Space dictates that only the overall findings can be presented here.

Children in Poverty: The Evidence

For the sample of countries noted above, we report a summary of our latest poverty estimates in table 1. Note that the national poverty estimates are population weighted sectoral estimates.

Table 1: Poverty Measures in SSA in the 1990s: A Summary

Head-Count Ratio (%)	61.09 (13.61)	47.42 (08.58)	56.75 (11.99)
Poverty-gap Ratio (%)	38.83 (10.46)	18.31 (06.38)	23.93 (08.92)
Squared Poverty-gap Ratio (%)	23.94 (08.20)	09.58 (04.91)	13.46 (06.90)
Poor's Expenditure ($/person/month)	14.80 (04.90)	26.20 (07.90)	18.3*
Mean Expenditure ($/person/month)	28.60 (10.60)	62.50 (21.10)	39.0*
Poverty Line ($/person/month)	25.20 (04.80)	41.80 (11.30)	30.3*
Gini Coefficient (%)	47.02 (09.41)	43.25 (06.94)	Na

Source: own results.

* Indicative only, being the weighted average of the sectoral means and as such they are not used in the calculations of the national poverty measures.

Concerning rural poverty, it is clear that poverty in rural SSA is very widespread: 61% of the rural population are found to be living below an overall (indicative) poverty line of about $25 per month per person (the mean of the distribution of the country poverty lines). As indicated, in SSA, rural poverty is also found to be both deep and severe. It is also clear that the experience of countries differs widely.

To further appreciate the depth of rural poverty, the average income of the poor amounted to only $15 per person per month. Thirteen countries had an income of the poor less than the recorded mean, with the lowest recorded for Guinea Bissau ($9.4) and Tanzania ($8.8). Seven countries had an average income of the poor greater than the overall average, headed by Cote d'Ivoire ($24), Ghana ($25), and Senegal ($22).

The spread, depth and severity of SSA rural poverty differ between countries. For all poverty measures Ghana ranks as the country with the least rural poverty (with a head-count ratio of 37%; a poverty-gap ratio of 8.5%; and a squared poverty-gap ratio of 2.7%). In terms of the spread of poverty, Zambia ranks as the country with the highest incidence of poverty (with about 77% of its rural population living below the poverty line). In terms of severity Guinea Bissau ranks as the country with the highest poverty (with a squared poverty-gap measure of about 32%).

Concerning urban poverty, it is also clear that poverty in urban SSA is fairly widespread with 47% of the urban population found to be living below an indicative poverty line of approximately $42 per month per person. Urban poverty is also found to be relatively deep, as reflected by a poverty-gap ratio of 18%, and moderately severe, as reflected by a squared poverty-gap ratio of about 10%. The average income of the poor amounted to only $26 per person per month.

The spread, depth and severity of SSA urban poverty differ between countries. Ghana again ranks as the country with the least urban poverty, with a headcount ratio of 34%, a poverty-gap ratio of about 10% and a squared poverty-gap ratio of about 4%. The highest incidence of urban poverty is recorded for Ethiopia with a headcount ratio of 65%.

At the national level the table shows that poverty in SSA is very widespread. About 57% of the population are found to be living below an overall (indicative) poverty line of about $30 per month per person (equivalent to the famous $1 per person per day) which is the weighted average of the sectoral poverty lines. Poverty is also found to be deep, as reflected by a poverty-gap ratio of about 24%, and severe, as reflected by a squared poverty-gap ratio of 14%. The average income of the poor amounted to only $18 per person per month (i.e. 60 cents per person per day).

For all poverty measures Ghana ranks as the country with the least poverty. In terms of the spread of poverty, Ethiopia ranks highest (with about 75% of its population living below the national poverty line). In terms of the depth and severity of poverty Guinea Bissau ranks worst.

Given the above results, and using information available on the population below 15 years of age we can estimate the incidence of poverty among African children. In a sense this is tantamount to defining a children head-count ratio as the number of children in poverty to the total number of children (say, H_C). Table 2 shows our results where we compare the children headcount ratio with the relevant headcount ratio in the population.

Table 2: African Children in Poverty: Children Headcount Ratio

B. Faso	69.67	71.79	45.95	50.60	65.40	68.72
CAR	75.44	78.52	49.63	50.02	65.74	67.33
C d'Ivoire	38.67	43.83	39.83	47.11	39.16	45.13
Djibouti	73.03	78.46	47.72	53.82	49.19	55.48
Ethiopia	76.91	79.89	65.01	71.03	75.11	78.73
Gambia	61.71	62.05	45.38	48.88	56.85	58.41
Ghana	37.08	42.93	34.35	41.74	36.22	42.61
Guinea	65.33	69.26	46.64	49.37	61.74	63.08
G. Bissau	73.00	74.14	54.44	53.24	67.42	67.55
Kenya	45.13	47.98	47.58	55.46	45.51	48.93
Madagascar	63.44	69.31	48.70	55.99	60.87	67.25
Mali	71.22	75.61	45.21	48.08	66.98	68.80

N						
Niger	62.25	64.33	40.27	42.12	58.72	60.57
Nigeria	51.43	51.43	37.77	36.23	46.18	45.58
Senegal	40.86	44.28	39.63	44.36	40.38	44.31
Swaziland	66.90	67.24	60.04	65.94	65.45	67.02
Tanzania	72.42	76.25	61.24	67.20	69.19	73.87
Uganda	57.78	62.89	48.22	54.98	56.60	61.98
Zambia	76.50	80.52	56.07	60.63	68.97	73.39
Average	61.09	64.36	47.42	51.70	56.75	60.08
(S.D.)	(13.61)	(13.42)	(8.58)	(9.43)	(11.99)	(11.52)

Source: own calculations.

From the above table, the average children headcount ratio at the national level is about 60 percent meaning that 60 percent of African children live in poverty. In the rural sector 64 percent of the children live in poverty compared to about 52 percent in urban areas. The distribution of countries with respect to the average children headcount ratio is worthy of observation. Twelve countries have a percentage of poor children above the mean; three of these record a percentage higher than 70% (Ethiopia, Tanzania and Zambia). Two countries have greater than half of the children as poor, but less than the mean; while six countries have a percentage of poor children in the range 40-50%. For both sectors—and the national level as well—the children headcount ratio is higher than the conventional headcount ratio. Overall the difference amounts to 3.3 percentage points for the rural sector, 4.3 percentage points for the urban sector and 3.3 percentage points for the national level. There is a higher proportion of children in poverty than poor people in general.

Reducing Poverty by Half by 2015

Given observation (f) made above on the calculation of the changes in poverty over time, we can look at the 'development duration' dimension of achieving the international development goal of reducing headcount poverty by half by 2015 where by poverty is meant the head-count ratio. In observation (f) we noted that changes in poverty over time can always be calculated as a product of the 'growth elasticity of poverty' and the rate of change in mean consumption. A direct calculation of the growth elasticity of the headcount ratio is possible if a Kuznets elasticity is available[2]. The remaining components of this elasticity include the elasticity of the headcount ratio with respect to mean consumption (which is provided by our estimates based on Povcal), the elasticity of the poverty line with respect to mean consumption (which is provided by our estimated equation of the poverty line) and the elasticity of the headcount ratio with respect to the Gini coefficient (which is available from our estimates based on Povcal). The only remaining elasticity is that of Kuznets and for the purpose at hand we follow Ali (1998) and use Sarel's (1997) estimate of the Kuznets curve[3].

Starting with 1998 as the base year, the international development goal requires the headcount ratio to decline by an annual rate of 4 per cent over the seventeen-year horizon. Thus the required rate of per capita consumption growth is given by [-0.04/ headcount growth elasticity] for each country. For a sample of 18 countries for which national consumption expenditure distribution data is reported in the World Bank (2000) World Development Report we have the required information. We use the growth rates of per capita consumption expenditure provided in the same source to arrive at per capita consumption for 1998 starting from the Summers and Heston 1988 base year. Table 3 reports our results on the required per capita growth rates and GDP growth rates to achieve the international development goal.

Table 3: Required Growth Rates to Achieve the International Development Goal and the Development Dimension of Poverty Reduction in SSA

	1998 Per Capita Expenditure ($$ PPP, annual)	Growth Elasticity	Required Per Capita Growth Rate (%)	Population Growth Rate (%) 1998-2015	Required GDP Growth Rate (%)	Actual GDP Growth Rate (%) 1999	Required Time (Years)
Burundi	294	-0.79	5.06	2.3	7.36	3.0	125
CAR	491	-0.30	13.33	1.9	15.23	5.0	74
C. d'Ivoire	623	-0.84	4.76	2.0	6.76	5.0	27
Ethiopia	216	-0.35	11.43	2.5	13.93	6.7	47
Ghana	636	-1.11	3.60	2.6	6.20	4.3	36
Guinea	356	-0.67	5.97	2.5	8.47	3.7	86
Kenya	569	-0.67	5.97	1.5	7.47	2.7*	86
Madagascar	347	-0.60	6.67	2.6	9.27	4.5	61
Mali	347	-0.44	9.09	2.6	11.69	5.0	65
Mauritania	668	-0.77	5.20	2.6	7.80	6.0	26
Mozambique	545	-0.81	4.94	1.7	6.64	7.8*	14
Niger	347	-0.46	8.70	3.0	11.70	4.5	100
Nigeria	474	-0.53	7.55	2.2	9.75	2.8*	261
Senegal	721	-0.77	5.20	2.5	7.70	6.5	22
Tanzania	232	-0.48	8.33	2.3	10.63	4.4	68
Uganda	422	-0.76	5.26	3.1	8.36	6.0	31
Zambia	313	-0.47	8.51	2.2	10.71	3.5*	113
Zimbabwe	673	-0.35	11.43	1.0	12.43	3.5*	79
Average	460	-0.62	7.28	2.3	9.56	4.7	73

Source: own calculations. Population growth rates are from UNDP (2000). Actual GDP growth rates are from ECA (2000). A * means the higher of 1998 or 1999 growth rates or an average of the two years.

The table shows that for the SSA sample of countries the reduction of poverty by half in a 17 year horizon an average annual per capita growth rate of 7 per cent is required. This, we suggest, is a very high growth requirement not only for SSA but in general. The required growth rates vary between the countries of the sample from low, and possibly reasonable, rates to very high and impossible ones to sustain. Achievable per capita growth rates are recorded for Ghana, Cote d'Ivoire, Burundi, Mozambique, Mauritania, Senegal, and Uganda. Extremely high per capita growth rates are required for CAR, Ethiopia, Zimbabwe and Mali. Taking into account projected population growth rates for the period 1998-2015 as reported in UNDP (2000) we get a confirmation for these required high growth rates for GDP. Overall an average GDP growth rate of nearly 10 per cent is required. Except for a few countries sustaining a GPD growth rate of this magnitude seems to be unrealistic. Achievable GDP growth rates of less than 8 per cent are required for Ghana, Cote d'Ivoire, Burundi, Mozambique, Senegal and Mauritania. High GDP growth rates in excess of 11 per cent are required for CAR, Ethiopia, Mali, Niger, and Zimbabwe. Comparing these GDP growth rates with the most recent record of growth in the countries of the sample with an average of about 5%, it becomes clear that indeed there is serious doubt of the feasibility of achieving the IDG for almost all of the countries of the sample. Indeed the table shows that the only country that has recently recorded a growth rate in excess of that required is Mozambique. Senegal, if it is able to improve its performance marginally, can attain the objective in 22 years.

Given the above results, the 'development duration' dimension of achieving the international development goal of reducing poverty by half in 17 years is obvious. The table shows our calculations for the time required to reduce poverty in half given the nature of poverty in the continent (determining the growth elasticity of the headcount ratio) and the structure of the economies (determining per capita growth rates). For the sample as a whole an average duration of 73 years is required, about four times the horizon for the IDG. The only country likely to attain the objective within the time horizon is Mozambique, while Cote d'Ivoire, Mauritania and Uganda could achieve the target in less than double the international time horizon.

Very long time horizons are required for the rest of the countries in the sample. The longest duration of 261 years is recorded for Nigeria (an oil country in the habit of recording negative per capita GDP growth), followed by 125 years for Burundi (a civil conflict country), 113 years for Zambia and 100 years for Niger. The rest of the countries of the sample require time horizons that range from 36 years on the low side to 86 years on the high side.

Policy and Children in Poverty

The impact of macroeconomic policy on children in poverty has been debated since UNICEF's incisive critique of adjustment policies (see Cornia et al. 1986). In the context of Africa the two sides to the debate were the donor community (represented in large measure by the World Bank, and to a lesser extent the IMF) and the Africans (supported by the UN system including UNICEF). The donor community argued from the position that 'policies that enhance growth must be poverty reducing, and reform policies are supposed to be growth enhancing'.

Perhaps due to the influence of UNICEF's critique of the first generation adjustment policies, a huge research programme on poverty has developed within the World Bank. This massive research output, which included theoretical contributions, model simulations and empirical studies, seems to have been directed at establishing the result that 'adjustment programmes' did not hurt the poor in Africa and that 'more adjustment rather than less adjustment' is needed for poverty reduction. Such an orientation, notwithstanding the rigor and the quality of its outputs, betrays an amazing ideological commitment to the economic reform programmes and an amazing insensitivity to the realities of the African case.

A sample of the arguments presented on behalf of the donors can be found in the World Bank (1990), 'World Development Report 1999: Poverty'; World Bank (1994), 'Adjustment in Africa: Reforms, Results and the Road Ahead'; World Bank (1995), 'Taking Action for Poverty Reduction in Sub-Saharan Africa'; and, Demery and Squire (1996), 'Macroeconomic Adjustment and Poverty in Africa: An Emerging Picture'. At the time of its publication the Demery and Squire piece was hailed as the last word on the subject upholding the position of the donor community. The authors declare that their objective was to provide 'the most convincing evidence to date that economic reform is consistent with a decline in overall poverty and that failure to reform is associated with increased poverty', and describe their analysis as 'solidly grounded' due to the recent availability of data from household sample surveys for six SSA countries at two points in time. Even earlier contributions, which used to be quoted by the World Bank in support of its contention that 'adjustment did not hurt the poor', are described by the authors as having been theoretical, or having used indirect evidence based on modelling exercises, or having relied on anecdotal evidence. Of the six countries considered only Cote d'Ivoire recorded a deterioration in economic policy with a corresponding increase in the head-count ratio. For Ethiopia, Ghana, Kenya, Nigeria and Tanzania policy improvements were associated with a decline in the head-count ratio. Thus, the authors conclude that their results present 'the most compelling evidence to date that improvements in the macroeconomic policy regime of the kind usually associated with World Bank and IMF-supported adjustment programs are consistent with a decline in the incidence of poverty overall. These results do not establish causality, but, at least in the six countries for which we have evidence, we can conclude that failure to implement an adjustment program has been doubly harmful to the poor'.

Like the World Bank and others the Africans were also constrained by the lack of data. They argued from their positions as participant observers in their countries, if not as victims of the impact of economic reforms on poverty. As one of their tools of analysis is the observed demise of the middle class, which comprised, among other groups, most of the civil service including the so-called African decision makers. In the economic reform literature all of these social groups came to be lumped together under the 'vested interests' that resisted the implementation of the reform policies. Some of them were identified as the 'rent seekers' who are distorting the allocation of scarce resources and hence causing the observed inefficiency of the African economies. But arguing from a participant observer position has recently gained respectability thanks largely to Professor Robert Chambers of Sussex University. Nowadays, participatory poverty assessment has become widely used even by the World Bank.

In this respect it is perhaps important to note that the adjustment policies implemented in Africa have been reviewed, from an African perspective, by Mkandawire and Soludo (1999). Three issues relevant to economic policy making that are highlighted by the review, and that need to be noted, deal with the ownership of policymaking processes, the capacity of Africans to make policy decisions, and the civil service reform component of adjustment policies.

Concerning the ownership of the policies, the authors note that 'the tragedy of Africa's policy making and policy implementation in the last several years is the complete surrender of national policies to ever-changing ideas of international experts.... The first attempts that Africans made at articulating a framework for their development were in the Lagos Plan of Action and the UNECA African Alternative Framework to Structural Adjustment... Most African governments signed the documents, and to date, none of these governments has publicly dissociated itself from the ideas espoused in them. But the World Bank virulently attacked the documents, and every African government that wished to have successful debt rescheduling or aid negotiations distanced itself from the principles in them' (Mkandawire and Soludo 1999:138). The point being made is the difference between the rhetoric and reality of the donor community when dealing with Africa.

Turning to the capacity of Africans, the authors note that one of the most disturbing outcomes of the adjustment period in Africa is the negative impact it had on the African capacity for doing things: thinking about the future, designing and implementing various policies to resolve conflicts or reduce poverty. The authors provide a very sensitive articulation of this problem in terms of a query and a joke and we believe that both are worth noting. The query posed by the authors is that 'much of the so-called lack of capacity in Africa is donor imposed. How can capacity develop when much of the financial aid is tied to technical assistance, which ensures that much of the money goes to pay for foreign advisors who have turned Africa into laboratories for testing their pet theories about development?' The joke, noted by the authors, is that somebody observed that 'there will soon be more foreign experts in Africa than there are Africans for them to advise' (1999: 111). We note in passing that while the joke is apt the consequences were tragic.

Turning to economic governance, the authors address the issue of civil service reforms initiated in the continent. In this respect it is noted that under adjustment programmes all economic ills were attributed to the 'poor policies' of the past and 'public servants were severely ridiculed for incompetence, lack of capacity, and proclivity for rent-seeking activities... The result, if anything, has been further demoralization and disillusionment. How anybody expected the remaining civil servants to be committed to implementing policies mostly designed in Washington beats the imagination' (1999:135).

Be the above as it may, we note that the African position is very simple. Granted that growth-enhancing policies will be expected to reduce poverty, the question that remains is: did the economic reform measures implemented in the continent enhance growth? The evidence does not support the contention of the donor community that economic reforms did not negatively affect the poor. Using the relationship between the rate of poverty reduction and the growth of per capita GDP, noted above, we can easily reflect on what did the economic reform process do for poverty in the continent basing ourselves on Rodrik's (1999) results[4].

For a sample of 32 African countries for which data was available for the period 1960-1973 Rodrik shows that the average growth rate of per capita income was 1.88% per annum. Thus, it is clear that the post-independence period witnessed a respectable reduction in poverty. This is not surprising given the struggle for independence and its political and socio-economic agenda. Only 7 countries in this sample recorded negative per capita growth rates and as such suffered from increased poverty. For the period 1973-1984 the sample included 37 countries. The average per capita growth rate declined to only 0.31% per annum. Thus, during this period poverty in the region continued to decline but at lower rates. The number of countries recording negative per capita growth rates increased to 17. For the adjustment period of 1984-1994 the sample included 40 countries. The average per capita growth declined to –0.31. Thus, during this period poverty started to increase in the region. The number of countries registering negative per capita growth increased to 21. Since the 1984-1994 decade corresponds to the economic reform period, then clearly adjustment 'did not help the poor' at this highly aggregative level of analysis.

As is well known, however, ordinary Africans, going about their daily lives of eking a living, have repeatedly expressed their views on the relationship between economic reforms and poverty. These are clear in the IMF demonstrations and riots. These African demonstrations have recently moved, perhaps due to globalization, to the seat of the Bretton Woods Institutions, (Washington, DC) and wherever the joint annual meetings are held.

Children and Conflicts

The highest form of conflict is civil war, defined in terms of the level of violence utilized by the parties (Collier (1998), Collier and Hoeffler (1998)). A recent compilation of civil wars finds that SSA has suffered 36 civil wars involving 20 countries (table 4).

Table 4: Civil Wars in SSA: 1960-2000

	Number of Wars	Total Duration (years)	Average Duration (years)	Total Population (million)	Share of Regional Population
Central	4	34.0	8.5	13.6	45.3
Eastern	20	105.0	5.3	220.7	80.8
Southern	6	69.5	11.6	52.7	74.1
West	6	26.0	4.3	144.9	61.8
SSA	36	234.5	6.5	431.9	71.0

The average duration of these wars was about 6.5 years, ranging from 2 years for the CAR conflict (1995-1997), to 24 years for the war in Namibia (1965-1989). The total population of the countries that experienced a civil war amounts to 431.9 million representing 71% of the population of SSA (excluding South Africa). By region, the share of population of countries in conflict varies from a low of 45.3% in the central region to a high of 81% in the eastern region.

The major characteristics of African civil wars as compared to those in other regions of the world have been identified by Elbadawi and Sambanis (2000-a). The study looked at the mean number of 5-year periods during which a war took place plus information on mean war duration, war-related deaths, democracy level and ethnic heterogeneity. On the basis of such information it is shown that (a) Africa has the highest incidence of civil wars among world regions; (b) the incidence of war has increased in Africa in the last two decades while it has fallen or remained constant in other regions; (c) African wars tend to be relatively short in duration but relatively intense in terms of casualties per unit of time (even excluding civilian war-related deaths and other loss of life caused by the fallout of war).

In a related work, Elbadawi and Sambanis (2000-b) estimated the likelihood of observing a civil war during any 5-year period during the period 1960-1998 for a sample of 161 countries. The likelihood of a civil war incidence is defined as the sum of two distinct probabilities, the probability that a civil war is initiated at a point in time and the probability that it is on-going at the following point in time, having already been initiated. The explanatory variables used included per capita real GDP (to proxy the opportunity cost of rebel labour), openness of political institutions, ethnic diversity, religious diversity, natural resource dependence, and population size. All of these variables were found to be significant at better than the 10% level of significance. The authors then used the estimated coefficients from the global sample (for the period 1960-1998) to estimate the probability of civil wars for the median country in the various regions of the world. Except for Asia (with a fairly high probability of 0.56) they find that SSA has the highest probability of civil wars among the remaining region of 0.1119. This compares with probabilities of 0.0046 for Europe and North America, 0.0205 for the Middle East and North Africa and 0.0048 for Latin America and the Caribbean. Using the estimated function for the period 1980-1998 the Sub-Saharan African probability increases to 0.155 while those for other regions decline or remains constant.

The Cost of Conflicts

The cost of civil wars can be looked at in terms of growth performance. Collier (1999, 1998) identifies five effects of a civil war: destruction of capital, disruption of transactions, diversion of public expenditure, encouragement of dissaving, and diversion of portfolios. 'Three of these effects, destruction, dissaving and portfolio diversion, reduce the domestic capital stock, and two of them, disruption and expenditure diversion, raise the costs of economic activity, especially transaction costs... in the aggregate the effect will be on the growth rate rather than being a one-off reduction in the level of output' (Collier 1998:21-22).

Collier (1999) quantified the effects of civil war on GDP growth both during the duration of war and during the five post-war years. The framework used is one of growth regressions where the dependent variable is the decade average per capita GDP growth rate of each country over the period 1960-1989. The source of the growth rates is Penn World Tables data base. The sample used included 92 countries of which 19 had civil wars. Civil war is incorporated in the analysis by three explanatory variables: the number of months of warfare during the decade that is designed to measure the concurrent effects of war (a variable called war-months); the number of months during the decade which fall in the first five years following the war (a variable called post-war months); and the product of the two (a variable called the legacy of war). The legacy of war is an interaction variable between the post war period and the total length of the previous war. It is expected that if there is a peace dividend irrespective of the duration of the war, then the variable 'post-war' months will be positive and significant whereas the variable 'legacy of war' will be insignificant. 'If, however, the duration of the war determines whether there is a peace dividend or a war overhang, then 'post-war' will be negative and significant and 'legacy' will be positive and significant. There will then be some critical duration of warfare below which peace yields a war overhang instead of a dividend' (Collier 1999: 174).

Structural explanatory variables included 'dummies for all three decades', initial 'level of schooling and the level of per capita income', and 'ethno-linguistic fractionalization and landlocked'. Policy variables were not included in the analysis 'because some of the effects of civil war work through policies'. This adjustment is in view of the fact that the duration of the war is measured in months while the dependent variable is the average rate of growth during the decade. Thus, according to the results during 'civil war the annual growth rate is reduced by 2.2%. During the five years following a war which only lasted one year, the growth rate would be 2.1% lower than had the war not happened. By contrast, after 15-year war the post-war growth rate is enhanced by 5.9% per annum' (Collier 1999: 176).[5]

Table 5 reports a summary of our calculations of the cost of civil wars, using per capita 1985 PPP dollars for each country after applying Collier's results noted above. We calculate the cost for 18 out of the 20 countries in Sambanis' (2000) sample: Djibouti and Liberia are excluded because some relevant information is not available. Our estimates provide rough orders of magnitude that help appreciate the implied cost of war. Table 5 summarizes the population-weighted per capita cost of civil war for each region and for Africa. According to our estimates civil wars have caused the continent to incur a cumulative per capita cost of $452 by the end of 1999. This means that had there been no wars we would have expected per capita income in conflict countries to have been $452 more than was observed in 1999.

Table 5: Per Capita Real Cost of Conflict in Africa ($ in 1985 PPP)

	Number of Countries	Region's Population Weight (%)	Observed Per Capita GDP 1999 ($)	No War GDP Per Capita in 1999 ($)	Per Capita Cost of War in 1999 ($)
Central Africa	3	3.23	861	1221	360
Eastern Africa	8	52.23	589	955	366
Southern Africa	4	10.80	878	1300	422
West Africa	3	33.74	1046	1650	604
Sub-Saharan Africa	18	100.00	783	1235	452

As the table shows the per capita cost of civil wars varies across regions. Country details show wide variation in the cost of civil wars from $4,022 for Namibia followed by Sudan ($1,039) and Nigeria ($667); to relatively low cost of $27 for CAR followed by Sierra Leone ($125) and Mali ($133).

To appreciate this further, we can examine the ratio of the costs to the observed per capita GDP at the end of the period. In terms of lost GDP due to civil wars the cost works out as 42% of GDP for Central Africa, 62% for Eastern Africa, 48% for Southern Africa and 58% for West Africa. These are very high costs to pay in terms of lost development opportunities. More dramatic details at the country level can be calculated: the cost of civil wars varies from a high of 176% of GDP in Ethiopia to a low of 12% in CAR. Costs exceeding 100% of GDP can be calculated for Sudan (113%) and Chad (103%). Other high cost countries include Namibia (90%), Burundi (87%), Angola (74%), Congo Democratic Republic (69%) and Nigeria (60%). At the other end, low cost countries include Zimbabwe (14% of GDP) and Congo Republic (19%).

Lost development opportunities are a major loss to children, current as well as future ones. In 1999 the number of children under 15 years of age affected by these lost development opportunities total about 211 million. Using our estimates of children in poverty, about 127 million children who were negatively impacted by civil war were already in poverty in 1999.

Given these lost development opportunities one possible question to pose from a 'duration of development framework' is 'by how much does per capita income in these countries need to grow if they are to recoup the loss, say in the time frame agreed upon for the achievement of the IDG?' To answer the question all we need to do is to calculate the required rate of growth to raise the observed 1999 per capita income to that which would have obtained had there been no war within a period of 14 years (using 2001 as the base). Our calculations show that for the sample of 18 countries an average per capita growth rate of 3.48% (with a standard deviation of 3.08 percentage points) would be required to recoup the lost development opportunities. This rate, needless to note, is much lower than that required to reduce poverty by half by the year 2015, so that by recouping the lost development opportunities the countries involved would not be meeting the international development goal. Our calculations also show that this required rate varies from a low of 0.78% for CAR to a high of 14.27% for Burundi.

Alternatively, we can ask the question of how long would it take a country to recoup the development loss if it were able to grow at the best-recorded decadal rate of per capita growth during the past four decades. Using the information on decadal growth rates, and excluding Burundi, Sudan and Zimbabwe, for which the best-recorded rates of growth were very low to result in exceedingly long durations for recovery, our calculations show that on average a period of about 14.6 years (with a standard deviation of 10 years) would be required. The duration varies among countries from relatively long durations of 38 years for Kenya, 31 years for Ethiopia and 23 years for Angola, to reasonably short ones of 5 years for Congo Republic and Nigeria, 6 years for Sierra Leone, and 7 years for Mali.

The above illustrative calculations confirm that there is an important 'duration of development' dimension that needs to be taken into account when thinking about initiatives relevant to children in countries in conflict, or countries that were successful in exiting from a civil war. According to the source we used for the compilation of our data on civil wars in the continent these 20 civil war countries are home to about 69% of the children in SSA (excluding the Republic of South Africa).

Children and Institutions

Economic historians such as Landes (1998) have investigated the causes of the wealth and poverty of nations. Alongside environmental and geographic factors, institutional and technological factors are found to be crucial. These have evolved over long periods of time, reflecting deeply-embedded value systems and social behaviour. Some of the core concepts of institutional development are reflected in the currently-popular notion of 'good governance.'

Key elements of capable institutions include promoting knowledge of how to operate, manage and build institutions of production and to create, adapt, and master new techniques on the technological frontier. In turn, these skills need to be imparted to the young. Institutions should afford opportunities for individual and collective enterprise. It is important to secure rights of private property and personal liberty; enforce rights of contract and provide a stable, responsive, honest, moderate, efficient and ungreedy government. Social structures should encourage geographical and social mobility and promote innovation, and tend towards an even distribution of income and wealth.

Empirical findings on the role of institutions in explaining the relative development performance of countries confirm the historical evidence. The major difference between the various analyses focuses on defining the institutional variable to be used in the regression analysis and in the sophistication used in running the regression where an indicator of economic performance is specified as a dependent variable. The most important recent contribution in this respect is that of Hall and Jones (1999: 97) who define a measure of social infrastructure that quantifies the wedge between the private return to productive activities and social returns to such activities[6]. 'A good social infrastructure ensures that these returns are kept closely in line across the range of activities in the economy'. They form a composite measure of social infrastructure that takes into account government anti-diversion policies and openness to trade. Hall and Jones (1999: 107) conclude that 'our results indicate that differences in social infrastructure account for much of the difference in long-run economic performance throughout the world, as measured by output per worker'.

The Political Environment

The political environment inherited by African children for the 21st century can be looked at in terms of a political freedom indicator produced by Freedom House. This is a composite indicator composed of two measures of political rights and civil liberties. These measures are scored on a scale ranging from unity (for free status) to 7 (for not free status). The composite indicator is the average of the two scores. The political rights component measures the extent to which a government is chosen by means of free and fair elections of representatives of the people. The civil liberties component measures the extent of freedom from government oppression. Freedom indicators have been compiled since the early 1970s.

Adopting ECA's sub-regional classification of countries with the slight modification of including Sudan in the East Africa sub-region and Mauritania in the West Africa sub-region, and excluding South Africa, table 6 below summarizes the state of freedom over the period 1972-1999 where figures between brackets are population weights.

Table 6: Political Freedom in Africa: Composite Index of Freedom

Sub-Region	1972 -1979	1980 –1989	1990 -1999	1998 -1999
Central (4.9)	6.1	6.4	4.8	4.8
East (44.9)	5.5	5.9	5.5	5.2
Southern (11.7)	4.8	4.8	3.9	3.2
West (38.5)	5.5	5.5	4.6	4.3
SS Africa	5.5	5.7	4.7	4.4

As is clear from the table in the 1970s and 1980s about 88.3% of the total population of SSA were living under conditions classified as 'not free'. The 1990s witnesses a marked improvement in the freedom status of Africans where the percentage of those living under 'partly free' regimes has increased to 55.1%. Only the Eastern Africa sub-region remained 'not free'. The last year of the 1990s confirms this improvement in the political environment across regions.

As usual, this aggregative picture hides a lot of variation between countries. Thus, for example, in 1998-1999, five countries were ranked as 'free': Sao Tome and Prinicipe, Botswana, Benin, Cape Verde, and Mauritius. These account for only 1.5% of the population of the region. Malawi and Namibia (each with a score of 2.5) are marginal cases of a 'free' status. At the other extreme, Somalia, Sudan and Equatorial Guinea each scored 7 ranking as the worst non-free political environment. Close behind them with a score of 6.5 are Burundi, Rwanda and the Congo Democratic Republic. With a score of 6 are Angola, Niger, Gambia, Cameroon and the Congo. These 11 countries account for about 24% of the population of the region.

Institutional Structure

As noted earlier a vast empirical literature linking the institutional structure to economic and development performance has developed over the past few years. The most commonly used indicators of the institutional structure of countries are the ones produced by the Political Risk Services group. In addition to this, Kaufmann, Kraay and Zoido-Lobaton (1999) identified an additional 12 sources from which institutional indicators can be constructed. Kaufmann, Kraay and Zoido-Lobaton (1999: 1) looked at the role of the institutional structure from a governance perspective where they identified six governance clusters where governance is defined as 'the traditions and institutions by which authority in a country is exercised. This includes (1) the process by which governments are selected, monitored and replaced, (2) the capacity of government to effectively formulate and implement sound policies, and (3) the respect of citizens and the state for the institutions that govern economic and social interactions among them'. The clusters include 'voice and accountability' and 'political instability and violence', to account for the process; 'government effectiveness' and 'regulatory burden', to account for the capacity of the government; 'rule of law' and 'graft', to account for the respect of institutions.

Using a standardization procedure the governance indicators are presented in such a way that each would have a mean of zero, a standard deviation of one and range from –2.5 to 2.5. Moreover, the indicators are oriented such that higher values correspond to better governance outcomes. In what follows use is made of the four sub-indicators related to government capacity and respect for institutions to look at the African institutional structure. Given the standardized choice of units used by Kaufmann et al. (2000), and assuming equal weights for the sub-indicators, the average of the indicators is used as a composite indicator of institutional quality. Table 7 summarizes the results.

Table 7: Governance Indicators of Institutional Structure in SSA: 1998

Region	Government Effectiveness (36)	Regulatory Burden (41)	Rule of Law (41)	Graft (35)	Average
Central	-0.763	-0.716	-1.019	-0.826	-0.831
Eastern	-0.905	-0.680	-0.813	-0.821	-0.805
Southern	-0.435	-0.014	-0.062	-0.141	-0.163
Western	-0.342	-0.504	-0.593	-0.508	-0.487
SSA	-0.611	-0.479	-0.622	-0.574	-0.572
Maximum	0.221	0.570	1.279	0.535	0.501
Minimum	-1.769	-2.340	-2.153	-1.567	-1.955

Source: based on Kaufmann et al (2000) data files. Figures between brackets are the number of countries for which the indicator is reported.

Given the methodology of constructing these indicators the table shows that for all indicators all regions have institutional structures of below average quality. The indicated numbers measure the distance from the average quality in terms of standard deviations. The ranking of the regions, in terms of the overall composite measure, is such that the best performing region is Southern Africa while the worst is central Africa. Botswana enjoys the best quality institutions in terms of government effectiveness and regulatory (with respective scores of 0.221 and 0.572 above the mean) while Congo Democratic Republic suffers from the lowest quality institutions in these two area (with respective scores of 1.769 and 2.34 below the mean). Mauritius ranks as the country with the highest quality institutions in terms of the rule of law.

For the purposes of looking at the development duration aspect of institutions use can be made of the Political Risk Services time series information. The PRS group publishes, and sells, the International Country Risk Guide (ICRG) that provides assessments of political, economic and financial risks for a number of countries around the world. Three major risk categories are reported: political, financial and economic. The scoring methodology adopted involves assigning risk points to each component including government stability, socioeconomic conditions, investment profile, internal conflict, external conflict, corruption, military in politics, religion in politics, law and order, ethnic tensions, democratic accountability and bureaucracy quality. The lower the risk points the higher is the risk: 0-50% of total points is very high risk, 51-60% is high risk, through to very low risk in the range 81-100%.

In what follows, use is made of the three categories of 'law and order', 'bureaucratic quality' and 'corruption' to look at the duration of change in institutional structure facing African children. The three categories are combined into a composite indicator with weights of 0.375 for each of the 'rule of law' and 'corruption' and a weight of 0.25 for the 'bureaucratic quality'. Further, the composite indicator is rescaled on a zero to ten basis and countries are ranked such that those scoring less than 5 are considered as having very low quality institutional structure while those scoring more than 8 are ranked as having a high quality institutional structure. Table 8 summarizes these results.

Table 8: Institutional Structure in SSA: 1984-2000

Region	1984-1989	1990-1999	2000
Central Africa	4.33	4.41	3.74
Eastern Africa	3.98	3.83	3.76
Southern Africa	4.38	5.13	4.74
West Africa	4.24	4.18	3.81
SS Africa	4.23	4.39	4.01

The table makes it clear that at the beginning of the 21st century the continent continues to harbour an institutional structure of very low quality. Indeed since 1984 the quality of institutions shows an overall deterioration for all sub-regions. However, a slight improvement is recorded for the period 1990-99 over that of 1984-89, focused on Southern Africa. If we consider such improvement as having been achieved in ten years, then this would imply an annual rate of improvement of 0.37 percent. With such low rates of improvements it will take the continent about 162 years to reach the lower limit of high quality institutions (i.e. a composite score of 8). This time dimension of the development process is an important consideration for the children of the continent.

Concluding Remarks

In agreement with UNICEF's approach to the major challenges that face Africa's children, namely poverty, conflict and institutions, this chapter has argued that given the initial conditions of the continent a 'duration of development' framework needs to be invoked to inform planned future initiatives to help African children.

The most pressing of the initial conditions is poverty. With 69% of Africa's population living in rural areas, rural poverty is widespread, deep and severe. About 61% of rural Africans live below a real poverty line of about $25 per person per month. The average income of the poor, summarizing the depth of poverty, amounts to only $15 per person per month (a mere 50 cents per person per day). The rural children headcount ratio, giving the percentage of children who are in poverty out of all children, is estimated as 64%. Urban poverty is also fairly widespread with 47% of the urban population living below a real poverty line of $42 per person per month. The average income of the urban poor is $26 per person per month. The urban children headcount ratio shows that about 52% of urban children are poor. Thus, at the national level poverty is also widespread and deep. About

57% of the African population is living below a real poverty line of about $30 per person per month (the famous $1 a day per person) with a mean income of the poor of about $18 per month only. The national headcount ratio for children shows that 60% of the children of the continent are in poverty—a higher proportion than the overall national poverty figure.

For a number of reasons, the continent is replete with civil wars and conflicts. About 70% of the population of SSA were involved in such conflicts between 1960-1999. We have shown that the cost of these conflicts has been a huge loss of 2 percentage points in annual per capita growth rates. The cumulative cost by the end of 1999 amounted to about 58% of GDP.

The 'duration dimension' of reducing poverty in the continent amounts to an impossible proposition in terms of achieving the International Development Goal of reducing poverty by half by the year 2015. In terms of per capita growth rates it requires an average rate of 7% per annum in a sustained fashion or—accounting for 3% population growth—an average GDP growth rate of 10%. In terms of duration, given the nature of mass poverty and the structure of the economies, an average of 73 years is required, nearly two generations.

The institutional structure of the continent, which defines the environment in which children rights are to be upheld, is characterized by a 'partly free' political environment and very low quality institutions. Given past performance, it will take the continent about 162 years (about five generations) to put in place an institutional structure of an acceptable quality.

Major progress in a reasonable time horizon, however, needs a new development orientation, if not a paradigm. An attempt at developing such orientation is to be found in the World Bank (2000b) collaborative report with a number of organizations concerned with the development prospects of the continent[7]. This attempt adopted a cumulative causation approach to development where four interlocking circles have been identified such that 'success in one element will make it easier to improve other elements. But Africa will not be able to claim the 21st century without progress in all four circles'. The circles, not very different from UNICEF's priority areas, are 'improving governance and resolving conflicts', 'investing in people', 'increasing competitiveness and diversifying economies' and 'reducing dependence and debt and strengthening partnership with the world community'. The report proposes a sensible set of development policies that can be accepted, adopted and owned by African governments and as such can be used as a new orientation for relevant development policies. However, given the developmental nature of the four circles, a major limitation of the report is that it does not identify sources of funds required to achieve progress under any of the circles.

Thus, we conclude that the 'duration of development' dimension for UNICEF's three priority areas is much longer than achieving 'major progress in one generation'. It is on the basis of this that UNICEF's major proposition on what can be achieved in one generation can be taken as unrealistic in the context of Africa, unless there is a truly dramatic change in the approach to aid and trade by the OECD countries. Indeed, reading the evidence on the continent correctly would suggest a need for establishing special institutions to cater for Africa including perhaps a special UN Children's Fund for Africa and a Global Fund for the Development of Africa.

1. One can allow for the changes in the distribution of income by estimating the Kuznets elasticity (e.g. the elasticity of the Gini coefficient with respect to per capita income), or simply by assuming that the distribution of income will remain the same! For a recent estimate of the Kuznets curve see, for example, Ali and Elbadawi (1999) and Barro (2000).

2. It can be shown that the headcount growth elasticity of poverty (say, h) is equal to: the elasticity of the headcount ratio with respect to mean consumption (say, p) multiplied by one minus the elasticity of

the poverty line with respect to mean consumption (say, (1 – e)) plus the product of the elasticity of the headcount ratio with respect to the Gini coefficient (say, m) and the Kuznets elasticity for the Gini coefficient (say, k). Thus, in notation, we have h = [p. (1 – e) + km]. Note that p is usually negative, while m is positive and e is positive but less than unity. The sign of k depends on which side of the Kuznets curve a country is, where at low levels of development k is positive.

3. The Kuznets elasticity based on Sarel (1997) is given by k = {-0.00145y+1940/y}/G, where y is the annual per capita income in 1985 PPP and where G is the Gini coefficient.

4. Results similar to those of Rodrik's are reported by O'Connel and Ndulu (2000).

5. The relevant ordinary least squares results, with heteroscedasticity-consistent standard errors, are reproduced below using our notation where A is a vector of other variables and b is the appropriate vector of their coefficients and where figures between brackets are the t-ratios (and the adjusted R-squared is 0.42) :

   DECPCGR = b A - 0.00018 WARMON – 0.00022 POSTWAR + 0.000004 LEGACY
   (-4.43) (-2.11) (2.25)

   To calculate the effect of the civil war on the annual rate of growth note that the coefficient on WARMON needs to be multiplied by 120.]

6. For the importance of Institutions in development see Rodrik (2000 and 1999-b).

7. The other collaborators include the African Development Bank, the African Economic Research Consortium, the Global Coalition for Africa and the Economic Commission for Africa.

4

Providing Education for Young Africans

JESSICA BRIDGES-PALMER

Educational achievement is one of the foundations of economic development. Comparative historical studies indicate that the transition to an educated populace precedes the transition to a healthy and more slowly growing population (Taylor et al. 1997). Meanwhile, international competitiveness in manufacturing and services in the coming decades requires an increasing level of educational achievement. It is those countries that have the highest level of secondary and tertiary education that will be best placed to take advantage of the changes in the global economy. The market for unskilled labour is dwindling on a global scale, as the unskilled jobs that had a niche in high-technology industries just one or two decades ago are increasingly replaced by mechanisation. The UN-sponsored 'World Conference on Education for All' held in Jomtien, Thailand, in 1990, reaffirmed the global commitment to universal, free, primary education, first stated in the 1966 International Covenant on Economic, Social and Cultural Rights. Even before that, the 1961 Conference of African States on the Development of

Education had aimed to achieve universal enrolment and thus eliminate inequality in primary education by 1980.

In the decade since the inception of the notably unconditional right to primary education laid out in Article 28 of the Convention on the Rights of the Child, there have been no less than 16 world conferences that had education as a sole or significant issue, culminating in the Dakar Forum of 2000 to review the progress of the global goals for education. In sub-Saharan Africa, the story is of a discouraging dichotomy between the laudable aims repeatedly agreed by the international community and the progress achieved by governments and international organisations. Yet, the stated goals are highly achievable. In order to reach the *global* Jomtien targets, the World Bank and IMF have estimated that an additional $8 billion per year would have to be spent across the world. This is by no means a vast sum: about 0.02% of global GDP, or about four days worth of global military spending. Its very achievability points to the lack of will in the governments of the developed and developing nations alike.

Education in Sub-Saharan Africa

A look at any of the figures regarding enrolment in education, dropout rates, gender ratios and affordability indicates that the crisis in education in developing countries in general is most severe in sub-Saharan Africa. A alone in the developing world, the region is not on course to reach the Jomtien targets for 2015. Currently, sub-Saharan Africa has an estimated 45 million of the 125 million children aged 6-11 out of school in the world, fully 40% of the school-age population (in South Asia, the next worst area, this figure is 20%). Region-wide statistics obscure the progress made by some nations, but also the deterioration in others. Uganda and Malawi have shown marked improvements in enrolment rates, others, including Mozambique, Tanzania, Nigeria, Ethiopia and Zambia, have experienced a net decline in the 1990s. The conflict-ridden nations of Sudan, Rwanda,

Somalia and Liberia have experienced either stagnation or declines in enrolment. Overall, by the 2015 deadline, if current trends continue, Africa will have a further 9 million children out of school, and three out of every four children out of school in the world will be African.

Simply getting children into school does not begin to address the problem—the average completion rate for four years of primary school is only 63%. In the worst-performing countries in Africa, such as Mozambique, fewer than half those who enrol in Grade 1 complete Grade 5. Furthermore, girls are both less likely to enrol, and less likely to complete the basic four years of primary education. Between one and two fifths of the entire education budget is spent on children who do not remain in the education system long enough to become literate.

In Ethiopia, with one of the worst enrolment rates anywhere in the world, one third of boys start school, compared with just one tenth of girls, and a quarter drop out in the first two years. Across Africa, average girls' enrolment stands at about 83% of boys'. The gender gap has narrowed since 1985, albeit far too slowly to approximate the Jomtien targets, and this improvement is unfortunately fuelled more by a relative decline in boys enrolment than an improvement in girls'. Female literacy rates remain very poor at less than 30% in many countries and at 50% overall (compared to 66% of men). As is well documented, educating girls has a profound effect on reducing infant mortality and morbidity.

Dropping out is affected by the costs of schooling, the poor quality of education that leads children to repeat years, increasing costs and class sizes, and the fact that poverty forces all members of the family to engage in income generating activities to pay for children's education. Underpaid or corrupt teachers may impose private tariffs on students for passing grades. Education reform requires that teachers are paid enough—and paid. African teachers' salaries are about five times average per capita income, compared with twice the average in Asia, but Africa's poverty means that this is a very low sum. Gender is also an issue here: many girls are withdrawn once they reach puberty. One study in Kenya found not only that enrolment levels were lower for girls, but that they did not enrol in the sciences, maths or vocational training (Mannathoko, 1999).

In this context, the HIV/AIDS epidemic has a regional impact both on the numbers of teachers available (and the constantly renewed expense of training them) and concurrently on the ability of households to survive without the labour of their children, either as income-earners or as carers. Many countries are losing teachers to AIDS more rapidly than they can train their replacements. Zambia is thought to have lost 1,000 teachers to the illness in 1999 alone.

Investing in People

Africa under-invests in education (Sachs 2001). As a proportion of GDP, Africa spends comparable amounts to other developing regions—around 5%. But with a per capita GDP so much lower than elsewhere, and teachers' salaries higher than average because of the shortage of skilled labour, 5% of GDP simply delivers far less than is required (Mehotra and Vandermoortele 1997). Because of rapid population growth, Africa also has a higher number of schoolchildren as a proportion of its overall population than other regions. Classroom materials are often absent: schools lack chalkboards, desks and other basic materials. Sub-Saharan Africa, with 10% of the world's children, invests 1% of the world total of public education spending. That amounts to $49 per student, compared to $4,636 in OECD countries. UNICEF has calculated the cost of bringing Africa up to universal primary education at about US$2 billion per year, but this does not include the costs of constructing new schools, or the costs of enhancing quality.

The heavily indebted countries of sub-Saharan Africa spend more on debt payments than on education, with Tanzania spending twice as much (after debt relief), and Zambia spending more on its debt than on health and education combined. In the region as a whole, military expenditure, at $7 billion, is twice that of education spending (debt servicing amounts to a further $12 billion).

Public expenditure on education has been falling in real terms since the 1980s. Loan conditions for one fifth of sub-Saharan African countries in the 1990s included explicit stipulations to introduce or raise tuition or materials charges. The justification for such levies was often that they introduce a 'participatory' element, or that households have demonstrated a willingness to contribute to improve facilities and content of education. Willingness, however, does not imply ability, especially in the fluctuating economic and political conditions that prevail in many African countries. Moreover, willingness may be restricted to less-poor households—and ability certainly is. The obvious differential impact of fixed fees on poor households hardly needs enunciating, but some particular features of poor households, such as incomes that fluctuate over the seasons, exacerbate these effects. Only recently has this policy been reversed, as national poverty reduction strategies emphasise the importance of universal primary education.

Konadu-Agyemang (1998) explores the effects of structural adjustment in Ghana on access to education and poverty and inequality, finding that the much-vaunted consistent GDP growth masks a reduced quality of life and public services for much of the population—leading us to ask: what is growth for? Despite improvements in many key macroeconomic indicators, real poverty is increasing, particularly in rural areas, but also in Accra, where it tripled in the period from 1988 to 1992. In this context, school fees become prohibitively expensive.

In most countries in Africa, parents are forced to meet substantial parts of the costs of schooling. Estimates indicate that almost 80% of costs are met by parents in Zambia, 50% in Tanzania and 35% in Kenya. Even when schools do not charge fees, parents often need to provide uniforms, books, pens, and desks, and may also need to organise collective activities to repair school buildings or fit out classrooms. The cost-recovery scheme in Tanzania has resulted in parents being prosecuted for non-payment of fees, with their children suspended from school. In one case study, registration for primary school only costs about 1000 Tanzanian shillings, however, the local school charges a 'desk charge' of 6000 Tshs, building improvements charges of 2000 to 5000 Tshs, a further 5000 Tshs for uniform and 2000 Tshs for books. A typical poor single mother can earn as little as 7000 Tshs per month, about 6500 Tshs of which will be used for rent, food and water. It quickly becomes obvious why enrollment rates are low. On average in Tanzania, while official fees were about $2, actual entry charges tended to be around $6, and parental contributions amounted to $38 over and above direct school fees, in a country where over half the population lives on under $1 per day.

Providing health and nutrition for students is a prerequisite for learning. Studies in numerous countries have found that educational attainment scores can be improved by a school nutrition programme that provides school meals (Kallaway 1996). The implication is that education for the poorest should not only be free, it should be subsidised by feeding students as well.

The dilemma of whether to focus on primary education or develop secondary and tertiary education remains unresolved. In the 1980s and '90s, primary education was the focus for donor policies, on the argument that this would maximise social gains. One reason for this was that the ratio of cost per student at the three levels respectively is something in the order of 1:10:100. However, social and political pressures have meant that domestic spending on secondary and tertiary education has been expanding more rapidly than primary.

We should not overlook the importance of secondary and tertiary education: basic literacy is simply not enough. The quality of education is key. In some areas of Africa where assessments have been attempted, education scores on multiple choice tests are close to the random level. Less than one third of pupils emerging from primary school qualifying for secondary school. In many areas, public schools are so woefully inadequate that there may be little or no advantage in attending them. Take the case of one public school in Shinyanga, which had ten classes to provide for over 1,000 pupils, most of which had no furniture or teaching materials. The teachers were generally only minimally trained, and the school had neither adequate water nor latrine facilities. They fared no better on formal assessment: a standard test at Grade 4 level had a mean score of 15%, lower even than the 25% pass rate (Watkins 2000). In Zambia, a reading test administered at Grade 6 showed that fully 75% of pupils were still illiterate at this stage. In Ghana, only 3% of Grade six pupils could pass a basic literacy test, and 1.5% a numeracy test. In rural areas, the pass rates were lower than 1%. Additionally, in Tanzania as elsewhere, national policy results in teachers being regularly transferred from area to area, creating constant flux in quality and no continuity, and little teacher commitment or accountability.

In the light of this it is not surprising parents are reluctant to allocate scarce resources to supporting state education. In these conditions, families' returns on investment in education may be minimal or non-existent, at least in the sense of acquiring learning skills, improving literacy and consequently alleviating poverty. High quality primary schooling is possible only with a major expansion of teacher training, which in turn requires providing more and better secondary schools.

Sachs (2001) estimates that providing universal secondary education to Africa would cost an additional $5-10 billion per year to scale up to this goal within a decade. Actual provision of education assistance to Africa by donor countries is well under $1 billion. These amounts are achievable. If donor assistance is targeted at providing this identifiable discrete provision to Africa, it is financially and politically possible for the major donors to scale up their assistance.

Non-Governmental Education Options

The experience of Tanzania illustrates the shortcomings of prohibiting private education in the absence of proper funding for state provision is counter-productive. If the state education system collapses in many areas, then there is no means for children to obtain any education at all. But universal education is a public good that can only be provided by the state. Relying on the private sector alone is not an option. Nor is it a realistic strategy for making up the shortfall in state education, when most people cannot afford fees. How can private schools generate a sufficient supply of trained teachers? How will the poor pay?

The recent trend of shifting substantial parts of the costs of education onto parents' out-of-pocket expenses, has abetted a de facto privatisation of education provision. Raising fees and charges for students in state schools is accompanied by the development of private sector schools that cater for Africa's middle classes. How is the private sector faring? In some areas, private schools are the only ones functioning. At the lower end of the market their fees may amount to much the same as the overt and hidden costs of state schooling. There is little evidence that similarly-resourced public and private schools differ in terms of quality. Where expensive, high-quality private schooling exists, it can only serve to exacerbate existing gross socio-economic disparities.

A major problem with relying on private provision to meet the shortfall in state expenditures is that it precisely excludes those poorest households who are most in need of education to break the cycle of poverty. In Zambia, between 1990 and 1996, the number of private schools tripled—without ameliorating falling enrolment rates. Privatisation is more widespread at the secondary than primary level, but enrolment in private primary schools often far outstrips official estimates.

Non-formal education provision is not a comprehensive alternative. It will always have the problem of diffusing the content and quality of education, when a core of standardised content and quality assessment is required. NGOs and religious organisations also have shifting priorities and their own agendas, and may lack the structural accountability that underpins state education.

Non-governmental providers have played a valuable role is sustaining education in many countries. Even with limited coverage, an NGO-run school can ensure that some students from a generation are not denied opportunity. In Somalia, the only education available is provided by NGOs, often with an Islamist orientation. Clearly there is a danger to this, as one of political extremists' favoured strategies is to target the young. The Afghani Taliban movement—the term itself means 'students'—was incubated in religious schools. State schooling can be an important guarantee of a secular and inclusive education system.

Where the political and financial commitment is made by a state, aided by drawing on innovations and knowledge developed by non-government providers, more can be achieved in a few years than in decades of NGO interventions alone. Likewise, participation works best as a means of improving an explicit, coherent national strategy for education, not as an end in itself. It should not be assumed that participation is tantamount to inclusiveness, or to the eradication of inequality. The recent shift in aid practices to embrace wider participation in setting goals and strategies is welcome, but severe structural obstacles persist to the inclusion of the poor in any participatory processes. This underlines the importance of maintaining universal access to education as a fundamental principle.

An African Curriculum?

Universal education can foster democracy as well as economic development. But the system needs to be well-designed and well-run. Too often educational policy has been based on notions of 'catch-up' to the necessary technological and business skills for the 'modern world', as if simply preparing people for this world would cause it to materialise across the nation. In fact, misguided curricula may create problems of over-qualification and unemployment, leading to population movements to urban centres and the abandonment of the agricultural sectors that might otherwise underpin a first stage in sound, indigenous development.

Sophisticated technological training at the higher levels in an economy with insufficient high-skill jobs simply creates fodder for the brain drain. Even in rural schools, the focus tends not to be on local life and occupational skills. That is not to devalue the merits of an academic education, an essential part of promoting lifelong learning, skills and social participation. The curricular legacy of schools to 'provide the human resources needed to run the colonial state at the lowest level' lives on (Banya and Elu 1997).

The choice of language of instruction has both economic and political implications. On the one hand, learning a European language is a necessity for participation in a global economy. On the other hand, for the majority of African countries that encompass a multiplicity of languages, official and educational multilingualism has clear value (Moodley, 2000). At various times, efforts have been made to promote African languages in schools and to develop indigenous curricula. These have rarely succeeded. Reasons for failure include, unrealistic goals for reform, reliance on macro-planning and difficulties of communication and contact with isolated rural areas, lack of donor support for research into indigenous learning, and lack of African teaching methodology in the formal system (Semali 1999). The problems with 'indigenous literacy', meaning studying indigenous technical knowledge and value systems and their transfer to school and work life, within a formal education and assessment framework, are apparent. As the required output of education systems is increasingly quantified and qualified at the international level, it is not surprising that local needs are misunderstood or ignored. Semali argues that indigenous knowledge has value even within the formal education system, suggests ways in which it might be incorporated successfully into curricula and highlights community involvement as key both in developing the educational content and as a teaching forum, noting that the community is often the principal educator: 'it takes a village to raise a child'.

The choice of language has political ramifications. In Rwanda for example, the question of the respective positions of French and English is freighted with political agendas. Government-sponsored attempts to foster civic pride can degenerate into frankly xenophobic nationalist agendas with odious consequences, as the current situation in Cote d'Ivoire reveals (We use the French appellation here so as not to break the law).

One prominent, if not totally successful, example of promoting 'relevant' education was the 'Education for Self-Reliance' programme in Tanzania, which focussed on local practical skills. The programme was perhaps undermined by its political, anti-colonial impetus, but it included an appreciation of local culture and customs, national identity and unity, cultural and moral values, preparation for both mental and manual work, and multilingualism including a local language.

Such vicissitudes aside, earnest programmes to foster indigenous knowledge should be considered as especially appropriate where the teachers themselves are ill-prepared to provide any more 'global' style knowledge or skills, and may be individually alienated from exogenous curricula, texts and 'national' languages. Language issues may also be credited with some of the drop-out problems: the highest drop-out rates (often after two years or so) may coincide with the introduction of English as a main or sole language of instruction, an experience which can be alienating. In Sierra Leone the community language is used in years one to three for this reason, to allow children to acclimatise to the school environment.

Africa is the victim of a 'digital divide' that hampers the development of the 'new literacy' in information and communications technology. At present, there is less than one computer per 1,000 people in sub-Saharan Africa. There are more telephone lines in Tokyo alone than in sub-Saharan Africa. In the developed world, functional literacy is being redefined to include technological capacity, while in Africa traditional definitions remain (Rasool 1999). Such a divergence can only reinforce existing disparities, and create a situation in which a few technological schools train students in information technology skills to be poached by industrialised nations. Technological education can be just a passport to a global labour market. Alternatively, Africa can develop a widespread ITC capacity, utilising computers and especially the internet as tools of learning, democracy and development.

The AIDS Crisis in the Education Sector

The AIDS pandemic is causing a structural and resource crisis in schools. Many teachers are infected with HIV. The loss of teachers has exceeded the new intake in many countries, leading to a reduction of staff members and the increase of class sizes. This has an adverse impact on the quality and quantity of teaching. In order to maintain existing levels of teaching staff—already insufficient—the worst-hit countries will need to double their teacher training programmes over the coming decade.

As for the pupils, many children come from families where a parent or close relative suffers from HIV-related illnesses. A substantial part of the care-taking has to be performed by children, mainly girls. Conventional wisdom holds that these duties will keep them from attending classes. In fact, the causal relationship appears to be more complex, with AIDS orphanhood or caretaking one factor among many that contributes to withdrawal from school (World Bank 1999: 226-7).

Overall, the AIDS pandemic is undoubtedly seeing a decline in the quality of education and probably it is causing a decline in the number of children attending school in the poorest countries. (Botswana, with its relatively high income and excellent school enrolment rates, but very high HIV levels, is a counterexample to this.) It is also likely that lower educational achievement increases the risk of contracting HIV. Among very poor, uneducated young women, high-risk sexual behaviours are particularly likely.

Increasing the resources available for education is therefore an important component of HIV/AIDS containment in Africa. It will directly and indirectly have an impact on the containment of the pandemic. In addition, schools may need to consider special responses to the requirements of pupils who have other onerous care-taking tasks to attend to.

Responding to the HIV/AIDS pandemic includes reaching children in school for sex education in the broadest sense to include training in life skills (see chapter 8). There is much accumulated evidence in support of the view that early and sustained sex education helps to cut down adolescents' sexual activities and especially reduce risks of HIV, other STIs and unplanned pregnancies. Nonetheless, conservative moralists continue to argue against sex education. Africa's schools face yet another complex challenge.

Mobilising a Campaign for Education

The benefits for Africa of free universal education are obvious, but even where the political will exists, African governments currently lack the resources to provide it. It is therefore necessary to mobilise the international donor community and international financial institutions, in support of this aim. For political reasons, the 'first dollar' of additional resources should be domestic. Given the limitations on governments, this requires a wider social mobilisation. Hence, a three-fold compact is required: first, a commitment by African governments to the goal of free universal education, second, a financial commitment by aid donors to support this goal, and third, a mobilisation of relevant social groups to help provide human and financial resources.

A campaign of this kind requires intermediate goals in order for it to become a meaningful and effective campaign rather than just a commitment. The formulation of the necessary intermediate goals is one of the main challenges of designing and implementing a campaign. This is especially the case where the global aim of the campaign cannot be achieved rapidly. Intermediate goals may include the following: The achievement of free universal *primary* education in specific countries or communities; the adoption of funded national plans of action to achieve this goal; and the mobilisation of necessary financial resources.

A campaign of this nature requires 'packaging'. In the case of free universal education, the following components can be considered in the way the campaign is sold, domestically and internationally. First, the issue is a *moral outrage*. The fact that so many children are denied an education is a scandal. Gender discrimination in education and literacy is equally scandalous. In addition, the issue represents an economic and a political disaster. Second, education is a *state responsibility*. Governments have committed themselves to providing education for all by ratifying the Universal Declaration of Human Rights and the Convention on the Rights of the Child. This reflects an evolution of global ethics: education is a basic right, and one of the basic responsibilities of a state is to deliver on this right. Third, it is a *discrete issue* that can be the focus for a targeted campaign. The campaign is not against poverty as such, or for human advancement, but for a single but vital strand in these wider goals. Next, the issue is *universal*. Free education is an issue that speaks to all people. It has been achieved in developed countries, but only within the last hundred years. Fifth, the issue is *relevant* to many different stakeholders, and so can become the focus of a *broad coalition*. Education feeds through into many aspects of national life. Girls' education is demonstrably the most significant factor in reducing child mortality, and linked to this, reducing very high fertility levels. A workforce's educational level is the single greatest determinant of economic development. Armed conflict is concentrated in countries with poor education levels. Lastly, the aim is *achievable*. It can be done. The cost estimates outlined indicate that the world can afford to fund basic education in Africa. The question is in fact; can the world afford *not* to fund education in Africa?

The campaign will require a broad coalition that includes the following four elements. It will demand *mass mobilisation*. The mobilisation of multiple grass-roots organisations and constituencies. The ordinary people of Africa must demand that their children are educated, universally and freely. It needs *professional advocacy*. The work of the specialist NGOs, domestically and internationally, is vital to any such campaign. These NGOs range from parent-teachers associations to churches to national branches of Save the Children Fund and UNICEF, to the international leadership of these organisations. It requires *material assistance.* Assistance agencies, ranging from local NGOs and community-based advice centres, to international NGOs, to UN organisations, to governmental donors, all will have a role here. These organisations must be an intrinsic part of the campaign: their educational services are essential, and should be supported to become higher quality, more accessible and, where possible, free. And it needs *coalitions with moral policymakers.* Sympathetic individuals in governments and in business, the UN, etc., will be key allies in this campaign. These 'policymakers with a conscience' will be strategic allies in terms of enacting legislation and policy changes. But it is important that they do not take the leadership of the campaign: this is for the grass roots.

All international agencies, policymakers and aid organisations should consider and reflect on the experience of the 1980s and early 1990s. Too often shifting political mores in the few industrialised, development policy-making centres of the world have dictated global policy that was directly contradictory to the international agreements sanctioned by the organisations that implement it. Policy formulations and prescriptions should be scrutinised and considered for their appropriateness to the individual and specific political, economic and developmental stage of the region. They must be based on their empirical, and not ideological, soundness.

It is tragic that Africa has made so little progress towards achieving the right of all African children to an education, and to implementing the World Summit for Children goals of universal enrolment in primary education. What has not been achieved in the past decade must become a priority for the coming years.

5

Child Victims of War in Africa

ALEXANDRA GALPERIN

'War-affected children are at a greater risk to grow into a generation of adults more committed to violence than peace. Commitments to war-affected children today will strengthen prospects for peace, human rights, and global security in the future.'

—Winnipeg Conference, Experts' Final Report 2000.

Children are victims of conflict. Unlike adults, who may be both perpetrators and victims, there is no question that children are solely victims—though they may also be surprisingly resilient survivors too. Even when children themselves become caught up in violence as combatants, they are not in control of their circumstances. This chapter provides an overview of children in war, as unarmed victims and (briefly) as child combatants, before turning to analysing how children can be protected by international humanitarian law and the Convention on the Rights of the Child. It is also necessary to look briefly at the nature of warfare in contemporary Africa, because this has major implications for the rights and welfare of children.

The Impact of Contemporary Conflicts on Children

All conflicts have a negative impact on children. Even limited conventional wars are likely to destroy basic infrastructure, disrupt services and injure or kill members of the family and friends who are active combatants. Moreover, the trend towards internal rather than international wars has meant that the battleground has been moved 'home' and that the fighting often takes place in villages or urban neighbourhoods. Civilians are thus more at risk. The additional trend towards low-cost technology and destabilization tactics has turned civilians into deliberate targets, further increasing the risk of their being harmed by violent acts. As 50% of Africa's population now consist of children, they are likely to be affected at least proportionately by this violence.

Levels of child mortality illustrate the vulnerability of children in African conflicts. The following table lists the world's worst-ranked ten countries in terms of their estimated under-five mortality rate in 1998:

Under-5 Mortality Rates

Country	Deaths/1,000 births	Rank
Sierra Leone	316	1
Angola	292	2
Niger	280	3
Afghanistan	257	4
Mali	237	5
Liberia	235	6
Malawi	213	7
Somalia	211	8
Congo, Dem. Rep.	207	9
Mozambique	206	10

The statistics above show that seven of the ten lowest-ranking countries for child survival unambiguously fit the bill of being affected by conflict. In addition, Mali suffered a long-running insurrection in the North. Of these, only Afghanistan is not in Africa. In all crises, children are the most vulnerable to increased morbidity and mortality. As a general rule, the largest number of excess deaths occurs in the age group from 12 months to 4 years, while children aged 5 to 9 also suffer from sharply increased mortality. The survival chances of infants are crucially dependent on the continuing ability of their mothers to breast-feed. Two converging factors are at work: malnutrition and public health crisis. In conflict, sanitation services break down, water supplies become exhausted or contaminated and primary health services become unavailable. All of these factors facilitate the rapid spread of communicable and water-borne disease amongst displaced and concentrated populations. More specifically, conflict contributes to malnutrition and the public health crisis through the destruction of food-supplies, preventing agricultural work and interrupting food-marketing, triggering population displacement, destabilising the public health infrastructure, over-burdening primary health services and interrupting immunization campaigns against communicable diseases.

Furthermore, internal conflict and deliberate attacks on civilians turn children into targets. Ethnically mobilized conflicts are especially prone to result in direct physical assaults against children, who are seen as the 'future enemy'. In Rwanda, propaganda over the radio station 'Radio-Télévision Libre des Mille Collines' explicitly encouraged the killing of children: 'To kill the big rats you have to kill the little ones' (Greitens, 2001: 149; African Rights, 1994: 34).

Displacement and separation from family and community are among the biggest contributors to conflict-related child suffering and death. Today, about half of the world's 45 million refugees and internally displaced persons are Africans, and about half of this affected population are children. Some are recently displaced, while others are a second and even third generation of uprooted people.

During flight, children are often in direct physical danger—of acute malnutrition, disease and physical assault. In addition to these dangers, girls are particularly exposed to sexual abuse. Depending on the conditions and services available, these risks may well continue once the destination of flight or displacement is reached. Because procedures and institutional responsibility for their protection and assistance are not clear, IDPs are often in a worse situation than refugees. In addition, displacement (especially for extended periods) may undermine traditional family and community structures, socio-cultural practices and the prospects of the child to acquire the necessary skills and knowledge to gain a livelihood once back at home or outside a camp (Evans, 1997).

It is estimated that about 3.5% of all displaced are unaccompanied children, who 'are separated from both parents and not in the care of another adult who, by law or by custom, has taken responsibility to do so' (Machel, 1996: para. 69). In Rwanda, by the end of 1994 an estimated 114,000 children were 'lost,' both internally as well as across borders (Evans, 1997). With no adult 'buffer' between them and a possibly hostile environment, such children are at an elevated risk from physical assaults, exploitation, educational deprivation and psychological trauma. The 'lost boys' of Southern Sudan are another case of a group separated from anything approaching a normal family environment (Human Rights Watch/Africa, 1995).

Conflicts increase the risks to girls and boys of becoming the victims of sexual violence (though cases of the latter tend to be particularly under-reported). Given the high infection rates with HIV in many sub-Saharan countries, and especially among soldiers (estimated to be 2 to 5 times higher than among the average population), such unwanted and unprotected sexual contacts bear the risk of infection with HIV.

Overall, the destabilizing consequences of war may further facilitate the spread of HIV/AIDS (and, eventually vice versa). Not only is rape common in war, but soldiers also frequently use the services of commercial sex workers. Half of the countries most affected by HIV/AIDS are also in conflict or heavily at risk from conflict. Given the fact that HIV now is the greatest threat to human survival in many African countries, children are becoming even more vulnerable to the consequences of sexual abuse (Machel, 2000).

The technology of war kills children, often long after the end of the conflict. Landmines have been widely deployed in African wars, often with the aim of terrorizing the civilian population and damaging their livelihoods. Because they are short, it is often more difficult for children than for adults to spot mines, and because of their lack of experience, children often fail to identify landmines when they see them. Sometimes, children's natural curiosity leads them to play with landmines. Moreover, while mines are designed to maim adults, they kill children, whose smaller bodies are much more exposed to the full impact of the explosion. Those who survive remain very severely disabled, often with little chance of obtaining proper treatment, and the fact that children are still growing complicates fitting artificial limbs.

Land mines have been laid at least 19 African countries over decades. Although estimates for numbers can be misleading, each one of the millions of mines has the potential to cause death and injury and clearance will take decades. In addition, literally millions of tons of unexploded ordnance are left exposed throughout the continent, attracting the natural curiosity of children. In many societies, children have tasks such as herding animals or fetching firewood that particularly endanger them, as they need constantly to explore new ground and cannot stick to established safe paths and fields. In addition, mines may have been laid years or decades before children were born, and thus have become part of their 'normal' environment. Constant reminders are needed to keep children aware of the risks these mines pose as they grow up. The increasing adoption and ratification of the Ottawa Convention of 1997 prohibiting anti-personnel mines marks significant progress, but un-cleared land mines are likely continue to kill and maim children for at least a generation.

Light weapons are inexpensive, easy to handle and have become easily available through illegal and legal trade, from sources both within Africa as well as from external suppliers, including Belgium, the United Kingdom and the United States (Clayton, 1999: 152-5,

Machel 2001). These cheap arms cause a high toll on human life in contemporary internal conflicts, and they kill thousands of children every year. Light weapons can also be used by children: the availability of light semi-automatic rifles such as the AK47 is a technological development that has made it possible for commanders to use child soldiers.

Chapter 3 has underlined the lasting economic consequences of Africa's wars. One of the mechanisms whereby it does this is through denying an education to children. In some wars, schools have been deliberately destroyed in a military strategy that is based upon destabilization and psychological warfare. In 1991, for example, approximately 45% of all primary schools in Mozambique were destroyed (Machel 1996). In their capacity as important members of the community, teachers also become prime targets (Garbarion et al., 1992: 23). In Rwanda in 1994 more than two thirds of all teachers were either killed or fled.

Education is especially important during conflict. It can inspire a sense of normality into the lives of children and help them to cope with psychological stress as well as raise their awareness of health and physical safety for the future. Lost schooling and vocational training over an extended period may seriously impair an individual's as well as a society's ability to recover after war.

Victims or Survivors?: The Psychological and Psycho-social Impact

The psychosocial stress of war goes beyond the direct impact that the experience of violence, loss and destruction may cause. The violent context of wars has probably contributed to an increase in intra-familial violence that renders children vulnerable to domestic abuse. Furthermore, children may suffer from losing their usual place and roles within the family or community. Sometimes they are compelled to adopt more 'adult' roles than usual for their age (increase of early marriages, child-headed households, child soldiers etc.). Sometimes, normal children's tasks cannot be carried out, because these have become too hazardous, such as herding animals and collecting firewood in mine-contaminated areas. Extended social networks such as friends, neighbours and peer groups may collapse because of displacement and separation (Boyden and Gibbs, 1997: esp. 87-100).

The fact that internal wars tend to last longer (spanning two generations in countries such as Sudan and Angola) means that many children grow up with the experience of a life-time of conflict. The healing of psychological and psychosocial stress may be much more difficult or even impossible under such circumstances, with unknown consequences for the longer-term impact on individuals and society at large (Machel, 1996, 2001; de Waal, 1997b: 309).

Views on the resilience of children against the psychological impact of war depend on whether children are seen as predominantly vulnerable or resourceful. Young children are strongly influenced by their environment. They are often disproportionately affected by the experience of anxiety in parents and adult caretakers, which may impact upon their ability to develop trust in others and themselves (Ressler, 1988). Adolescents, on the other hand, will have less difficulty understanding what happens around them and giving events a 'meaning' which will help them in coping (Boyden and Gibbs, 1997, Argenti 2001). But their experience of violence may also leave them much more conscious of the risks that they face and may make it difficult for them to imagine a positive future, possibly leading to depression (Ressler, 1998). A child's age, gender, social status, cognitive development, personality and health, alongside contextual factors such as the nature of the stressful event, and the extent of social networks and economic resources, will determine that child's level of resilience or vulnerability (Boyden and Gibbs, 1997).

Children can show resilience to conflict, depending on their age, the socio-cultural context and individual personality. They sometimes even cope better than adults with certain situations, for instance in adapting to new environments (de Berry and Boyden, 2000: 3). But children can also be especially vulnerable to the direct and indirect impact of conflicts. This vulnerability has physical, psychological and social dimensions.

Western scientific tradition has long emphasized the physical and mental vulnerability and incapacity of children (Boyden and Gibbs, 1997; Argenti, 2001). Within this tradition, childhood is described as a succession of various developmental steps that mark the development of physical strength as well as the development of cognitive and social skills (Ressler et al., 1988, chapter 11). However, these depend to a significant extent on the amount of care and protection that a child receives from its immediate environment, i.e. its family and the community. In times of disruption and unrest, the risk is high that children may not get the attention and care they need. This may lead directly to bodily harm and emotional distress, or indirectly to longer-term consequences for the overall physical and mental development of the child.

Such a vulnerability-focused view of childhood has several weaknesses. It ignores specific capacities and strengths that children may have. It also assumes a unitary and almost deterministic process of development, which risks ignoring social (gender, class, birth order etc.) and cultural differences (Argenti 2001). Whereas Western societies often exclude their children from certain social and economic processes (most prominently from production activities) other societies view their participation as essential for the learning and development of children (Boyden and Gibbs, 1997). Some societies prepare their children to resist physical and emotional stress. Pastoral societies are an example (Boyden and de Berry, 2000). Such social and cultural differences entail diverse paths to development which in turn influence the way children experience and cope with violence. Undeniably, children are victims of war—but they are also survivors whose resilience can allow them to emerge from conflict and build their lives.

Contemporary Warfare: Patterns and Methods

Evidently, contemporary wars in Africa have serious impacts on children. One reason for this is that the number of wars has not decreased, and another is that the nature of most of Africa's wars expose children to particular risks. Most of today's wars are internal, protracted, and cause mostly civilian deaths. Following a series of explosions of violence in Africa in the early 1990s—especially in Somalia, Sierra Leone and Rwanda—some analysts have suggested that we are witnessing a 'new' type of war rising from the ashes of the Cold War marked by a 'coming anarchy' (Kaplan, 1994). By contrast, instead of irrationality, other analysts have been able to identify elements of 'functionality'. In a reversal of the famous Clausewitzian characterization they have identified a dominant function of new wars as 'the continuation of economics by other means' in environments scarce of (alternative) opportunities (Keen, 2000: 27; Reno, 2000). A third view emphasises that predatory states and irregular resource-based wars targetting civilian populations were not a new phenomenon in the 1990s, but rather existed during the Cold War though gaining less attention from scholars and journalists (de Waal, 1997b).

One legacy of liberation struggles and the Cold War period in Africa has been the militarisation of the continent. Arms and experienced fighters are in abundant supply. Several conflicts, such as in Angola or Sudan, have been going on for decades. Many of today's conflicts in Africa can be linked to 'wars before' in the same country or 'wars next door' i.e. spill-overs from neighbouring countries at war (de Waal, 2000: 5; Ali, 2000). The disengagement of previous superpowers after the end of the Cold War led to heavy cuts in military and economic support to African governments. As a result, massive conventional armies became hard to sustain. But only a few countries have seen peace and demilitarisation as a result (Mozambique is a rare example). Instead, the nature of militarisation has changed with a focus on decentralised war strategies and low-cost war technologies. While heavy weaponry has become unaffordable for most African governments, light and small weaponry are available through many channels and at very low prices—supplying insurgents and other armed groups (Volman, 1998: 158; Machel 2001). Self-financing technologies of warfare include the involvement of armies in licit and illicit commercial activities, the use of militia, the mobilisation of fighters along ethnic lines, the forcible conscription of men and children, the use of anti-personnel land-mines and looting and pillaging from the local population. Destabilisation tactics based on terror against and intimidation of the local population is widespread. They include indiscriminate killings, rape, torture, population displacement and the creation of famines. One of the most significant outcomes of these kinds of war is the creation of groups that gain substantial economic benefits from war. A number of African wars appear to be run in part for profit, with a 'mercenarisation' of conflict (de Waal 2002: chapter 6). The recent looting of the rich natural resources of the Democratic Republic of Congo by several foreign armies is a case in point.

Tactics of irregular warfare are not new, and were not only practised but refined by both guerrillas and counter-insurgency strategists during the Cold War period (de Waal, 1997b). What is new in the post Cold-War era is that such tactics can no longer be linked to right- or left-wing ideologies. In many places, soldiers and rebels have become increasingly indistinguishable—in Sierra Leone the term 'sobel' was coined for precisely such people (Richards 1997: 14). These are methods of warfare that directly inflict damage on civilians, including children.

Child combatants are present in all of Africa's wars, both internal and international. They are found both in regular and irregular armies. They are in fact a diverse phenomenon. There are a number of different patterns of recruitment of children as soldiers.

One pattern is the extension of the recruitment pool to younger and younger conscripts due to shortage of eligible young adults. This appears to have been the case in the Ethio-Eritrean war of 1998-2000, on both sides. The Angolan and Sudanese governments have done likewise. Differing cultural definitions of adulthood, mean that any person who has entered a certain age grade can be eligible for military services despite being 'underage' according to law. Teenagers recruited into the SPLA are a case in point, some of whom are adamant that they are 'adults' and should be allowed to fight. Crises in schools may cause schoolchildren to volunteer for rebel movements, either in search of education and general advancement, or specifically to fight. Again, the SPLA is an example. Abandoned children may be taken on by an armed force as a benevolent patron, initially as camp followers who subsequently graduate to combatant status. This, for example, occurred with the NRA in Uganda. Lastly and most disturbingly, there is the phenomenon of preferential recruitment of children as combat troops or for specialist duties because of their pliability, lack of realistic assessment of risk and readiness to kill. This is made possible by the availability of light weapons that children as young as 6 can use, and the disruption of communities that facilitates recruitment of children. Charles Taylor in Liberia was the continent's foremost exponent of this kind of mobilisation, but it is also practised by the Lord's Resistance Army in Uganda and the Revolutionary United Front in Sierra Leone.

Legal Protection of Child Civilians during Armed Conflict

Any conflict, even one that is fought in strict compliance with the existing International Humanitarian Law (IHL), is likely to affect the rights of children as laid down in the Convention on the Rights of the Child (CRC). Full compliance with children's rights is only attainable in peace (Kupers, 2000 b). When we discuss legislation applicable to armed conflict, we therefore talk about *mitigation* rather than full protection. Unfortunately, as described in the previous section, the last decade has seen the persistence of failures in mitigating even the grossest impacts of war on children.

This section reviews the legal protection that the Geneva

Conventions of 1949 (hereafter GC), the Additional Protocols of 1977 (AP) and the CRC provide for children in internal conflict. Currently, 186 states have ratified the GCs of 1949, while 154 and 147 states, respectively, have ratified the APs I and II of 1977. It is important to remember that these instruments are the result of a compromise between military 'necessity' and humanitarian motivations. The 'protection' of civilians as defined in these documents therefore is never absolute, but conditioned by the customary military doctrine of 'proportionality'—i.e. the provision that 'civilian casualties ought to be proportionate to the concrete and direct military advantage to be gained by the attack' (Hamilton and Abu El-Haj, 1997: 19).

Within these limitations, children enjoy two types of protection in the GCs and APs: general protection as 'non-combatants' or civilians, and specific protection as children (Krill, 1992; Best, 1994: 281). Detailed rules confirm that children should not be arbitrarily killed, tortured or ill-treated (including by means of sexual abuse). Children should be given priority in receiving necessary assistance and care. Specific provisions exist for the handling of unaccompanied children, evacuation and the reunification of children with their families; all guided by the right to family unity. Finally, children's education and the cultural environment must be preserved (Stavraki, 1996; Kupers, 2000a; Krill, 1992).

Looking at these provisions, it seems that the GCs and APs have the potential to counter most of the breaches against children's well-being and rights that we have reviewed above. But critics emphasize important weaknesses of the law. First, the Conventions and Protocols are inconsistent in the way they set age limits, and on the whole, they do not extend specific protection to children over 15 (Hamilton and Abu El-Haj, 1997). This reflects the fact that children are not really protected *as children* but as individuals *within specific contexts* (unaccompanied, detained, interned, or simply as non-combatants).

Secondly and more seriously, the CRC lacks specificity and clarity with regard to the protection of children in conflict. Just one article out of 54 deals with the rights of children during conflict (Article 39 treats issues of post-conflict recovery and reintegration). This article (38) has been criticised for 'watering down' absolute provisions in the Aps (Hamilton and Abu El-Haj, 1997; Krill, 1992). Article 38 obliges State Parties to take all 'feasible' measures (instead of the stronger 'necessary') 'to ensure protection and care of children who are affected by an armed conflict.' (CRC, article 38.4). However, the ACRWC, Article 22.3 is much clearer in extending rules governing international warfare to internal conflicts.

Child combatants are illegal under international law and international humanitarian law. The CRC and the ACRWC both prohibit the recruitment of children and their use as combatants (Articles 38 and 22 respectively). In this context, it is important to note that the CRC gives some latitude for countries to vary their definition of childhood, and in fact applies two standards itself. Article 1 of the CRC defines a child as anyone under 18, adding the proviso, 'unless, under the law applicable to the child, majority is attained earlier.' Article 38 specifies that children under 15 years should not be recruited into armed forces and should not take a direct part in hostilities. This clearly permits the recruitment and utilisation of children as young as 15. However, the ACRWC clearly and unequivocally states, 'a child means every human being below the age of 18 years' with no provisos (Article 2), and its article concerning armed conflicts does not qualify this in any way. The ACRWC came into force in December 2000. This situation has been redressed by the adoption of the Optional Protocol on the involvement of children in armed conflict in May 2000, which requires states to take a number of measures to minimize the involvement of children aged 15-18 in conflict. Critics say it these provisions are not as strong as one might have hoped (Helle, 2000). Both the CRC and the ACRWC also require that children be protected during armed conflict in accordance with international humanitarian law. The ACRWC also adds, 'Such rules shall also apply to children in situations of internal armed conflicts, tension and strife' (Article 22(3)).

The greatest challenge for any legal instrument concerned with conflict is monitoring and enforcement. This is a problem for both the CRC and IHL, in different ways. In both cases, the primary responsibility for implementing the law lies with states. They need to create appropriate national legislation ensuring that those who breach the law can be held accountable. Within states, laws need to be disseminated amongst those who are expected to apply it and/or comply with it. Conventions such as the CRC, the GC and APs are of concern to the wider public, and should be made known to it. Moreover, the compliance with law needs to be monitored and there need to be mechanisms to bring breaches to the attention of appropriate authorities. Finally and most importantly, there needs to be a will for the actual prosecution of violations.

The following article heads each Geneva Convention: 'The High Contracting Parties undertake to respect and to ensure respect for the present Convention in all circumstances.' This obligation includes not only the application but also the dissemination of the law to both military and civilian audiences. It also implies that signatories should monitor each other and express their concerns about possible failures to apply the law. In practice, the ICRC has often stepped in as a neutral and impartial humanitarian actor and has used its 'right of initiative' (Best, 1994: 155) to offer its services to parties at war, supervising the compliance of belligerents with IHL (amongst other tasks entrusted to it by the Geneva conventions). This has included action in numerous internal wars. The ICRC's interventions are limited, however, by the fact that it cannot enforce the observance of the conventions. In acting as a neutral and impartial 'assistant' of IHL and its implementation, ICRC has preferred a style of confidentiality, reserving itself the right to speak out in cases where breaches were 'major', witnessed by the ICRC, and if all diplomatic efforts to stop violations had been exhausted (Moorehead 1998). Critics have claimed that this style of cautious secrecy makes the ICRC incapable of effectively working in situations of genocide (de Waal, 2000: 169).

The CRC has created mechanisms for monitoring progress on

the implementation of the rights of the child. First of all, it has set up a committee consisting of ten experts in order to monitor the progress made by State Parties in implementing the Convention (Article 43). States are obliged to report on their progress to the Committee and the Committee may make 'suggestions and general recommendations' to State Parties based on the information received. But reporting has been very uneven in quality. The CRC is also criticized on the basis that it 'lacks a formal complaint mechanism and has no effective sanctions it can impose on under-performing governments' other than publicity (Save the Children, 1999: 18) (unlike the UN Human Rights Commission). There are both similarities and important differences with IHL, which does not possess effective sanctions on non-complying parties other than prosecution in the yet-to-be-established International Criminal Court. The CRC has different objectives. It is a body of 'soft' law depending on the goodwill of states and international co-operation (Stavraki, 1996). While IHL is a realistic minimum to which belligerent parties have agreed to abide, the CRC sets out ambitious aspirations and norms for 'state practice as it is expected, intended or hoped to become at some future date' (Best, 1994: 7).

Conclusion and Recommendations

The current legal and actual protection of children from the consequences of war is unsatisfactory. This is especially true for the majority of contemporary conflicts, which are internal wars. Where the CRC lacks specificity on conflict situations the IHL lacks a specific focus on children. Where it is not clear whether CRC actually applies to conflict situations, the provisions of IHL for internal wars are relatively weak. But as with all bodies of law we have to remind ourselves that law is nothing but paper as long as there is no commitment to put it into action. It is therefore rather disputable whether new legislation will provide a remedy to the dilemma.

With regard to the CRC, we have seen that the effort to come up with innovative law for children affected by armed conflict (in Article 38) has led to a step back from the protection granted by the Geneva Conventions and Additional Protocols. This is not to question the enormous progress the adoption of the CRC has meant for the overall promotion of children's rights and interests. But based on our analysis, it seems that the CRC has a rather lesser role to play in the actual protection of children during a concrete conflict situation. With all its faults, IHL as a body of 'hard' law seems more capable of providing children with the protection that would mitigate (and sometimes even prevent) the worst war-related consequences on children.

As discussed above, IHL suffers from some obvious weaknesses. Critics claim it is not specific enough in detailing the protection of children. However, IHL is categorical in the protection it extends to non-combatants, and this includes children in almost all circumstances.

In this context, progress is best made by moving forward on both IHL and the CRC. There are a number of incremental steps that will help to entrench IHL across Africa, including wider and deeper dissemination of the relevant laws, adoption of national legislation and ratification of relevant international conventions and protocols including the Rome Statute of the International Crime Court (ICC) for the prosecution of the gravest war crimes. Another range of measures includes supporting national humanitarian organizations that have the capacity to intervene as neutral and impartial respondents in humanitarian crises.

The CRC has an important role to play as well. As any war will violate the rights of the child, the ratification and implementation of the CRC testifies to a country's commitment to peace. This can be seen as a crucial part of a determined effort of African countries to demilitarise and to 'transform cultures of violence and militarism into more peaceful societies by implementing measures to end all violence against children' (Winnipeg 2000, expert's final report). Children's rights and interest should be central to this agenda, and children's views and needs need to be included in peace accords and plans for post-war recovery and reconstruction. Finally, there is a need for an 'ethical renewal' of the commitment to the protection of civilians and particularly children (Kupers, 2000) that envisages linking traditional value systems with international norms.

6

Youth in Africa: A Major Resource for Change

NICOLAS ARGENTI

This chapter explores the important but little-studied area of youth in Africa, relating it to key phenomena on the continent including mobilisation for violence, religious resurgence and the informalisation of economic activity. It asks, what are the key cultural and social aspects of Africa's youth today? What are the implications of the transformations taking place in the values and expectations of youth?

The question of youth in Africa is huge and under-explored. There is a wealth of personal experience available about all the issues raised in this chapter, both with individuals and institutions, but there is a marked lack of scholarly or policy-oriented writing on the subject. In recent decades, scholars have begun to switch research focus away from the structures of power towards marginalised categories such as women and the 'subaltern'. But young people have yet to receive the scholarly attention that they warrant. Policymakers too have been shy of studying youth. Even UNICEF, an organisation whose mandate includes young people up to the age eighteen, has tended to neglect teenagers. This is unfortunate not only because of the intrinsic importance of young people, but because they also provide a bridge to younger children.

For this reason, this chapter cannot be a comprehensive overview, but instead must be an exploration of some significant themes, chosen somewhat arbitrarily. Unfortunately, this entails neglecting other important themes, including for example the Mouride Brotherhoods, the Roman Catholic Church, the role of music, sports clubs, and student unions.

Africa's Paradox: Understanding 'Youth' in Africa

Debates on 'youth' in Africa—both academic and popular—tend to take for granted the assumption that 'youth' are a simple demographic group whose identity can be taken for granted. We must begin by questioning this. Our understanding of young people and the roles they play, and can potentially play, requires us to look at how ideas of 'youth' have emerged from concepts of childhood that prevailed in pre-colonial African societies, and also from western concepts of youth as applied and disseminated by colonial and post-colonial governments. This history helps to reveal the extent to which the 'problems' regarding young people in Africa today are not simply the result of successive inexplicable 'crises'. Rather, they are the comprehensible results of important historical changes that have occurred in Africa over the last few generations, so that the social systems that exist today have been substantially transformed from the local-level kinship-based systems that existed a century ago. The roles of young people have been dramatically and irreversibly changed, and, as often as not, young people are orchestrating these changes themselves.

While African governments may tentatively sing the praises of youth as the 'promise of the future', they equally often fear them as the source of today's instability (Durham 2000; Mbembe 1985: 17-

18, 30). Two stereotypes have thus simultaneously emerged, one portraying youth as 'heroes', the other as 'villains' (Seekings 1993). A long-term view of young people's contribution to Africa's social, political and economic life should help to place this paradox in perspective.

Young people's relationship to traditional social orders

It is impossible to generalise about the rich diversity of social groups that make up the continent and the positions that young people have historically occupied within them. But there is no doubt that young men and women played markedly different social roles in pre-colonial societies than they do today. While understandings of 'youth' in Africa today are powerfully based on western concepts, the means whereby governments engage with young people in practice is strongly influenced by the social history of young people's role in pre-colonial societies and in contemporary rural settings. This rural history continues to influence the modern role, the expectations, the problems and the potential of youth in Africa today.

There is tremendous diversity in Africa's traditional rural societies. But the fundamental point in this context is a common theme: in traditional hierarchies, young men and women in pre-colonial Africa were subordinate to the power of male elders. This subordination was expressed and played out at the local level by treating all social subordinates as children, or 'social cadets' (Bayart, 1985). Men were therefore not classified as 'children' as a result of their biological age, but rather because they had not achieved the level of economic importance that would permit them to acquire wives, build their own compounds, and become economically viable agents. Childhood thus refers to a position in a social hierarchy more than it does to biological age. 'Children' become 'adults' when they ascend this hierarchy. The category 'youth' is therefore a moveable feast, a category used by different interest groups to define ever-shifting groups people.

Colonialism wrought profound changes, some advantageous to

young men and women, others not. The main advantage of the onset of colonial authority for a minority of young men stemmed from the need of the new bureaucracy for skilled labour: literate clerks, secretaries and low-ranking officials who could keep the machinery of government working at the national and local levels (Banya and Elu 1997). Gaining an education (typically in a mission school) thus came to be seen as a ticket to freedom from the protracted subordination to one's elders. As Bayart (1989: 151) puts it, for the elders, 'The era of the Whites became the era of insolence, when "children", "their mouths on fire", came out of their silence'. For the first time, young men did not need to wait for half a lifetime to acquire status: they could take a short-cut through salaried employment, and even come to wield power over traditional elders. The moment when many African countries achieved independence, and many educated young men moved into positions of bureaucratic power, taking over the jobs of the departing colonial administrators, marked a major shift in domestic power relations. 'Youth' had become a major political force. It is no accident that a number of nationalist movements identified themselves as 'youth' — the Somali Youth League even incorporated the term into its name.

Of course, only a minority of the emerging youth of Africa became overnight success stories of emancipation, enrichment and political empowerment. The serious problem that arose was that the great majority of young people who sought entry to the new order were not granted it. These young people—mainly men—were deeply frustrated by the false promise of emancipation represented by mission-school educations that led to nothing. Some were coerced into forced labour by the colonial armed forces and their proxy chiefs, and were then unable to find salaried employment in the urban centres (Bayart 1989; Geschiere 1997; Kilson 1966; Mbembe 1985; de Sardan 1984). Overall, Africa's children began a huge exodus from the rural areas to the cities, that continues to this day (Banya and Elu 1997). Dissatisfaction was manifest in millenarian movements and revolts, petty crime and attacks against traditional elders, whose positions the young men wanted most often not to obliterate, but rather to accede to (Bayart 1992; Joset 1955; Seekings 1993; Warnier 1993).

Africa's young men (and still more so women) found it difficult to accede to power as represented by the modern state, but were also still marginalised in the gerontocracies that controlled so much of life, especially in rural areas (e.g. Geschiere 1997:164; Goheen 1996: 145, 161). 'Youth' thus became a problem for both sets of authorities: a negative category that referred neither to children nor to adults. Not only for colonial authorities, but for many policy-making bodies and academics today, 'youth' has come to denote a liminal category. As a result, 'studies of youth are too often studies of deviance or of problems needing programmatic intervention' (Durham 2000: 116), rather than studies of opportunity. Some post-colonial regimes have reproduced this prejudice at the local level by reinventing 'traditional' hierarchies in the political sphere under the guise of 'authenticity' campaigns, with heads of state identifying themselves as traditional elders and the nation's youth defined as problem children needing strong paternal leadership. In this context, the notion of the 'Father of the Nation' serves to reduce 'youth' to the status of infants who owe allegiance, obedience and gratitude to their 'father' (cf. Bayart 1992, Geschiere 1997, Mbembe 1985, Toulabor 1992, Van Dijk 1998).

Young people's exclusion from national political orders

Rather than resolving the problems faced by young people in African societies, then, colonial and post-colonial governments have exacerbated them. Meanwhile, population growth has created societies in which young people are an absolute demographic majority. Young school and university graduates' opportunities for employment in state bureaucracies have not expanded, and have commonly shrunk on account of economic crises and structural adjustment programmes. Most of the young, educated or uneducated, who have been drawn to Africa's cities have not succeeded in finding jobs in government employ or opportunities in the formal business sector;

many have been forced into the informal sector, which at its lowest end provides only for crime and prostitution.

The style of education in much of Africa has not helped. Too much of Africa's schooling has been based on distorted and debased versions of traditional age hierarchy. Reinventing the role of village elders, the political elite have commonly adopted the ingrained tradition of preaching to one's people as one would to recalcitrant children. Schoolteachers and even university professors have adopted the same attitude of didactic condescension. At all levels of the educational system, students are therefore compelled to memorise, to repeat, to recite, and thus to embody their subjection to the authority of the master. Efforts to develop a critical understanding in the student are jettisoned in favour of a purely disciplinary exercise aimed at the '*encadrement*' (regimentation) of the young population and the reproduction of the national hierarchy (cf. Mbembe 1985; Cruise O'Brien 1996; van Dijk 1998). It is little surprise that those members of the elite who can afford to send their children abroad for education do not hesitate to do so.

This should not negate the significance of student movements in Africa, although it is arguable that these represent an historical phenomenon of decreasing relevance. Across the continent, the educational system prepares people for jobs that overwhelmingly do not exist. As Cruise O'Brien (1996: 65) points out, students now see themselves as an abandoned generation. The 'high order of built-in frustration' that results from this system has led to three distinct problems: a rural-urban imbalance, the educated unemployed, and the so-called 'brain drain' (Banya and Elu 1997). In addition to these problems, one should underline the fact that the high level of education of a small minority, while contributing to the development of a new class of elites, has not led to the devolution of opportunities for participation to the majority of the young. Furthermore, those university students who attempt to participate in the national debate by organising in groups that do not come under the aegis of the party youth wing are harassed by the paramilitary police (gendarmerie) and subjected to arbitrary acts of violence and incarceration without charges. Student uprisings are consequently frequent, though the extent to which these represent struggles for the rights to free speech and to education or mere attempts to appropriate a slice of the 'national cake' and entry to the circle of the new elite is questionable (Cruise O'Brien, 1996; Mbembe 1985).

For example, in Sudan, the Khartoum University Student Union was instrumental in the 1964 uprising that brought down the military government of General Ibrahim Abboud. Subsequently, the Islamist movement sought to mobilise among the student body, culminating in a wave of strikes and protests against the then-secular and leftist government in 1972-3. Although crushed by the Nimeiri government, the value and potential of mobilising students was not lost on the Moslem Brothers (Al-Effendi, 1991). However, while university students remain disproportionately influential as a socio-political group in Sudan (and indeed elsewhere in Africa), their ability to rock the government is massively reduced. The multiplication of universities, the decline in quality of these universities which is matched by the lower career expectations of students, and the strict and heavy-handed policing of campuses, have all contributed to the marginalisation of student politics. The government also sought to mobilise its own youth party, sometimes in paramilitary style, and intimidate alternatives. Meanwhile, the SPLA also received much of its impetus from the feeling that young people were excluded and marginalised by their elders, whose politics they decisively rejected. The leadership of the Nuba division of the SPLA was drawn from members of an underground organisation called 'Komolo', whose name means 'youth' (Yousif Kuwa 2001). But the youth orientation of the movement has declined over the nearly two decades of continuous warfare. A similar trajectory can be seen in Ethiopia: the radical students who brought down the Emperor and set in train the Revolution (Balsvik, 1985) have been replaced by a sometimes militant and angry student body, but a much less influential one.

The ambiguity of these uprisings points to a typical pattern by which the persecution of a section of society (in this case the student body) leads to the disillusionment of its members, and then to their adoption of increasingly Machiavellian world views. Since their experience of the state is of a place in which democratic ideals are of no value save as a rhetorical device, they stop striving for such ideals, and become instead pragmatists who simply seek advancement within the status quo, adopting the 'politics of the belly' of the ruling class as their only guiding principle (Bayart 1989). This mis-education of the student produces at best a class of passive and silenced academics and government functionaries, and at worst a faction of cynical pragmatists who reproduce the conditions of their own de-skilling (see Bayart 1989).

But this scenario applies to autocratic regimes capable of absorbing a substantial proportion of their educated population. In the post-recession scenario of economic crisis that prevails in Africa today, the Machiavellian pragmatism that the students absorb in secondary or higher education is insufficient to lead them straight into formal employment. Students therefore sometimes pass through a period of uprisings, protests and insurrections that assume various degrees of violence. Intended as a form of control over the youth, the tactics of pacification and the ideal of cynical self-preservation promulgated by the state ironically lead to further protests. The state thus ultimately bears the fruits of its persecution of the student body in its outright criminalisation. This is the reason why some do not think of young people straightforwardly as victims of state authoritarianism: when all other forms of agency are denied, young victims tend in turn to become perpetrators themselves. This desperate form of self-preservation then leads to further violence against young people as it justifies further government oppression. The situation regarding students can thus be seen as a microcosm of the aggravated case regarding the militarisation of youth.

Young People and Public Policy

The fact that government bodies are widely perceived to exist for the benefit of their functionaries rather than the people they are meant to serve seriously affects their ability to function effectively. As a result, there are major problems with the implementation of public policy in Africa. Since colonial days, lack of consultation and insensitivity to local realities have routinely undermined trust in public policy. This has left a deep legacy of distrust in governmental interventions. Ordinary African citizens routinely suspect that any initiative from a government department or international agency may have a hidden agenda, or may be a passing fad that will soon be superseded. For many ordinary people and low-level bureaucrats alike, the established modus operandi is to try and survive despite public policy initiatives, paying lip service to them and going through the motions of implementing them, but in fact either ignoring them or subverting them. Africa is littered with development or environmental programmes that failed because local people were not meaningfully consulted.

This problem exists for some public health programmes as well. During the 20th century, many draconian policies were enforced in Africa in the name of public health, including the forcible bulldozing of shantytowns and relocation of their inhabitants, and the movement of villages to contain tsetse flies. The ethics of some colonial medical practices have also been questioned. Leaving aside the current debate about whether the origin of HIV can be traced to the use of infected chimpanzee livers as a culture for developing polio vaccines, it is apparent that some European medical scientists may have relaxed their ethical standards when operating in Africa (Hooper, 2000). In Apartheid South Africa there is a disturbing and sometimes bizarre history of medical experimentation conducted with the aim of finding pathogens that will selectively attack Africans. Our point here is not whether these allegations are true, but that many Africans—and the young and the disenfranchised in particular—have deep suspicions of national health policies. For example, many young people believe that advocating condom use and educating people about the risk of HIV infection is a Western attempt to limit Africa's population.

Research in Nso', Cameroon, has revealed that local interpretations of AIDS are being assimilated within just such a conspiracist notion of government and of the wider world. In a region that has suffered in the recent past from exploding volcanic lakes that engulfed communities in deadly carbon monoxide, natural disasters and misfortunes are interpreted as being man-made and intentionally caused (Pool 1994, Quaranta 2001). Having suffered for decades under an autocratic regime, local people now interpret natural misfortunes in terms of witchcraft beliefs, according to which there is no such thing as a natural death. While inexplicable deaths are routinely attributed to witches thought to be living in the community, natural disasters that kill on a large scale are understood in terms of the 'witchcraft' of the state. The state is thus seen as a predator, preying upon its people for its own benefit in much the same way as witches gain their power by forfeiting their own children to their co-conspirators in the supernatural world (Rowlands and Warnier 1988; Geschiere 1997). The grotesque disparities in wealth and power between the United States and Africa, or between local villagers and urban elites within Cameroon, are also interpreted in terms of this local idiom. Hence, for example, the Lake Nyos disaster that led to the deaths of thousands as they slept was widely blamed upon U.S. and Israeli secret testing of a neutron bomb in which the Cameroon government was said to be complicit.

In the same way, AIDS is now attributed by many in the Cameroon Grassfields to the covert testing of a biological weapon or to a Cameroon state-sponsored conspiracy to wipe out the minority Anglophone population of the North West Province. Other conspiracy theories similarly put the talk about AIDS down to government or U.S. propaganda designed to frighten people from having children (Quaranta 2001). While these theories can easily be dismissed as unfounded, it is important to point out that they can only thrive due to the hostile political climate of suspicion and terror in which the people of the North West Province perceive themselves to be living. Where there is political repression and no democratic transparency, citizens need to double-guess the real reason for any policy decision, so that conspiracy theories become allegories explaining the opaqueness of the state and the apparently insatiable appetites of its functionaries (Mbembe and Roitman 1995). This has bleak implications for the treatment and prevention of AIDS. Once the illness has been subsumed within a wider sociological understanding of the misfortunes brought on by the state, local sufferers believe that treatment needs to be directed not at them, the victims, but at the state which is seen to be the source of the illness.

We cannot afford to wait for the state in Africa to become truly democratic and transparent and to have regained the confidence of its citizenry before implementing HIV/AIDS treatment and prevention programmes (van der Vliet 1996). We should merely underline that any programme that fails to include research and consultation regarding the often strongly politicised local understandings of AIDS (or any other disease) will inevitably fail to achieve its ends. Greater effectiveness of treatment and prevention programmes will be assured in the long term by working hand-in-hand with young people to gain their trust and ensure their willing participation.

Young People's Quest for Alternatives

African governments' problem with young people stems from the fact that the young are numerous, energetic, and seek alternatives to their plight. Young people do not simply succumb to the domination and repression of authoritarian states; they do not accept their limited life options but actively seek alternatives. Despite the disillusionment and the criminalisation of the young described above, the fact should also be underlined that young people very often do not simply reproduce state violence—even when they might seem to a casual observer to be doing so—but rather find ways of appropriating and subverting it.

We must see young people not just as victims of the misfortunes of Africa over recent decades, but as a powerful force for change. Analysing youth and student movements, we see new practices that have often been ignored, stigmatised, or even persecuted by governments and policy-making bodies. But it is in such fields of action and innovation that one can find one of the wellsprings of young people's innovation and hope in the present.

Ever since colonial contact, African people have abounded with grassroots methods for appropriating the forms of power with which they were confronted, and subverting them for their own ends. Many of these social movements have been reviled by colonists and postcolonial elites alike for their alleged 'irrationality', for the disturbing elements of satire they seemed to evince, and for the passions that the leaders of such movements were able to arouse amongst their young acolytes. The widespread Mammi Wata cults of coastal West Africa and the Bori cult of Niger (Drewal 1988; Masquelier 1992)—not to mention countless witchcraft associations such as the *famla*, the *msa* or the *djambe* of Cameroon (Warnier 1993; Geschiere 1997) and more recently the *feymen* phenomenon of fraudulent 'sorcerers' who promise to reproduce wealthy people's money while in fact stealing it (Malaquais 2001)—are typical of such movements. They represent the powers of seduction of the material trappings of western wealth and modernity, seemingly making available to their devotees the fabulous riches that the majority of Africans can only dream of, and yet which are regularly paraded in front of them by the elites of their countries. While these cults are believed to be of great social value to their adherents, however, they are the subject of suspicion and anxiety to outside observers, encapsulating as they do in the seductive persona of the siren or the witch bearing gifts both the attractions and the dangers of the pursuit of wealth without regard for social norms.

If these forms of worship have a dark side, then, it is because the history of capitalism in Africa has also shown a dark side in its failure to spread wealth evenly and to promote social justice. Such cults permit their adherents to express not only their desires, but also their misgivings about the social consequences of capital accumulation and the means by which this force has been harnessed by the few at the expense of the many in Africa. Denied more open forms of participation in civil society, young people have exploited the invisibility, the creativity, and the humour of such movements to elude repressive manifestations of power. One of the points often overlooked by those who deplore the lack of political participation by African peoples is the degree to which overtly political activity is quite simply not practicable under authoritarian regimes. Often, young people's organisations and meetings are prohibited unless they explicitly represent the youth wing of the party in power (often the single party). In this context, young people and the disenfranchised in general seek participation in mundane practices that can pass for religious, theatrical or folkloric when the need arises, thereby avoiding state censure.

An example of the tendency of the young to develop informal or even covert forms of participation in national politics, is provided by the young participants in the Ode-lay masquerades of Freetown, Sierra Leone. They cultivate close links with the city's politicians at the same time as they implicitly satirise them by appropriating their titles and exaggerating their forms of attire and wealth (Nunley 1987). A list of some of the militaristic titles adopted by the young members of an Ode-lay society includes the 'Director for defence and communication', the 'Representative to the United Nations', and the 'Special envoy from the OAU.' (Nunley 1987: 64). This masquerade group and others in Freetown have abandoned the use of masks altogether in favour of military dress. As Nunley makes clear, this military aesthetic underscores the close contacts that politicians have with such masquerade societies, and objectifies the political power that these groups and their supporters wield by way of their symbiotic relationship. Here, as in every other case one cares to examine, the use of masks has nothing to do with 'backward' rural practices mired in 'tribalism', nor with timeless 'folk' traditions or even with 'art' as popularly understood in the West. On the contrary, the practice offers young urban people a rich medium of expression that transcends local identity and fixed, timeless notions of tradition to represent a true picture of the changing social relations of young people in an African city. These dances do not try nostalgically to hide the clientelism, the crime, the violence or the desperate survivalism of life in Africa's cities today. Nor do they pander to the nostalgic (or merely cynical) folkloric search for an 'African authenticity' in an imagined utopian past to which so many African elites and foreign observers alike devote themselves.[ii]

The young marginal and unemployed 'Sapeurs' of Brazzaville are another case. They are regularly referred to as 'delinquents' by the elites whose exorbitant European designer style of clothing and general hedonism they mimic. But their real and sartorial 'adventures' similarly entail a subtle political commentary that is all the more incisive for its implicitness (McGaffey and Bazanguissa, 2000). The young *aventuriers* or *sapeurs* have developed a desperate culture of extroversion around the cult of the foreign. This leads them to travel to Paris where they undergo extremes of penury in order to save the money with which to buy the necessary set of designer outfits with which to return to Brazzaville. There, they display their new *gamme*, the complete range of outfits that they hope will gain them entry (however illegitimate and fleeting) to the space of the elites. The famous pop musician Papa Wemba has sung about the dream of reaching Paris and seeking the coveted articles of clothing known to initiates as *griffes*:

At Roissy-Charles-de-Gaule
My Love, chérie
Know that I am waiting for you
That day, chérie
This griffe, *it's Torrente*
This griffe, *it's Mezo-Mezo*
This griffe, *it's Valentino-Uomo...*[iii]

Gandoulou (1989) makes the point that the *sapeurs* of Brazzaville are not involved in an act of mere parody of the Europeans or the Congolese elites they emulate, but in an appropriation of the trappings of modern power. While this may amount to nothing less than 'a subversion of the cultural classification of a political order' (Friedman 1990: 318), it must also be kept in mind that its critical element only consists in the fact that the *sapeurs* are excluded from the wealth they so desperately desire. In other words, such movements are not to be read in simplistic Marxist terms as the rejection of the capitalist system from which their adherents are excluded, but as a plea for social inclusion and participation by a section of the population that has been marginalized by poverty, unemployment, rapid urbanisation and social change, and state paternalism and authoritarianism. Like the Mami Wata and *bori* adepts and the Ode-Lay maskers, the *sapeurs* are not ridiculing the elites they imitate so much as seeking a subversive means of entry to their circle.

The innovative social movements spearheaded by the young such as those described here represent the tip of an iceberg that has received very little attention indeed so far, either by social scientists or by governments and NGOs. When academics have studied African masked performance, dance or possession rites, they have tended until recently to approach the subject from a largely unreconstructed Western art-historical perspective. This has led to a prejudice against studying change and innovation in Africa, and to a marked preference for emphasising 'tradition', understood as a classical body of timeless 'art' that can only be degraded by contemporary developments and the contributions of today's young participants (see Argenti 2002b). If we are to understand the reasons for which young people still eagerly contribute to the development and invigoration of their performance traditions—and the invention of completely new ones as well—then we need to jettison such prejudice and look at the social and political importance of young people's contemporary participation in their cultures.

The same point applies with respect to government involvement with the 'national cultural heritage'. As mentioned above, the post-colonial state—like the colonial state—has historically been ambivalent about performance; seeing in it as often as not a source of potential critique and derision of the state rather than a positive contribution to the fabric of civil society. As a result, when governments have become involved in local performance or musical groups, it has tended to be in a heavy-handed and clumsy manner aimed at harnessing the popularity of a group to the ends of the party in power. Inevitably, such adventures have failed, leading both to the devaluation of the performance group in the eyes of its supporters, and to frustration with the meddling of the party in power in cultural affairs (see e.g. Steiner 1997 for an example from Cote d'Ivoire). While such cynical party-political ploys are to be avoided, there is presently a window of opportunity for governments and NGOs to develop a relationship with performance groups that would not be programmatic or censorious, but open-ended and open-minded, thus helping to foster and to learn from the forms of participation that young people are so innovatively developing on their own initiative. Policymakers and others concerned with children ignore this tremendous source of energy and innovation at their loss.

Young People's Participation in New Religious Movements

Sport, performance, education and religion are the chief non-militant channels for youth organisation. Of these, organised religion deserves special attention because of its immense impact across Africa. As a case in point and without pretending to be exhaustive, this section focuses briefly on Pentecostal Christianity.

The recourse of more and more young people to Pentecostal churches (and equally to Muslim brotherhoods, see O'Brien 1996, Tozy 1996) throughout the continent represents a social phenomenon closely related to the aims and aspirations sustaining young people's participation in performance. On the one hand, Pentecostal churches have to be given credit for what they do in many cases offer to young people. Far from representing a means of opting out of society, they offer opportunities for participation in civil society that are so often denied to young people both in political life and the established church alike (Gifford 1995; O'Brien 1996). On the other hand, however, there is a cloud to this silver lining. The emancipation from elders, the state and the established clergy offered to young people often comes at the price of an appalling level of competition between churches, the 'Satanisation' of everyday life, and the pressure to reject one's kinship ties and—overtly at least—one's cultural beliefs and practices (Meyer 1998; O'Brien 1996).

In many ways, the positive aspects of Pentecostal churches have a lot in common with the innovative performances discussed above. Like these performance groups, they are almost entirely run by young men and women. Like them, they are experienced by their adherents as a new phenomenon and a radical break with the past. Like them, they often seem to outside observers to be incompatible with a modern way of life, but are experienced by their adherents as a means of coming to terms with modernity. Finally, like them, these religious movements have important social and political ramifications that might easily be overlooked—not least in that they offer their participants a means of participating in civil society that they might otherwise be denied.

The following paragraphs illustrate these points with examples gleaned from a few specific Pentecostal churches in Africa. Van Dijk's (1998) analysis of the Born-Agains, a Pentecostal movement that emerged in Malawi in the 1970s, highlights first of all the youth of its participants. The preachers—themselves ranging in age from nine to thirty—emphasised to their followers the need to make a break with the traditions of their elders. They even ridiculed elders in public and satirised their rituals. Elders and their whole way of life were equated with a distopian, Satanical past that it was essential to repudiate if one was to free oneself from the powers of evil. The rites of the church therefore emphasised immediacy and the present above all, linking the suddenness of the moment of conversion to a future-oriented religious ideology. This temporal orientation was aimed at attaining a society in which power and authority would be resituated 'beyond the clutches of tradition and its gerontocracy' (van Dijk 1998: 166). The militant nature of this message and the forceful style of its communication (often using military metaphors) amounted to nothing less than a 'flagrant protest against gerontocratic authority' (ibid. 168).

The 'cultural amnesia' of the young Pentecostalists not only contrasted with the practices of their elders, however, but also with those of the state. Just as elders had always justified their monopoly of power according to time-honoured rituals and the links to the ancestors that these secured for them, so too the Banda regime of the day was actively reinventing a traditional Chewa past and putting it to work in the national, public sphere to legitimise its rule over all Malawians (Kaspin 1993; Vail and White 1989). The advantage of this policy was that it gave Banda claim not only to party-political legitimacy, but to eldership over his subjects. Young people were thus made submissive to the Banda regime in the same manner that they were to their traditional elders. Within such a political context, the Pentecostal rejection of everything the elders stood for was a double-edged sword: it simultaneously marked emancipation from gerontocratic structures and from subjection to a totalitarian regime. Throughout the continent, Pentecostal churches evince an anti-nostalgic element that plays a role in protecting young followers from the perceived abuse of power by their elders, and this same rejection of nostalgia also acts as a critique of the state that so often models itself on pre-colonial cultural models of authority and legitimises itself according to historical memories of nationhood.

The Pentecostal cry to make a complete break with the past and to be *born again* also clashes directly with the current cultural policies of the Ghanaian state (Meyer 1998). There too, the state aims to instil in its ethnically diverse population a sense of national pride by celebrating certain traditional rites as aspects of Ghana's 'national heritage'. A 'Ghanaian culture' is thus created with which to oppose the globalising cultural influence perceived to emanate from a neo-colonial west. In contradiction with this project, the upwardly mobile young men and women who join the Pentecostal churches emphasise the 'global' character of their religious practices and reject 'traditional' practices as sinful. Behind this religious doctrine lie the frustrations that emerge when these well-educated and economically successful young people come up against the demands of a gerontocratic structure that blocks their progress and seeks to confine them within an age-based hierarchy. This is the sense in which Pentecostalism can be understood as a modernist movement. It focuses on achieving a continuous state of rupture with the past by means of continuous personal renewal, and thereby to establish and a life of freedom from enslavement by Satan—where Satan can be seen as an embodiment of the gerontocratic structures that so alienate the young.

However modernist the Pentecostal message is, however, the young Ghanaian members of these churches in fact evince an ambivalent relationship to modernity: Many of their beliefs, such as their very literal belief in the satanic powers of traditional spirits, are directly inherited from their elders. By emphasising the Satanical powers of traditional spirits, Pentecostals incorporate these spirits into their cosmology under a new guise (Meyer 1992; 1998). The very power of these demons as experienced by Pentecostals emphasises not how they have broken with their cultural past, then, but just how difficult it is for them to do so. In this way, the Pentecostal message can be seen as one that addresses young people's need on the one hand to break free from the onerous demands of extended family structures and the limits to personal progress that they impose, while simultaneously accounting for the links to family and locality that remain important to them despite their modernist aspirations.

Pentecostalism is therefore best understood not simply as a unidimensional break with the past in thrall to globalising Western influences, but rather as yet another example of the creativity with which young people develop new practices from elements of foreign and local sources to address the tensions they experience in situations of rapid social change. These include tensions between tradition and modernity, old and new hierarchies, abilities and opportunities, and social aspirations and social reality. In other words, what young Pentecostals actually do in practice is not to reject their cultural context but to use it as a means of apprehending the global. In the hands of the young, 'traditional' and Pentecostal rituals alike are thus equally modern and transformational (cf. Werbner 1997).

As mentioned at the outset, however, there is a price to pay for the 'liberation' that Pentecostalism offers its members. Pentecostal churches such as those in Kinshasa described by DeBoeck (2000) offer to exorcise 'possessed' children, and demand for their services grows daily in what seems in many Central African cities to be a witchcraft epidemic. As children and young people, especially those in urban centres, become increasingly socially and economically marginalised, they accordingly become a source of anxiety and suspicion to their elders. Children and adolescents living in the streets, on the margins of society and on the fringes of the law, are accordingly more and more often accused by adults of being witches, nocturnal cannibals or agents of Satan who feed on unsuspecting adults. Tragically, some adults are willing to believe traditional healers who tell them that their own sons and daughters, some of them no more than four years old, are the cause of their misfortunes and their illnesses, and may be the first to accuse their very own children of witchcraft.

By lending credence to the alarmist scape-goating of street children, these churches encourage the growing fear of children and adolescents and their consequent further marginalisation and maltreatment, contributing to the 'Satanisation' of everyday life and the further impoverishment of civil society (O'Brien 1996). But it must also be recognised that Pentecostal churches are the only organisations willing to get involved in this serious social problem. Governments and NGOs alike stand by idly as tens of thousands of children in Kinshasa alone are ostracised and chased out of their homes by their own parents, who thereby displace their fears of the apocalyptic social environment of war, hunger and generalised '*multicrise*' that they inhabit onto their own children. Pentecostal churches confirm parents' worst fears when they 'diagnose' young witches by the hundreds, but they also take them in and treat them, attempting to return them to their homes as 'good Christians,' thus protecting them from further abuse and helping to reintegrate them to their families.

Nor are children mere victims in this process, injurious to their well-being as it is. As is the case amongst adults accused of witchcraft throughout Africa, children accused of Satanical witchcraft in Kinshasa paradoxically tend to concede that they are indeed witches, and will describe in detail the cannibal feasts in which they have allegedly been involved. Some of these confessions are extracted from children under duress, the interrogators happily using violence against children to obtain the results they seek. But it is also the case that the power to travel to the other world has become a powerful allegory of their marginal social situation for these liminal young people. These neglected urban children thus actively transpose the rural myths of Africa's village communities to their contemporary setting, using metaphors of nocturnal transformation and supernatural alter-egos to explore the crushing reality of extreme poverty and powerlessness that is their lot in a social setting of extreme disparities in wealth. Their allegories of cannibalism thus describe the bodies they feast on in modernist terms, each mouthful of forbidden flesh representing some aspect of Western technology and power that their poverty precludes them from obtaining. As with the Mami Watta or the Bori cults, these allegories of cannibalism evoke not only the unfettered appetites unleashed by modern capitalism, but the devastating effects of the free market economy on the social fabric of Africa's imploding cities.

In Senegal, where the public sector has been shedding jobs ever since the beginning of structural adjustment programmes in the mid-1980s, just 5% of young people now coming on to the job market after completing their secondary educations find jobs in the formal sector (Cruise O'Brien 1996). The rest go into the informal sector, with a significant impact on crime in the urban centres. In such an extreme setting, the conditions conspire to make a criminal life nothing less than a rational choice. Likewise, in Bamako, Mali, the route to economic independence is effectively blocked for the young, leading to the sorts of tensions within the family that one currently finds in Kinshasa. In Senegal, as in Kinshasa, adults express fear of the younger generation ever since the widespread killing of migrant Mauritanians in 1989 (Brenner 1994, Cruise O'Brien 1996). In Kinshasa too, adult suspicion of children and youths is indelibly connected to the unprecedented scene of Kabila's recent march from the bush in to Kinshasa with bands of young soldiers armed with assault rifles. In Mali, where students have taken to pilfering from market stalls in marauding bands, traders have formed vigilante self-defence groups to protect themselves against the scourge of the young (Wigram 1994: 36). Under such pressures, Pentecostalist churches and Sufi Brotherhoods such as those in Senegal offer young men a distinct youth identity and a modicum of protection, representing a field of civil society capable of pressurising the state by threatening a withdrawal of support (Young and Kanté 1992).

Innovative forms of dance and performance, possession rituals, new religious movements: all of these are fields of activity that are being pioneered by young people today as they struggle on the fringes of society, engaging in the informal sector to try to make a living against the odds. As we have seen, many of these informal activities, be they religious, theatrical, political or economic, tend to push young people into the nether region between legality and illegality, between the worlds of fiction and reality, between petty crime and outright organised crime and military violence. Nevertheless, analysts, aid agencies and policy-makers ignore young people's innovative informal activities at their peril, missing a vital field of political activity and social renewal in a context where legitimate political platforms and formally recognised youth groups are all-but-impossible to maintain. For one thing, these groups display extraordinary ingenuity in the creation of fields of action that offer the young victims of imploding states a platform within the fabric of civil society where they might otherwise resort to violent crime and militarisation. This tremendous source of energy is ignored at our loss. The next section examines what happens when young victims see no recourse but to become perpetrators themselves.

Young People and Militancy

Where would warmakers be without youth? The co-option of the energy and devotion of young people for the personal advancement of a few military elites in situations of political insecurity is the single greatest reason for the pejorative connotations associated with the category of 'youth' in Africa today. As opportunities for advancement and success in national government or legitimate economic pursuits fade away, and as local traditional orders become increasingly intermeshed with national political orders that have lost all legitimacy, young people are challenged to find alternative forms of representation and economic opportunity. Many young people, like some of their elders in the public sector, have recourse to criminalised forms of exchange in the informal sector and to petty crime as a means of making a living. Their suspicion of both local hierarchies and national governments alike make easy prey of them to those promising radical reform and seizures of power on behalf of the disenfranchised, or simply for those in need of a band of mercenaries for frankly self-serving ends.

In other words, the conditions of economic collapse, of free market restructuring programmes, and of crises of legitimacy all affecting Africa's nation states, coupled to the compromised authority of local elites seen to be either 'mired in tradition' or in league with a criminal state, are fertile ground for the mobilisation for violence of youths with few other life choices (de Waal 2002, Richards 1996, Bayart et al. 1999, Vidal 1995). In the Great Lakes and elsewhere, both governments and insurrectionists have mobilised youth into armed forces (Bayart et al. 2001: 192).[iv] On the ground, it is often difficult to divide the field into 'legitimate governments' on the one hand and 'rebels' on the other. In Sierra Leone, the term 'sobels' has been invented to encapsulate the merged identities of soldiers and rebels (Richards 1996). The recent multiplication of armed militias fighting each other on the basis of invented ethnic cleavages in Brazzaville, for example, demonstrates the extent to which political elites, the military and disgraced ex-military officers can be involved in the creation of militarised gangs as 'third forces' for the pursuit of personal gains on the political stage. In such situations, the fragmentation of political parties (or of the single party) into narrowly personal or patrimonial interests leads in the first place to the collapse of the social fabric and the abandonment of the young to their own devices. By building fear, hatred and paranoia into daily life, the groups competing for control of the resources of the state then orchestrate the ethnicisation of politics as a means of facilitating the recruitment of the young for violence (Bazenguissa-Ganga 1996).

The reading of 'youth' as a social problem has a grounding in reality that must be addressed, but it also has become a pretext for repression for some autocratic regimes bent on silencing legitimate dissent and alternative visions of social inclusion. The violent reactions by many single-party regimes to the struggle for democratisation of the '80s and '90s was justified (when justification was sought) according to the need to protect the nation against the threat of treasonous insurgents. Often in fact this threat was no more than the expedient hallucination of a paranoid regime using violence and other forms of coercion to perpetuate its existence. Inevitably, state violence and state-sponsored 'third forces' used to incite ethnic conflict and legitimise the imposition of states of emergency followed by military intervention have bred resistance amongst those young people most affected by such violence, which is in turn used to justify further and greater state repression.

Some African states are now little more than shadow plays (Reno 1995, Bayart 1999), providing opportunities for a few elites to monopolise state resources for private gain—an activity known as 'straddling'—without managing to exercise much real control over their putative territories. In such conditions, the state is as much to blame for the conscription of young men and the forced labour and sexual favours of young women as are the marauding militias that they fail to control. It is undoubtedly the case that military factions abduct young people and coerce them to become fighters. However, it is very often the case that young people are not simply abducted against their will, but that the environment in which they struggle to survive leads them to see military service in a government army or rebel force as a rational choice: along with Pentecostal churches, war is today Africa's biggest industry (Cruise O'Brien 1996).

Some young soldiers join from hunger or homelessness, others to seek revenge on those who have killed their families, others for political reasons. Young people are disillusioned with the broken promises of democratisation and development. They are exposed to the wealth and modernity of the global economic system in videos, the national press, 'high life' posters, cartoon strips and pop music, but these aspirations are sliding out of their reach. Stood-down boy soldiers in Liberia speak longingly of their guns not as weapons, but rather as the first piece of modern equipment they have ever possessed (Richards 1996: 29; Hodges 1992).[V] Youngsters in the RUF who do not obtain real assault rifles will carve wooden replicas of them, as did the young Shona men in Zimbabwe involved in the independence struggle of the 1970s (Dewey 1994). The fact that these imitations of real weapons are not functional points to their symbolic properties as keys meant to facilitate entry to a world of modern wealth and power that these young men are otherwise totally debarred from.

As we have seen with respect to Pentecostal religious movements and performance groups, therefore, mobilisation for war does not represent a return to the past for its young participants, but rather a 'blind leap into a dreamed modernity' (Marchal 2000: 174). While foreign observers may be tempted to equate the recourse to violence with 'medievalism', 'barbarism' or a lack of 'civilisation', the personal adornment of young fighters tells a different story. For the impoverished young men who take up arms around the continent, the symbolic connotations of the gun are part of an attire designed to connote urbane power and sophistication: a sign of what they desire if not of what they possess. Hence it was not only their guns, but also the golden ear rings and necklaces and the wigs worn by the young looters of Mogadishu known as the Mooryan that marked their identification with an American modernity, as did their preference for imported products and clothing, and the *noms-de-guerre* they adopted, such as Rambo, Clint Eastwood, etc. (Marchal 1993).

And here we are also reminded of the connections between the motivation for outright militarisation and young people's search for alternative life-ways by means of performance. The Ode Lay masquerades of Freetown described above have been interpreted as emerging from the links that developed between disillusioned students and marginalized young men—links arising directly from the rarefaction of opportunities for young graduates, the collapse of public institutions, and the emergence of a political culture of intolerance. Ultimately, then, it is the same factors that gave the Ode-Lay its specific politicised configuration that would also see the emergence of the RUF and its failure to articulate any clear political agenda, but to descend instead into extreme violence as a substitute for popular support (Marchal 2000; cf. also Abdallah 1997; Bangura 1997; Rashid 1997). The point here is not that Ode-Lay masquerades and their like should be treated with phobic aversion as evidence of sublimated violence, but that they could be interpreted as a more successful response to the same factors that eventually led to the all-out militarisation of certain sections of the young in Sierra Leone.

The emancipatory significance of militarisation in the popular imagination of marginalized young men is too widespread a phenomenon to ignore in Africa. For young men in the Democratic Republic of Congo, diamond smuggling across the Congo-Angolan border has become a means of transforming traditional rites of passage to manhood into a quest for wealth in the capitalist economy that replaces the allegory of the adventure of the hunt with the modern struggle for cash

(DeBoeck 1996, 1999). While these young men do not themselves usually become soldiers, passage through the militarised no-man's land of the border region constitutes a form of risk-taking similar to conscription, and evading the soldiers of the various armed factions during smuggling provides a source of danger associated with the hunt for big game and other rites of passage that once marked legitimate entry to adulthood. The complex contemporary reality of economic and political insecurity coupled with the rising aspirations of young people exposed to the desires that drive the free market economy results in a series of contradictions that young men may try to resolve by means of armed struggle or even simply of exposure to danger.

Youth—or, to be precise, male youth—are seen as militant, rebellious, impatient, malleable, and risk-taking. If these energies cannot be channelled into a courageous commitment to a national cause (national liberation or something similar), then it becomes possible to mobilise young men in a violent and anarchic way. Some writers, observing the apparently uncontrolled and irrational violence of the wars in Sierra Leone and Liberia, have hypothesised that Africa's youth are now out of control; that a combination of frustration, lack of education, access to drugs, and the readiness of cynical warlords to provide them with weapons, has created a dangerous new class of armed thugs with no agenda other than enjoying themselves at the expense of civilised values, and that the continent is now falling prey to a 'new barbarism' (e.g. Kaplan 1994).

This is of course an alarmist exaggeration. The majority of young combatants across Africa have rather conventional aspirations for their future lives. They would like an education and a useful job. Like young people across the world, they rebel against their elders, ignore advice, and enjoy taking risks. In addition to poverty and the collapse of the state, the advent of the AIDS pandemic has shortened time horizons, narrowed expectations, and heightened risks. But, given the option, most young people would prefer a future of security and domesticity. It is striking how little research there is on this area. There are very few surveys of the background and aspirations of young soldiers in Africa. There is very little sociological or economic analysis of youth and their needs and strategies for survival.

Conclusion

In recent decades, young people in Africa have become a political force in societies where they were previously by-passed in favour of adults and elders. However, the promise of participation in governance made by nascent democracies to their young people—underscored by schooling, meritocratic civil institutions and multi-party politics—is now being frustrated as economic crises restrict opportunities for employment. In many cases, anxious national and local leaders feel threatened by disaffected young people. The definition of young people as 'youths', with its negative, threatening implications, may become a self-fulfilling prophecy. Obviously, youth is not a monolithic or homogeneous category (Bazenguissa-Ganga 1996; Durham 2000; Seekings 1993), and it has been observed that 'there are predators among the young as well as heroes and victims, criminals in the shanty towns and military entrepreneurs in the war zones' (O'Brien 1996: 56-57). Youth are often cynically mobilised by political leaderships in pursuit of taking and retaining power. But what the overriding majority of the analyses available to us suggest is that young people do not turn to crime or violence *ex nihilo* by some obscure magnetism, but in response to the particular historical, economic and political conditions outlined above. Violence is not an end in itself for young people any more than it is for anybody else, but a means to an end learned by young people from their elders and used by them when denied all other means.

Given the chance, young people do not vent their frustration in the form of anarchic violence. On the contrary, all the evidence suggests that young people only become involved in warfare or other forms of violence as a rational choice in a zero option political and economic climate. The remarkable thing to consider is not why some of Africa's youth have embraced violence, then, but why *so few* of them have. The great majority—even amongst those subjected to military violence themselves—are proving to be extremely skilled and inventive in responding to the successive crises piled upon them by local communities, national governments, 'third forces', and the adverse effects of free market capitalism. Local populations in Africa's nation-states are often confronted with centralised governments that hide their fragility by imposing themselves violently on the people that are supposed to be their citizens, and as violence, extreme disparities in wealth distribution and out-migration invalidate adults' and elders' models of bounded community, it is young people who are increasingly taking the helm and, against all odds, peacefully constructing alternative social orders. Unlike some of their elders, young people throughout Africa today embrace alternative social formations and create new translocal alliances that challenge bounded views of community and fixed notions of ethnic or national identity (Appadurai 1990; Argenti 2001; Bayart et al. 2001; DeBoeck 2001; Ferguson 1999).

While the authorities look the other way, young people are reaching a critical juncture in Africa, silently becoming key figures in their communities in the promotion of socio-historical change. The innumerable informal means by which they are doing so—desperately under-studied though they are—make them crucial potential partners in the formulation of development programmes. There is increasing evidence that Africa's young people often seek to contain conflict and avoid confrontation by informal means that address the sources of disagreements elliptically without exacerbating violence. This is an approach at odds with Western views that political disagreements should be explicit and confrontations overtly addressed if they are to be resolved. There is evidence that gender relations are being reconfigured, especially by religious movements. Such youth-initiated processes are ignored at our peril.

Teenagers are the role models for younger children. The organisations and social relations pioneered by youths will be emulated, taken over and adapted by their younger siblings and indeed their own children. The social revolutions innovated by Africa's young people have just begun: if we want to see the future of Africa's children of today, we should look at Africa's young people, and imagine the possibilities.

As young people lead societies to change and adapt to new circumstances in increasingly bold and imaginative ways, it becomes ever more imperative that they should be widely consulted and honestly invited to participate as equal partners in the formulation and implementation of programmes. Of particular importance today is the question of how people adapt to the difficult circumstances presented to small-scale communities by the larger entities into which they are required to fit: nation-states and global economies. A focus on young people—until recently often left out of social studies and the development of policy alike—will reveal the extent to which youth truly is a major resource for change in Africa.

i. I would like to thank Jean-Francois Bayart for his comments on a draft of this chapter that was presented as an Issue Paper at the Pan-African Forum on Children held in Cairo in May 2000. The time to conduct the research was provided by Brunel University's Centre for Child-Focused Anthropological Research.

ii. For further analyses of innovative contemporary performance, see Argenti 1998, 2001, 2002a, and for attempts by the state to appropritate them into rituals of nationhood, see van Dijk 1998; Steiner 1997; Vail and White 1997; Kaspin 1993.

iii. From *Matebu*, by Papa Wemba, author's translation.

iv. The factors precipitating young people into violence in the Great Lakes region has been said to differ from other parts of the continent in that it was the government (at both the national and local levels) that succeeded so tragically in mobilising the youth to violent ends, and not an insurrectionist force (Bayart et al. 2001: 192; Human Rights Watch 1999; Marchal 2000).

v. Richards has been criticised for his description of the role of the RUF in the Sierra Leone war as 'rational'. As Bangura (1997) points out, the sort of atrocities committed by the young RUF cadres does not fit easily within any normal understanding of rational action. Furthermore, the fact that violent acts may have a rationale is no guarantee that they are defensible on ethical grounds. My point here, however, is not to suggest that the horrific atrocities committed by the RUF cadres can be rationalised, but rather that, within the political and economic context in which rural young Sierra Leoneans found themselves at the time, the choices that led them to join the RUF were rational—and hence that young men are not simply drawn into violence by some entropic urge, but as a result of specific conditions that can be addressed by governments, international policy-making bodies and NGOs.

7

Reflections on Youth and militarism in Contemporary Africa

Okwir Rabwoni

The problems of young people and war in Africa are indivisible. There cannot be peace in Africa unless our societies address the needs of young people. As a social group, youth in Africa today find themselves a desperate social group, hanging without roots, and without realistic political participation. This is a root cause for the militarisation of young people. African governments and civil society have a duty to analyse the problems of youth and put in place policies which in the long run can provide a sustainable solution to the problems facing youth. This chapter examines some of the dimensions of the crisis of youth in war and the ways in which young Africans can contribute to peace. I start with my personal experience of war, which began when I joined the National Resistance Army (NRA) in Uganda at the tender age of fifteen.

Personal Experience

My first experience of war was terrifying. As a boy, when you join an army, you think you are going to see war as it happens in the movies. It's not like that. In my first combat, I thought I was going to die. I thought, my mother will never see me again. We were attacking a heavily fortified garrison in Western Uganda. I was 15, coming on 16. Despite the training and discipline I had received, that first battle was a very traumatising experience. Then later on as I acquired experience I was able to steel myself.

The experience of war has a permanent impact on you, and affects how you relate to others. One of the principles of serving in the army, is the harsher you are on your comrades, the better it is for all of you. As a commander of even the smallest unit, it becomes part of your character to enforce discipline on your subordinates through strict measures. Of course, the aim is to make your comrades survive, but this harshness becomes part of your character, and after the war it takes time to remove it. Now imagine that you are not imposing your harshness on adult men but on children who are still growing up. These children become traumatised because their instructors and commanders do not show them kindness at an age when they really need it. When you join the army nobody cares for you. You are alone in the world, and either you are strong and survive or you are weak and you die, it's as simple as that.

In war, young children are really scared. Some of them miss their families. While they pretend outwardly to be brave, in reality they are lonely and afraid. You can hear them talking about daddy, mummy, and other things about home life. As their commander you have to be sensitive to that. Some of them would come to you and treat you as their parent. But some of these children go to the other extreme. For example they may become very violent, and be uncontrollable and want to kill prisoners of war. After the war, some of them become criminals and have to be arrested. In most cases the outcome depends on the approach taken by their commanders. Poor commanders allow them to smoke drugs and become indisciplined. The use of drugs arises from fear. When children become casualties they are also traumatised. When they suffered injuries, they become children again, and they cry like children. At other times, they relapse into childish behaviour, they put their guns aside and play like children.

The other part of being a fighter with the NRA, was the political education. I liked this more. Often this is called 'indoctrination' but in reality it was quality education including learning the political history of our country. Museveni was one of our teachers. Political education gave the fighters a sense of motivation. We learned that we were not just there to fight, but we were fighting for a cause. Also this education gave us a sense of discipline. Most important it removed that rabid hatred of the enemy that you have as just an ordinary soldier. I reached a point at which I would pity the enemy prisoners of war, because I knew they were being misled by the political echelons at the top. By the end of the conflict I could see the bigger picture. The higher I rose in the command structure, the more I realised that fighting is just part of the struggle, and the bigger task is building the social and economic infrastructure of the country.

I became a section commander. As a corporal, in a section of 12, we had five who were below the age of 15. Normally, the *kadogos* (child soldiers) were assigned to guard duty, which was a way of training them and keeping them away from the front line. But in our case we were forced to do combat duty, because we were guarding General Fred Rwigyema who used to command from the front line. So we were involved in many combat encounters.

After end of the war in 1986, I stayed in the army and went for training in Libya, Cuba, North Korea and Tanzania. The war carried on in northern Uganda and even into Sudan. I became a platoon commander, ranked as a sergeant but appointed as an officer. For some time after our victory, the *kadogos* were not yet demobilised—it took until 1989 to demobilise them all. As the army rolled on, the child soldiers who remained in Kampala and the peaceful parts of the country were demobilised and put in schools. But others stayed in the front line, they grew up and become men and stayed on in the army. In 1990 I was allowed to go back to school to complete my formal education. I enrolled at Makerere University.

But later in that year I was persuaded by General Rwigyema that the time to liberate Rwanda had come, so I left and crossed the border on 1 October 1990 with the Rwandese Patriotic Front (RPF). This issue of Rwanda had been with me for some time and I had many Rwandese as my friends. During my primary and secondary schooling I studied with Rwandese and Burundian refugees. These were traumatised children. They Rwandese youth looked and behaved like adults because of the problems of exile. They were very serious, and didn't play sports or dance. At that time I did not really understand what the problem was. They were always talking on their own with a conspiratorial air. Later I discovered that they were feeling insecure and talking about going home. They failed to integrate with other children of Ugandan background. Many of them left school before finishing and ran to the bush. They wanted to use the skills of the rebels in Uganda to go and resolve the problems in their own countries later. Because the generation of their fathers had failed to solve the problems they felt it was their duty to do it.

When we invaded Rwanda, we thought it would take a short time to achieve victory because the Rwandese army was weak. But after President Habyarimana received reinforcements from Zaire and France, it took us three and half years before we achieved our goal. In theory I left in the army 1996, when the RPF demobilised its non-citizens. But in fact I remained in the army to finish the Zaire operation before going home. In Zaire I was elevated to acting brigade commander, taking command of a full strength brigade. We started in Kindu, then went to capture Lumumbashi, and finished as one of the brigades that captured Kinshasa in May 1997. I was 28 years old.

After Kinshasa, I returned to Uganda and became an MP in May 1998. I was elected as Youth MP for Western Uganda under the system that reserves seats for 'youth'. Only those aged under 30 can stand for these seats. As a youth MP, I was active in activities to give the youth of Uganda a higher profile and a stronger engagement in national politics. I set up elected youth committees at village level, and put through the legislation for funding them, so that they would have a regular financial support. Then I was able to push through a scheme for youth who have completed tertiary institutions to access micro-credit, called the Youth Entrepreneurial Scheme. Then, we initiated a programme of conflict resolution seminars to teach the dynamics between youth and conflict. This went ahead with donor support. Also we organised an anti-corruption crusade. We formed a pressure group, the Young Parliamentarians Association which aimed to check excesses, and we censured ministers of state for education and finance. These were positive experiences for youth participation, but only a beginning.

When it came to the elections for 2000, I organised the youth campaign for Dr. Kizza Besigye who was standing against President Museveni. During that campaign I was arrested and forced to leave the country.

It is now 17 years since I joined the NRA. Of my comrades in the army from that time, few are still alive. Every name is prefaced by 'the late' so-and-so. Very few of us have remained, and most of those in the army, now holding senior positions as colonels and lieutenant-colonels. A few are in politics. Most of those who started as child soldiers ended up as adult soldiers. Many of them died in combat, and AIDS has taken many.

Root Causes of Child and Youth Soldiers

So long as we have societies that are not economically sustainable, conflict is almost inevitable. When armies are in the bush they will use all available means to pursue their war aims. They recruit as much as they can. War is a phenomenon which moves with its own momentum. It is very difficult to determine the momentum of war and to keep it limited. When the aim is winning, the commander cannot decide to use one type of weapon and not use another. When people are angry, whatever they have in their arsenal they will use. This applies to using child soldiers as much as it does to other weapons.

When a rebel army enters government it is always under pressure to demobilise. But if it demobilises without provision for where these troops will go and what they will do, it is storing up problems for the future. The only skill these boys have is their capacity to fight. If they do not turn to organised robbery they may create a new rebel force.

The political reasons for young people to take up arms must not be overlooked. First there is the despair and frustration of young men at the failures of post-colonial African leaders. Independence came with many promises. The youth movements took a prominent role in many independence movements. But along the line the youth contribution was hijacked by politicians. The youth are mobilised when they are needed by political leaders to enact change, and after that they are abandoned. Their contribution is not institutionalised. For example, in Uganda the youth formed the core of the NRA at both the political and military level. The NRA grew out of the Uganda Patriotic Movement, led by Yoweri Museveni at the time of the 1980 elections, which was a youth-based movement, including university students, secondary school students and unemployed youth. It was envisaged as a third force to the two existing sectarian parties, which were seen as discredited. Throughout the struggle, youth were the backbone of the NRA.

When we came from the bush in 1986, the army continued its pacification of the country, but the NRM did not have a youth wing to address the problems of the youth. So the young people of Uganda were leaderless and not organised. Even the election of youth MPs to the national assembly came only in 1998, two years after the 1996 general elections, because there was no law to govern the youth elections. So this frustration at not being integrated in the decision making of the country can lead youth to the armed forces, which is an area which they can dominate, make decisions and rise to the top.

This situation also means it is easy for the youth to be manipulated. Whenever there is an election, the youth are remembered. They are given T-shirts and are deployed around the country singing slogans, making demonstrations and intimidating the other parties. They are energetic and easy to deploy and do not demand much. Everywhere we turn in Africa, political parties have youth wings that are organised with these tasks in mind. So even civilian governments militarise youth at the level of party organisation. Young people are politically idealistic and ambitious and are attracted by quick solutions to their problems. With good leadership they can make a major contribution to development, democracy and nation-building, but with the wrong leadership they can become a powerful force for destruction.

Youth are marginalised at the level of policy. When national development programmes are being drawn up, youth representation is not considered. We find in many countries that the youth are placed in a department in the ministry for sports or labour. There are very few cases in which the youth ministry and the youth budget have been administered by the youth themselves. Instead, politicians have a condescending attitude of doing things on behalf of the youth. Older people assume that young people have no ideas of their own. Even as a youth MP in parliament I faced this problem.

Another aspect of the political problem is the general rise of militarism and militaristic ideology in sub-Saharan Africa and notably in the Great Lakes. This pattern has its roots in leaders deliberately refusing to trust institutions. However young and weak, institutions are not allowed to develop. Whenever there is a dispute between leaders and institutions, the leader takes over and dismantles the institution. This is dangerous. Most of these institutions exist to create credible democracy, participation and rule of law. But when leaders dictate from on high and destroy these institutions, it is difficult to persuade the youth to negotiate with such leadership. Instead young people prefer to shoot the leaders out of office. They have the experience of violence and the example of successful coups and revolutions. So violence becomes a means of resolving political conflicts as they arise. The chief failure is on the part of the leadership to deny society opportunities for conducting dialogue, as a way of providing safety valves for pent-up pressure.

We have a political culture of militarism in which many people think there is no alternative to violence. In any situation where people don't agree, their first option is to go for war. Violence is very attractive to people who have used it to solve problems. It is decisive and above all it is quick, and many political leaders are impatient and are not ready to sit down and go through long processes of talking. This turns fighting into a version of ordinary political business. The youth are sucked in. After a while we have a generation of people whose only skill is war, so that war becomes a permanent feature of national political life. In many countries have a highly combative society with youth who have only one skill, fighting.

Where there has been a long history of people being trained and armed, existing social problems become militarised. For example in Uganda, cattle rustling used to be carried out with spears and shields. Today, cattle rustling involves forces that are properly regimented with command structures and logistical support and equipped with rocket launchers. They are no longer raids but military operations. Cattle rustlers in Karamoja and Turkana can hold the national army at bay for some time.

The availability of weapons and trained youth means that the raw material exists for creating an army. Any trained officer can obtain enough funds to purchase a thousand automatic rifles, and then with elementary organisation he can form the nucleus of a guerrilla army that can bring a government to its knees. So long as the youth are economically dispossessed they are fertile ground for manipulation by political forces that can afford to recruit them, irrespective of ideology and programme.

HIV and AIDS has brought another dimension to conflict in Africa. The psychology of war leads people to be reckless. They become disrespectful of death, which means that they are unconcerned about the dangers of HIV. The thinking is, 'so-and-so died the other day, this one is dying of a bullet, I am likely to die tomorrow, so why should I take precautions?' I have seen soldiers in combat become very reckless, risking their lives, especially when they see their comrades dying. But many have survived combat only to die of AIDS later. Post-victory jubilations cause soldiers to behave irresponsibly, after a town has fallen or a war has been won. AIDS has cost the cream of the Ugandan army and now is taking the same toll of the Rwandese.

As someone experienced in war, I believe that it is not possible to isolate the problem of child soldiers from the broader context of the African political crisis. It is important to tackle the fundamental causes that bring these children to be soldiers, rather than identifying these children as a separate problem. Sometimes, those who try to analyse conflict in Africa pick out elements that are symptoms of a deeper phenomenon. Also, it is necessary to understand the positive aspects of youths' involvement with war. Why is war attractive to young people and what do they gain from it? In many cases, such as our case in the NRA, young people gain skills and contribute to nation-building. If there are good reasons for young people to volunteer to fight, then they will do so, and no amount of special programmes and laws will be able to prevent them from taking up arms.

Dealing with Child Soldiers

Every conflict in Africa includes child soldiers used by one side or the other, or usually, both. In theory, it should be possible to ban child soldiers. Governments have a legal responsibility to only recruit adults. Under normal circumstances all children should be in school, and it is an abrogation of their rights to recruit them. After a war it is the duty of a guerrilla army to demobilise any child soldiers immediately and put them back in school or train them in skills other than fighting. Guerrilla armies that control large areas and can carry out other activities in the rear, should give children non-combat duties.

But often the reality can be less simple. Many guerrilla armies do not face a situation in which they can simply say that they have nothing to do with young people under 18.

In my own case, I joined as a volunteer. I had been exposed to politics and I was ready to join the struggle when I was 15. This is common in Africa. Many African teenagers think like adults, they have had life experiences that force them to mature quickly. This was the experience of many children in Uganda. In some cases the parents would send their children to join the guerrillas, usually for political reasons. For example this was common among the Tutsis in Rwanda, who sent their sons to fight for the RPF. But the most common reason for children to join is that they had lost their families and were orphans. Others were trapped in schools in the war zones and had nowhere to go.

The NRA had a policy to look after the children who joined. When this was followed, the outcome was relatively good for the child recruits. The policy was for them to be attached to a senior officer, who would have the responsibility of looking after them. Some of them, who were well handled by good commanders, could then become good citizens. For example if the commander was well-educated, the children would admire him, and as soon as the war was over they would be eager to go to school and obtain an education. On the other hand, if children were not looked after in this way, they could become delinquent and violent.

For many children in the NRA, their role was not to be involved in combat, but to carry out the ordinary chores that are needed to sustain an armed force in the bush. If a force is to survive, it needs labour to carry food to the front lines, to cook and clean. If children stayed in their homes they would have similar responsibilities. So, if children in the army were kept out of danger and well looked after, their experiences would not have been too different from normal.

The bottom line is that war is not good for children, whatever circumstances they are in. The key question is not whether they are at home or in the army, but how they are treated, what kind of training they receive and what happens to them afterwards. Once they have attached themselves to an army, it is difficult to withdraw them from that situation. Where do you put them? You may have nowhere to take them that is safe. Even if they are far from the front lines they may face aerial bombardment.

In other conflicts, the experience of child soldiers has been extremely poor. For example, the way that child soldiers were handled in the SPLA is not impressive. Child soldiers were moving with adults and doing everything that adults were doing. They were not attached to commanders and were not given any special treatment. They were leaderless. It is important to treat children in a way that is commensurate with their capacities and needs. Many of them are tender and vulnerable and can pick up the wrong traits. For example, if there are commanders who take drugs, the children will be attracted by such kind of behaviour. Inasmuch as children are contributing to the army's tasks, it is important to recognise that they are still children and assist them as children. It is also important to know that sometimes they will behave as children. First of all, they sometimes are not able to persistently stand the rigours of long marches and carrying heavy loads. Then there are some situations they cannot handle. For example, there are instances in which children have shot prisoners of war, because they have seen their families killed, and they do not possess restraint and so they tend to overreact. Similarly, they should not be given delicate duties like field engineering, such as dealing with landmines. What children excel at is guarding their commanders, when they are working and at the same time are being supervised and trained.

If any children came to the NRA during the war, we did not send them back home. All were welcomed, even the very young. Looking back, this was an error and the youngest should have been forced to return. But in many cases it would have been difficult to reject them, because orphans had no home to return to.

Demilitarising Africa's Youth

Demilitarisation includes economic and psychological aspects. The two are inter-linked. For example, one of the functions of economic rehabilitation is to give former soldiers a sense of self-esteem, so that they can have the confidence to live in society without carrying a gun. For a young man who has always carried a gun since he was a child, it becomes an essential part of his sense of who he is. A boy like this will feel that in order to get a girlfriend he needs to appear in his village carrying a gun, wearing a uniform and walking with a swagger. The same with getting drinks free. But if a young man can get these things without carrying a gun, and can get society to recognise him as a man, then he will have the self-confidence to be a civilian. This is a complex issue that involves the entire society and all kinds of leadership. Everyone has to be part of creating a leadership that does not glorify violence. This does not happen quickly. It will be a long drawn out process to demilitarise the mind.

One part of this will be developing the right kind of education. At the moment, schooling does not include education for peace. On the contrary, the style and substance of education, supported by the wider popular culture of the youth, reinforces a military mentality. Young men in general glorify the heroism attached to military adventure. Films and books also glorify violence. Schools are often run along military lines, based on principles of giving commands to the students, ensuring conformity through intimidation. Education for peace needs to be designed in this context. Schooling is a training for life, and a young person's experience at school is second only to family life in terms of preparing him or her for future life. Education for peace should have elements that teach peaceful coexistence, dialogue and restraint. As well as teaching these values, schools should practice them too. Democracy can start in the classroom. This may be a revolutionary agenda for African education, but in light of the predominance of youth in our societies and their potential to either create or destroy the future of the continent, this is not too much to demand.

Africa's young people should be mobilised for peace. Our political experience is that young people are forgotten except when politicians need to mobilise them for war or for electoral campaigns. It is very rare that young people are mobilised in pursuit of other ideals such as peace. If young people are provided with better education and skills and the prospects of a better future, they will be less likely to be cannon-fodder for war-makers. Churches and boy scouts have reached young people, but politicians in peacetime have left the youth as virgin territory.

Both individuals and whole societies are traumatised in the aftermath of war. One element in this trauma is the readiness to use violence. Individuals who have experienced war can be irritable and impatient with little time for dialogue and compromise. The experience of Uganda demonstrates this. Those who served as soldiers are decisive, but become dictatorial if they do not immediately succeed in getting their way. They find a quick solution but do not think about the aftermath. By contrast, politicians who have not practised violence show more patience.

Part of the brutalising experience of conflict is an intolerance for civil society, humanitarianism and human rights. Youth who have participated in military conflicts tend to have contempt for human rights in general, as well as human rights activists. They identify human rights contemptuously with people who are 'not serious' about 'real' political change. It is very difficult now to convince the youth, especially in the Great Lakes, that human rights organisations can be serious partners for social development, and not just a western industry for generating employment. This attitude needs to be seen in the context of the brutalisation of these youth by war and their absence of any experience of their own human rights being respected. In many places there has been genocide and revenge killings. They think that the best judge for cases human rights abuses is the Kalashnikov. While these attitudes remain we cannot expect to emerge from our current crises of war and poverty. African governments should invest heavily in human rights education.

Part of the broader search for solutions must be to create a new sense of citizenship among young people. With the commitment to building the African Union this has assumed particular importance. The issue of a common citizenship should start with educating the youth about their common African identity. Our experience has been that parochial nationalism can be very dangerous. In a context where there is tension between different groups, whenever there is a problem of any kind, it will always turn into an issue of foreigners versus locals. For those who are refugees, the experience of exile can also create serious problems. Many people who have lived in exile grow up feeling that they are not welcome. Combined with militarism, the outcome can be deadly. They may believe it is better for them to eliminate their adversaries, even if it means risking being destroyed themselves, rather than face going into exile again.

One of the most immediate means for bringing young people into civil democratic politics is to lower the voting age, perhaps to 16. This is the age at which many African youth are joining high school. They are highly active politically and may act as advisors to their less well-educated parents. If we are serious about winning young people away from armed militancy we must open up avenues for civil and democratic participation instead. Legalising their entry into the democratic decision-making process will encourage young people to be more responsible citizens with a greater stake in their countries' democratic processes.

Conclusion

While the Convention on the Rights of the Child should be lauded for its potential to advance the condition of Africa's youth and children, experience has shown that the realisation of the rights it includes relies on a genuine commitment by African governments, civil society, rebel armies and citizens—including young people themselves. This in turn calls for re-examining the real causes of conflict in Africa, the resolution of which will deny the politicians the opportunity and the need to recruit children and youth as soldiers. Serious efforts should be made in the area of peace education and inculcating values of peace, tolerance, restraint and dialogue among African youth by developing primary school curricula so as to ensure that peace education becomes part of our national cultures and psyche. In areas where people are suffering post-war trauma, comprehensive rehabilitation and demilitarisation is needed, to instil a sense of hope. We need to final ways and means for effective youth participation in decision-making processes at parliamentary and local level, decreasing the attractiveness of militarism for young people. Finally we need to build a culture of respect for human rights. This will arise out of sustained relationships between civil society and the state, especially the security forces, so that the two can overcome their mutual suspicion. It is through these kinds of participation by young people and civil society, that we can move towards the realisation of human rights for children and young people in both peace and war.

8

HIV/AIDS and Young Africans

Alex de Waal

All Africa's children and young people, and all concerned with them, must concern themselves with HIV/AIDS. In this chapter our overwhelming concern is with teenagers who are sexually active.

Most of sub-Saharan Africa is suffering a generalized epidemic of HIV/AIDS in which almost all sexually active individuals are potentially at risk of contracting the virus. Factors such as high levels of commercial sex, high prevalence of untreated sexually-transmitted infections, early age of onset of sexual relations, and dense sexual networks, have contributed to fast-growing epidemics with high saturation levels in many populations.

HIV/AIDS is the single greatest threat facing Africa's young people today. In the worst-affected Southern African countries, the current statistical likelihood of an individual teenager today dying from AIDS-related causes during her or his lifetime is approximately 60% or more. The pandemic also affects young people through the crisis in the educational system, and the wider disruption and impoverishment it causes. Containing and rolling back HIV/AIDS is the single action that will have the greatest impact on African children's life chances.

More than 16.3 million Africans have died due to AIDS or HIV/AIDS-related causes since the pandemic began twenty years ago. Approximately one quarter of those deaths were among children under the age of 15, most of them infected at birth or shortly afterwards through mother-to-child transmission, with a smaller but significant number infected through sexual abuse at the hands of an HIV positive adult man. This figure of four million child deaths attributable to AIDS is profoundly shocking: it represents a huge toll of preventable deaths.

But this number is exceeded by the number of teenagers infected by HIV who will subsequently die of AIDS. The median age of infection for women is about 20-22 years, implying that a third of Africa's 14 million HIV positive women contracted the virus while in their teens. The average age of infection for men is somewhat older—in their mid- and late-20s—but substantial numbers of young African men are also infected while teenagers. Millions of Africa's youth are infected with HIV before they turn 18, that is, while they are still defined as children. And for most of those young people of both sexed who are not (yet) infected at 18, sexual practices have already become established by this age.

HIV and Teenage Girls

Almost all African young people become sexually active as teenagers, including a high proportion as young teenagers (here defined as those of 15 or under). Studies in many countries indicate a high proportion of girls of 15 or less who have engaged in sex—over 20% in many cases. At this young age, girls are more biologically susceptible to contracting HIV because of their incompletely developed genitalia. Seropositivity rates for teenage girls are often shockingly high. Studies in Kisumu, Kenya, found HIV positivity rates among girls of

8% at age 15 rising to 33% at age 19. Rates among boys were substantially lower, but still significant (Pisani 2000, UNICEF 2001a).

These very high rates reflect a mixture of biological and social factors. Women are more biologically susceptible to HIV infection than men, and the gap is wider for younger ages when girls' partly immature genitalia increase susceptibility. Hence early sexual activity is a high risk factor for HIV infection. Many girls become infected almost as soon as they have their first sexual encounters, and female age-specific incidence peaks in the early twenties, about ten years earlier than for men. Research suggests that the age of her sexual partner is a major risk factor for a young woman: a partner of her own age is much less likely to infect her with HIV than one who is five or ten years older. A typical infection scenario is that an older man infects a teenage girl. She will later infect a steady boyfriend or husband, and possibly her children too.

Why are teenage girls engaging in high risk sexual activity? The first, partial, answer is that there is a certain amount of rape and non-consensual sex. This is exceptionally difficult to study, and the problems of obtaining an accurate estimate of the incidence of sexual violence is compounded by the fact that it may well be most common in areas of acute conflict and social breakdown, where health services are non-functioning, health data reporting systems are non-existent, and epidemiological studies are not undertaken. In non-conflict areas there is some evidence that suggests that young women are most at risk from sexual violence, and that a majority of rapists appear to be young men and boys (including students). In some countries, notably South Africa, the incidence of rape has become exceptionally high, while reporting remains low and successful prosecution rare. Data from conflict zones is much poorer in quality, but suggests that specific locations have an extremely high incidence of sexual violence. For example one survey in post-conflict Mozambique (Nordstrom 1997) revealed that 'every women and girl' had been sexually assaulted while their town was under Renamo occupation, be it rape or being forced into acted as a concubine. The author cites estimates that, over 80% of girl and women refugees will have suffered sexual abuse. Investigations in refugee camps for Somalis in Kenya in 1993 found also found extremely high levels of sexual violence against refugees (African Rights 1993). Older men, especially soldiers and policemen, were responsible for a substantial number of these rapes. Given the much higher seropositivity rates among these older men (and especially those in the military), and the likelihood of the sex act itself being violent, HIV infection is much more likely to result from such acts.

Girls are very vulnerable to coercion and pressure of various kinds. They may have sex with teachers, employers, or other men who can wield power over their lives. There is a strong link between alcohol consumption and high-risk sexual activities, and girls are likely to be unused to consuming alcohol and estimating their tolerance levels. In conflict zones, young women may seek out the 'protection' of a soldier.

Poor women and girls often engage in sex as an economic coping strategy. One extreme of this is 'survival sex', where they engage in prostitution at the lowest end of the market. This is the most dangerous in terms of the likelihood of HIV infectivity, because of the number of sexual partners, the probability of contracting another STI, and the likelihood that clients will insist on not using condoms—or pay less for protected sex. Commercial sex work is another variant, which ranges from a survival strategy to a means for social mobility. A third variant, which is particularly significant in many parts of Africa, is having multiple liaisons with 'boyfriends' or sugar daddies, in return for some financial benefits (Manjante et al. 2000). Students and girls who work as maids may be compelled to trade sex for grades or employment. Refugees and workers in insecure occupations such as waitresses, food sellers, barmaids and domestic work are likely to have to engage in these kinds of sexual liaisons to obtain some economic security.

Many African teenagers are married. This is particularly the case in more traditional societies and in rural areas, where custom dictates that a girl is married as soon as she reaches puberty. Girls may be younger wives in a polygamous household. In these circumstances the woman is likely to be poorly educated and subject to a high degree of pressure and control from her own family. Their husbands are older. A young woman in these circumstances has virtually no freedom of action. She cannot question her husband's sexual practices, either with her or with other women. Brideprice will have been paid so her family will put her under pressure to stay with her husband. In such cultures, domestic violence is considered acceptable. Fortunately, to date, the societies with the youngest age at marriage (e.g. the Sahelian countries) have relatively low levels of HIV prevalence.

There is little doubt that the great majority of young peoples' sexual encounters are consensual. Most sexual activity and most HIV infection arises from adolescents exploring their sexuality, and their ability to use their sexuality to gain advantages—money, good grades, a fun night out. Young women are frequently reported to prefer older men as 'sugar daddies' (Nduati and Kiai 1997).

It is important to note that if girls were simply having sex with boys of the same age they would be at much lesser risk of HIV. They mainly contract the virus from older men. Mature adult men's preference for sexual liaisons with teenage girls is likely to be the single most important factor in the transmission of HIV to a new generation of newly-sexually active young people. These older men are an integral and dangerous part of teenagers' sexual networking.

The older man-girl sexual liaison has wider implications: young people are following an example set by their elders. As soon as teenagers are sexually active, many of them are presented with a model of frequent partner change and casual sex, often with economic rewards attached for the younger female partner. Sexual habits acquired during adolescence tend to influence sexual behaviour patterns during a lifetime. High-risk sexual behaviour in the teenage years are likely to predispose to continuing high-risk behaviour later in life.

Changing Teenagers' High-Risk Practices

Changing the high-risk sexual behaviour and practices of young people—both girls and boys—is perhaps the most important challenge in overcoming the HIV/AIDS pandemic. Africa's best hope is that the generation that will become sexually active in the next five years will have much lower rates of HIV infectivity than the current generation.

How can the necessary change come about? The UNAIDS survey of behavioural change concludes, for young people, that,

> Skills training, attitudes, norms and self-efficacy have all proven effective in predicting behavioural change among young people. In intervention research, these constructs have been useful in mediating actual risk behaviours. Results have shown that young people who have already initiated sexual relations must be treated very differently than those who have not, and that interventions have to as well target specific behaviours rather than risk reduction in general (UNAIDS 1999b: 30).

This section will examine different aspects of behavioural change, but first examines two questions: transmitting information about AIDS and its prevention, and the making available the necessary means for prevention—chiefly condoms.

The great majority of African teenagers know that AIDS exists. This is particularly so in high-prevalence countries, where most young people have seen older people dying of AIDS. But the mystery that surrounds HIV/AIDS in many African communities remains a profound problem. Leclerc-Madlala (2000) comments, 'The mystery has to do with the stubborn and multi-layered AIDS silence... that has consistently characterised the AIDS pandemic in Africa from the very beginning.' She further argues that the silence has much to do with heterosexual power and sexual lifeways, the structure and meanings which are contoured by culture. This was a persistent theme of interventions at the Africa Development Forum 2000: African adults, including parents, teachers, religious leaders, cultural figures and politicians, need to break the silence about HIV/AIDS and sex. This means confronting and overcoming deeply-held cultural obstacles to inter-generational discussion of these issues. Conservative moralists, especially associated with religious establishments, continue to object that sex education programmes and social marketing of condoms encourages immorality. In fact, there is powerful evidence that sex education for children tends to delay the start of sexual activity, reduce numbers of partners, and raise contraceptive use among those who are sexually active (World Bank 1999: 149).

Many misconceptions remain even at this mature stage of the epidemic. The long period in which an HIV positive individual remains healthy but potentially infectious, and the fact that a recently-infected individual can be highly infectious, is still not widely understood. Many young people still believe that they can assess a partner's status by looks alone. In addition, messages may be mis-interpreted. For example, it appears that many teenagers interpret the message, 'sticking to one partner' to mean 'sticking to one partner *at a time*'.

Knowledge about how to protect oneself from HIV/AIDS is extremely variable. Surveys that ask young people to identify means of protection come with highly variable outcomes. Levels of knowledge about condoms, abstinence and fidelity to an HIV negative partner tend to be greater in urban areas, and among better educated populations. In many countries—including even Uganda, which has run model public education programmes—awareness of the efficacy of condoms remains surprisingly low.

One of the key targets for policymakers is making information available about HIV/AIDS. For example the 2000 UN General Assembly Special Session on HIV/AIDS reiterated the target that by 2005, at least 90% of young men and women aged 15-24 should have access to the information and skills required to reduce their vulnerability to HIV. Those who drafted the target knew well the gap between 'knowing' and acting. Unfortunately the nature of public policies is such that the most readily implementable and measurable elements of any policy are those that are prioritized. Thus, in practice, most prevention interventions 'rely on the assumption that giving correct information about transmission and prevention will lead to behavioural change. Yet research has proven numerous times that education alone is not sufficient to induce behavioural change among most individuals' (UNAIDS 1999b: 5).

Meanwhile, potentially important means of risk-reduction are insufficiently developed, disseminated, available or practised. This may be due to lack of research or failure to disseminate findings and relevant technology. We can identify three that have important potential. The first is the use of microbicides. These have been shown to reduce vulnerability to infection among women, but have been unaccountably neglected by pharmaceutical companies. The second, already mentioned is a young woman's increased risk associated with the increasing age of her partner. Discouraging these age-gap liaisons could substantially cut HIV incidence. Third is the very high risks associated with 'high transmitters', that is individuals who are exceptionally sexually active with multiple partners. In all communities these individuals are known. Avoiding sexual contact with them is an obvious and important step towards protection, as is targetting them for behavioural change interventions.

Knowledge is little use without the availability of the means of protection. In many cases, condoms are simply unavailable or are too expensive. Or they are not available at the right times and places where young people are likely to have sex. Even if they are available, there may be tremendous socio-cultural barriers to obtaining them. In a conservative Moslem society, a pharmacist may ask a customer who wants to buy condoms, 'are you married?' Many young people would not even walk into a pharmacy in their hometown, where the pharmacist knows them or their parents, with such a request. The difficulties are greater for girls than boys. The problems of easy and discreet access to condoms are greater in rural areas than in towns and cities. Female condoms are virtually unavailable anywhere. Meanwhile the comprehensively-discredited view that condom availability encourages promiscuity remains tenacious among conservative moralists.

The greatest challenge is translating 'knowledge'—whether theoretical or personalized—into practice. It is clear that the 'abstain, be faithful, and condomise' ABC strategy has glaring inadequacies (Airhihenbuwa and Obregon 2000), even where HIV awareness is high. This problem is not unique to HIV/AIDS. Young people around the world continue to engage in risk-taking personal activities such as smoking or driving fast, even when both their theoretical knowledge and personal experience indicates that they should not. Similarly, even when patients 'know' what treatment regime is necessary, treatment compliance studies concerning diseases such as TB and leprosy consistently show that patients tend to discontinue treatment as soon as symptoms disappear. This is a major problem—perhaps *the* major problem—with HIV/AIDS prevention programmes. Awareness and knowledge, plus the availability of protection, are simply not enough. Many who say that condoms are protective still have unprotected sex. Many who know the risks have multiple partners. They 'know better', but they still do it.

This problem still persists in the at-risk community most heavily saturated with safer sex messages, namely gay men in Europe and North America. In an analysis highly relevant for African adolescents, Walt Odets notes, 'Too many men now simply dismiss the pertinent messages of prevention because prevention feels irrelevant to their circumstances, and too many others lose prevention incentive because they feel that infection has somehow already occurred or surely will' (1997: 137). Odets' basic arguments are that prevention messages aimed at the general heterosexual population in Britain and the U.S. are simply irrelevant to the specific risks faced by gay men, while a general public health strategy that fails to distinguish between the situation and needs of HIV positive and negative men fails to establish the required incentives to promote prevention. He concludes, 'Contrary to the assertions of many AIDS educators, gay men have not grown "complacent" in the epidemic, they have simply become acclimated to the personal irrelevance of prevention's "universal" messages' (p. 140). In this respect it is interesting to note that the most significant changes in sexual practices among gay men were entirely initiated by activists and occurred in the early and mid-1980s, before public funds and programmes were devoted to the issue. 'Contrary to popular wisdom, this unprecedented mass behaviour change owed little or nothing to the actions of governments or others outside the gay community, or to HIV antibody testing, or to the application of theory-based health educational models.' (King, 1993). It is deeply unfortunate that the homophobia so prevalent in Africa has stood in the way of learning lessons of activism and public policy from the community with most to teach, namely western gay men.

There is much research by psychologists on the gap between knowledge and behaviour and between stated intentions and actions. An overview (UNAIDS 1999b) identifies several individual-based models: the health belief model, social cognitive (or learning) theory, theory of reasoned action, stages of change model and the AIDS risk reduction model—the last one developed specifically for AIDS. In addition, there are several social theories and models for behaviour change, based on the fact that sex requires two people, and that motivations are complicated, unclear and may not be thought through in advance. Another group of theories focuses on the structural and environmental constraints such as individual and social empowerment and socio-economic factors. Lastly some theories focus on the perception of risk and communication about sex. The multiplicity of theories alone forces us to confront the complexity of the challenge of changing sexual behaviour—it is because change is not easily achieved that researchers have investigated so many hypotheses.

Unfortunately, almost all the studies on sexual behaviour and practice change have been undertaken in North America, with very few in Africa. Given the importance of social factors such as peer pressure and social networks, which are extremely sensitive to the cultural and social context, it is difficult to generalize the extensive research on health behaviour from these American contexts. Moreover, Africans in Britain have complained that they are rarely involved directly in AIDS research—in contrast to the gay community, whose members are usually full participants in any studies (Mukasa 1997). Excepting a handful of 'gold-standard' monitored intervention programmes (Campbell and Williams 2001), there is a striking lack of research into how knowledge translates into behaviour in the African context. However, the general frameworks are useful for pointing potential problems, and for reorienting interventions towards social change rather than focusing exclusively on behavioural change.

The first problem is that of context and relevance. Information assimilated in one context is often not applied in another. Knowledge absorbed in a classroom is simply not part of decision-making in the bar. A second question is the social environment of behaviour. Behaviour is strongly influenced by peer pressure and conformity to example. Being part of a group can also convey a sense of invulnerability. Role models are important, both from among young people's peer groups and their elders.

Attitudes to risk are also important. Many individuals have a predisposition to risk-taking. Young people (especially) like the adrenalin rush that comes from risk-taking. Or, whenever there is an increase in safety in one area, they seek greater dangers elsewhere to maintain a certain level of excitement. (For example it is well-demonstrated that as cars become safer, drivers go faster.) Some male occupations are also inherently risky (e.g. soldiers, miners, construction workers on high buildings), and those who practice them gain a sense of self-worth and masculine identity from these jobs. For these men, engaging in 'unsafe' sex may be seen as either irrelevant (because there are other greater risks in their lives) or as part of their entire high-risk lifestyle.

Many young people, especially girls, face no real option but to run the risk. A parallel with environmental degradation is instructive: poor people across Africa engage in environmentally destructive practices, not from ignorance, but from lack of alternative sources of income. Poverty forces them into short-term practices that undermine their long-term prospects. So it is for many poor youth in Africa, especially young women: their entire lives consist of uncertainty and risk, playing off one set of immediate pressing concerns against another, less visible and less immediate risk. Commercial sex workers may engage in unprotected sex because their clients pay more for it, and they cannot afford to forego the business. For some women, the possibility of angering their husbands by demanding the use of a condom, implies the immediate risk of violence. In this context, the risk of loss of status must not be neglected. For a woman, the risk of being seen purchasing condoms may involve an immediate loss of status in the community (Wallman 1996: 229).

Questions of self-esteem, and negotiation and life skills have received attention from researchers and policymakers. Young people often lack the social skills to retain control in a situation that can lead to sex. This is particularly true of young women who are dealing with older men. It is particularly difficult for a girl to insist on an older partner using a condom.

The consumption of alcohol (and other drugs) is a major factor in high-risk behaviour. All the above problems of risk-taking and ignoring 'knowledge' are compounded by alcohol consumption.

The above implies an important agenda of interventions aimed at young teenagers specifically targetted at changing sexual practices. In most areas of life, young people learn by doing. Their knowledge is what they have successfully done and mastered. Compare how teenage recruits in the military are trained to respond in battle: not by education and awareness but by intensive drilling that alters their instinctive reactions to situations, and by simulated combat with real dangers, and by real combat itself. Compare also how people learn sexual technique. In the past, young men had a similar approach to STIs—which were sometimes known as 'diseases of the brave.' With HIV/AIDS, trial and error doesn't work. The implication of this is that young people themselves must be the practical educators of their peers in matters of sexual practices, and that the key sites for learning must be the locations where teenagers are likely to have the chance of sexual encounters.

Another dimension to the knowledge-behaviour gap is the question of how HIV/AIDS fits into the world-view of African teenagers. Paul Richards (1999: 1) gives an intriguing insight into this:

> When youthful fighters of the Revolutionary United Front first attacked the town of Pujehun in SE Sierra Leone in April 1991 they shot dead the hospital pharmacy storekeeper because he was slow in opening the drug store. Give us the key, the young fighters clamoured, because we are all dying of AIDS. At the time, Sierra Leone had one of the lowest seropositivity rates of any country in the region. How did these troubled young insurgents get the idea that they were doomed by AIDS? And what does this tell us about their state of mind and prospects, fuelling a conflict that has since become a by-word for atrocity and destruction of agrarian communities?

What this illustrates is that for many of Africa's youth, the future is seen as profoundly uncertain, and their horizons are short. They simply have no life plans, and little expectation that they will be able to achieve the goals of a good education, a well-paid job, a stable family, etc. If many of Africa's youth see themselves as excluded, undervalued and doomed, what incentives do they have to avoid risky sexual activities? They ask, 'Why should I change my behaviour when I see little hope for improvement in life's opportunities?' (Collins and Rau 1999). Or, if people see the public authorities failing to take actions such as cleaning water supplies and removing rubbish, which would protect them from environmental health risks, this may reinforce a sense of non-control over privately-contracted infections.

AIDS prevention messages need to pay special attention to this context. Messages that spread fear, such as 'AIDS kills', may simply be counterproductive. On the other hand, messages that focus on the normalcy of people living with HIV/AIDS run the risk of failing to distinguish between those who are HIV positive and negative, in effect putting all at-risk people in the same category.

Young people have many reasons to distrust those who are transmitting anti-AIDS messages. Apartheid South Africa is an extreme example but a revealing one: even if the pre-1994 government had wanted to mount an HIV/AIDS prevention campaign among blacks, it simply lacked the credibility to do so. Some radical activists believed that the virus was deliberately manufactured by racist scientists to eliminate the black population—and indeed one right-wing MP publicly is quoted as having said, 'if AIDS stops black population growth, it would be like Father Christmas.' (van der Vliet 1996: 50). This echoes U.S. activists' charge that the Reagan Administration was quite happy to preside over 'genocide' in America's gay community. Young people elsewhere may see HIV as a political conspiracy by either gerontocratic elites or foreign powers, to prevent them having sex or to eliminate whole populations. Such views are not discouraged by the public statements of some African leaders.

There is also a danger that the lifetime chances of contracting HIV are so high—in countries such as Botswana today they are in the region of 60% or more—that young people simply fail to see a means of realistically protecting themselves and may cease to engage in protective strategies. This has been shown for gay men in the west. In Kampala, individuals may not seek treatment for STIs, for fear of finding out that they are HIV positive (Wallman 1996: 176). Becoming HIV positive may be so over-determined that huge and unprecedented changes in sexual behaviour are required to have a significant impact on lifetime chances of infection. In these circumstances, young people may simply plan to have a shorter adult life than their parents—maybe ten years instead of twenty or thirty.

HIV/AIDS and Schools

Most African children attend school. It is the place where they are most easily accessed. Schools are an important place for imparting knowledge about HIV/AIDS. Classroom AIDS education should not miss the opportunity to teach wider social issues that may shape young people's behaviour: 'AIDS education more broadly conceived promotes exploration of stereotypes and biases, fosters compassion for people in need, and examines how social and political institutions shape the epidemic' (Silin 1997: 168).

Too often, however, schools in Africa are organized in an hierarchical and authoritarian way that reinforces the very same power structures that have helped make the epidemic so intractable. Messages transmitted in schools can be contradicted by the behavioural example of the school itself—or even by a command-based, gender-biased 'participatory learning group.' Sex in schools, among pupils and between teachers and pupils, is a sensitive issue but it cannot be avoided. Schools can set standards for responsible sexual practices.

It is widely recognized that young people, especially girls, need education in 'life skills', especially negotiating sexual encounters. Many teachers are hesitant to teach an issue as difficult and controversial as HIV/AIDS and often this results in the minimum teaching of basic facts on transmission and protection, without the necessary life skills and negotiation skills that can enable students, especially girls, practise safer sex. Formal lectures alone are unlikely to have much impact on behaviour change: role-playing, peer educators, and other participatory methods practiced over a long period are required. But does Africa possess the trained sensitive teacher-facilitators who can provide this kind of education? Or will the continent be marked by a few, high-profile 'gold standard' projects run by visionary leaders, which simply cannot be replicated and scaled-up?

In all secondary schools and many primary schools in sub-Saharan Africa there is sexual activity among pupils and between teachers and pupils. Some of this is the normal process in which young people explore their sexualities (often starting at a very young age). Sexual harassment and violence is also common (African Rights 1994b). It is not uncommon for some male teachers to trade grades and special treatment in return for sexual favours from their girl students, including young teenagers. There have been well-publicised incidents of mass rape of girl pupils by their male peers, one of the most notorious being the incident at St. Kizito secondary school in Kenya in July 1991, in which 19 girls died and a further 71 reported being raped. Such cases are certainly just the tip of the iceberg in terms of coerced sex between students. As well as teaching young people about HIV/AIDS in the classroom, it is important that schools become a locus for setting an example for responsible and safe sexual attitudes and practices.

Despite the ubiquity of sex in schools, sex education is still rare and opposed by many religious groups. It is unheard of for schools to provide condoms. Any head teacher who tried to do so would immediately incur the wrath of conservative religious moralists. This task might best be undertaken by an independent international organization.

As micro-cosmoses of wider society and the locus for the socialisation of the young into the values of that society, schools are an important location for forging social and individual behaviour. This may extend from sexual activities to include wider changes to socio-cultural values, that may promote transparency, gender equality, and social mobilisation. The institutional culture of schools may have to change to allow more active involvement of students in issues of governance and responsibility. Jonathan Silin comments, 'The AIDS curriculum may be more about life than about death, more about health than about illness, more about the body politic than the body physical' (1997: 178).

The education sector across Africa already faces a large number of difficulties. National resources for education are often over-stretched already and adding HIV/AIDS education will only add to the strain. One of the main tasks will be investing in human capital: training teachers and peer educators in the complex and sensitive tasks they must undertake.

Sexual Abuse of Children

For too long, the sexual abuse of children in Africa has been a taboo subject. When the issue was raised in public, for example with reference to well-publicised scandals in Europe and North America, the common African response was, 'it doesn't happen in our culture.' Unfortunately, this response has been shown to be incorrect.

The number of young children infected by HIV on account of rape by an adult cannot be known. There are virtually no statistics on HIV prevalence among children aged between 3 and 14. These data are simply not collected. However, there is evidence on a small scale from the Family Support Trust clinic for sexually abused children in Harare, Zimbabwe. These point to an alarming picture, hidden from view. Over half the child victims of sexual abuse who were seen in the first two years of the clinics activity were under 12, and 16% under 5. High rates of HIV were found: 8% among the 5-8 year olds who presented at the clinic. We know two factors predispose to HIV infection that are present in such cases. One is that immature female genitalia are a major risk factor, and the second is that violent sex greatly increases the chance of HIV infectivity. Note also that boys are victims of sexual abuse too. Street children are particularly at risk from child sex abuse (UNICEF 2001a).

Other snippets of data are also suggestive. Data from HIV surveys in Kisumu, Kenya shows about 8% of 15-year-old girls are HIV positive (Pisani 2000). A study of rape in Senegal found that 60% of rape victims were schoolgirls and students, with an average age of under 15 (Mottin-Sylla 1993). This indicates a high rate of sexual encounters with adult men. Even when the girl of this age consents to intercourse, it qualifies as statutory rape.

There are some indications that sexual abuse of children may have risen on account of the AIDS pandemic. In Zimbabwe, some men are reported to believe that having sex with a virgin is a method of 'cleansing' the body of HIV. This, however, is a 'fact' that has gained currency through circulation rather than verification, and it has not been either fully investigated nor reliably reported from elsewhere.

In some African societies, women are married very young, often before they reach puberty. Their husbands may have sex with them before puberty. In some such cultures, the 'punishment' for raping or defiling a girl is marrying her. The rights implications as well as the potential for HIV transmission in these circumstances do not need to be stated.

Child sex abuse during wartime is a special problem. The extent of rape during war is well documented. Increasingly, research is revealing the extent of sexual abuse of children too. For example, Nordstrom found that children were often the victims of sexual violence in Mozambique. Government soldiers and even troops serving with the UN peacekeeping mission, were also responsible for the sexual abuse of children. She adds that 'it is estimated that underage boys are sexually assaulted with a frequency that is close to that of girls.' (Nordstrom 1997) If the sexual abuse of girls and boys is as epidemic and as liable to come from any quarter as the above suggests it may be that sexual abuse is also a frequent part of the experience of child soldiers. Additionally, for many children it may be the attempt to escape sexual abuse that leads them to a position where they are easily enrolled into fighting. It may even be the case that some children regard soldiering as preferable to prostitution.

Responses to this set of problems should start with public debate and information. These issues need to be brought out into the public realm. Research needs to be undertaken. Open debate needs to be initiated. Recent publicity over baby rapes in South Africa have given the issue a high public profile, but in a sensationalized and extreme way.

Legal measures need to be enforced, and where necessary, enacted. Most countries have laws providing for a minimum age for marriage; often this is not enforced especially in rural areas. Most legal codes prohibit sex with under-age children, though some do not distinguish between under-age children having sex with one another and statutory rape by an adult. These laws are only intermittently enforced. Often, the matter is settled in a customary civil court by the payment of compensation to the victim and her family. Particular attention needs to be given to schools, where many instances of sexual abuse of minors occur.

Enforcement of laws against child sex abuse require sympathetic handling by the police, courts and concerned welfare organisations. Important steps in this regard include special police departments where children can be treated sympathetically and seriously, and child-friendly courts.

The HIV/AIDS pandemic shines a spotlight on many of the most shameful secrets of a society, exposing hypocrisies that most would prefer to remain hidden. The extent of child sex abuse is one of these. It is an issue that can no longer be avoided.

Conclusion

The HIV/AIDS pandemic is now in its third decade. At the 1999 UN General Assembly Special Session, governments adopted a target: to reduce the incidence of HIV among young people aged 15-24 by 25% by 2005. This is an extremely ambitious target which may not be met. But it underlines the priority of targeting youth for HIV/AIDS prevention programmes, focussing on behaviour change. Almost a decade ago, UNICEF highlighted precisely this. James Grant wrote,

> Most of the human faces of this epidemic are of children and youth. As many as two thirds of all HIV infections occur among young people before their 25th birthday. For young women in their teens, the rate of infection is twice to three times that of young men of the same age. (UNICEF 1993: 1)

Indeed adolescents are one of the favoured target groups for national and international programmes. There are some clear instances in Africa where HIV rates among young people have come down. Uganda, the first country to recognize an AIDS epidemic, is a well-known case. Senegal has acted early and decisively to prevent the emergence of a generalized epidemic, and infection rates in Kinshasa remain relatively low. But unfortunately there are too few examples of a countrywide success in rolling back the pandemic, and many obstacles to scaling-up the successes that have been registered.

Reversing a generalized epidemic is intrinsically difficult. In concentrated epidemics (such as in Asia and Europe), the highest-risk groups can be readily identified—commercial sex workers and their clients, certain occupational categories such as truck drivers and soldiers, men who have sex with men and intravenous drug users. In such cases, focussed programmes can be highly effective, while programmes aimed at the general populace have been cost-inefficient and ineffective at reducing HIV in the highest-risk categories.

In most of sub-Saharan Africa, the generalized nature of the epidemic dictates programmes aimed at the majority of the sexually-active population. This does not rule out targetted programmes aimed at groups engaging in high-risk practices—in fact the best general programmes consist of overlapping targetted programmes tailored for specific groups and sexual practices. This requires a level of mobilization several orders of magnitude greater than anything that has been attempted so far. The scale of this task must not be underestimated. At the African Development Forum 2000, 'Leadership at All Levels to Overcome HIV/AIDS,' several African leaders compared the degree of mobilization required as equivalent to war. This is if anything an understatement. The HIV/AIDS pandemic is a survival issue for Africans, African countries and the African continent. AIDS education is a first step. Participatory health promotion is emerging as a 'best practice', but much remains to be learned about translating textbook theory into practice (Campbell and Williams 2001). In the 1980s, the gay communities in the U.S. and Britain were galvanized by AIDS activism and achieved major behavioural changes even before official programmes were initiated: some African countries need to mobilize their *entire societies* to the same degree.

Unfortunately, once an HIV/AIDS epidemic has become generalized in the population, its transmission is over-determined. Extremely high levels of consistent safer sex and other preventive behaviours are required for any significant reduction in HIV incidence.

In such an epidemic, reaching youth and children is imperative. This is dictated by the high rates of HIV infection among young women and the way in which patterns of sexual activity are set at an early age. The pandemic will be rolled back only when a cohort African youth grows to adulthood largely free of the virus. But for authorities to reach youth is intrinsically difficult, especially in societies which are polarized by the politics of age. Much greater effort and imagination is required.

With high rates of high-risk sexual activity among teenagers, it is tempting to define youth as a 'problem' with regard to HIV/AIDS. In fact, this is a variant of blaming the victim: the 'problem' is the behaviour of adult men, especially those in positions of power. It is important to reach target the mature men who have sex with teenage girls—and change their sexual behaviour. More widely, those in positions of power and authority should use their leadership to set an example, to break the silence and encourage behaviour change. At present this is rare, and it is unsurprising that young people are suspicious of those in authority. Those who are preaching abstinence, faithfulness and use of condoms may be indistinguishable from those who are seen to be responsible for the epidemic in the first place. Practice must change at the top.

9

Pentecostal Christianity and Young Africans

CHARLOTTE SPINKS

For many young Africans, 'youth' is not serving as a transitional phase to a more established social status, but is an enduring limbo. This is a source of tremendous frustration. Instead of leaving youth behind and entering adulthood by marrying and establishing an independent household, an increasing proportion of this 'lost generation' (Cruise O'Brien, 1996) are unable to attain any other social status. Often only partially educated, these unwilling youths often remain without employment and forming a category of social 'cadets'—in wealth and power if not in age. Hence they lack the resources to shed junior dependence and attain economic independence and achieve effective participation in the social and political life of their communities and nations.

The frustration arising from protracted 'youth' is magnified at the national and regional level by demographic changes: youths now form a large section of the population (even a majority in some areas), and are increasingly urban. Living in economic uncertainty and frustrated at their often incomplete education and social marginalisation, African youths are ripe for mobilisation.

In this context, many young people respond by turning either to violence or to religious commitment (or both). As a consequence, two kinds of new social organisations with strong youth identities have emerged outside of the traditional kinship lineage. Both groupings provide an expression of youth identity beyond the constraints of their elders: armed movements (addressed in other chapters in this volume), and new religious movements, of which Pentecostal Christianity is the leading example. This chapter charts the modern rise of Pentecostal Christian movements in Africa to assess their impact on young people in Africa, and thus on the future of Africa.

Background

There is a vast and confusing array of terms and labels for modern Christian movements in Africa, including: Pentecostal, charismatic, (neo-)fundamental, cults, 'born-again'; and numerous Church groupings such as 'Assemblies of God' (AoGs), and 'African Independent Churches' (AICs). Although there are differences between the specific meanings of each term, all essentially refer to a similar Christian ethos based on the personal experience of spiritual gifts and 'Baptism in the Spirit', rather than to specific theological and religious doctrines. For the purposes of this chapter, the different labels will be used interchangeably. In fact, these new movements adapt so rapidly that many specific labels are now obsolete or far-removed in practice from their initial definition (Hunt et al, 1997: 2).

There has been a rapid growth of charismatic movements worldwide, and whether indicators that 16,400 Africans become Christians everyday are accurate or not, it is clear that 'Christianity is a significant force in the lives of a good part of the population' (Gifford, 1995: 2, 1988: 103). Although this Pentecostal growth has occurred gradually since the 1970s (partly a result of the influx of American evangelists), the late 1990s witnessed an explosion of radical Christian activity amongst young Africans, aided by the increasing use of electronic media (Maxwell, 1998: 255). This occurred in the context of national crises. The absence of a strong state or civil society, and the perceived irrelevance and double-faced actions of mainstream churches, have led Africans to turn elsewhere for solutions to their problems. Pentecostal movements are especially attractive to young adults because of the contrast they offer to youth-despair; for this reason they are frequently labelled 'youth Churches' (Gifford 1998).

Rather than representing a global Americanisation, these churches are better seen as a radical and highly spiritual indigenous African trend. While mainline churches and state structures have failed to meet the modern needs of African people, Pentecostal Christianity has filled the void in 'answering needs left entirely unaddressed [elsewhere]' (Gifford, 1998: 329). In the context of the rights of the child, these churches provide a means for young people participate in social, economic and political life in a way that is personally meaningful. Whether or not this is a meaningful realisation of 'participation rights' is a different question.

Charismatic 'born again' movements emphasise the personal experience of spiritual gifts (e.g. prophecy, healing, speaking in tongues) and Baptism by Spirit, rather than formal theological and religious doctrine. This stresses the personal conversion experience (becoming 'born again') as the key identifying factor. In practice, this has led to a focus on personal inspiration, prosperity teaching, spiritual power and miracles, extreme commitment, church planting, and strong methods of zealous evangelism. The ultimate aim of the Pentecostal movement is to convert the entire population, and thus shape the 'destiny of the nation ... after their image' (Marshall, 1995: 245). The strict Pentecostal moral code, which includes abstention from alcohol, tobacco, drugs, and sexual promiscuity, is promoted within an emotional religious atmosphere (e.g. singing and dancing), in which members can be re-birthed by receiving an infilling of the Holy Spirit (often symbolised by speaking in tongues).

The Gospel of Prosperity teaches that God desires every Christian to be wealthy, and that true Christianity leads to prosperity. It also confirms the converse: that poverty is a self-inflicted sin, or a consequence of insufficient faith. This doctrine of prosperity has an obvious attraction for those engulfed in poverty as well as for those seeking to legitimise their wealth. The prosperity ethos hails from North America and has been criticised for opposing mainline church teachings that treasures cannot be stored on earth,[1] and traditional African cultures which teach against accumulating more than one's neighbour and view wealthy individuals with suspicion (Gifford, 1990).

There is controversy over the origins of the Pentecostal movement. Some writers argue that African 'charismania' is U.S.-originated and controlled, while others see modern Pentecostal movements as responses to the successes and shortcomings previous African churches (e.g. AoGs and AICs). Whichever interpretation one favours, the modern African charismatic renewal is a dual response to the bureaucratisation, religiosity and irrelevance of the mainline churches (Hunt, 1997: 3) on the one hand, and to states perceived as corrupt, authoritarian, shirking its welfare responsibilities, submitting to Islam, and unable to maintain societal order on the other (Marshall, 1993: 214-5).

Pentecostal Christianity in Africa is 'youth-driven in a way which is almost unimaginable in Europe', with young Africans initiating and leading churches (Ward, 1999: 235). The main age group of both leaders and members of one prominent Ghanaian Pentecostal church is 18-35 (Gifford, 1998: 82). Pentecostalism meets youthful desires for reality and independence by providing spontaneity, close bonding, instant communities, and simultaneously offering mystery and meaning to life (Quebendeaux, 1983: 218). Young people easily identify with the charismatic movement in two key respects. In the first place, Pentecostal movements' rejection of the status quo appeals to youthful aspirations to escape the routinisation of modern life to find the supposed reality and purpose of living. Secondly, prosperity teaching supports and legitimises ambitious young men and women seeking to break traditional bonds (e.g. family ties and traditional forms of wealth distribution) to achieve economic independence.

The success of the new churches is accounted for by a combination of *push* factors (away from the racism of mainline Church missionaries and the perceived irrelevance of their teachings, and away from the disinterest of the State in meeting youth needs), and *pull* factors (toward Pentecostalism as identifying and meeting youth needs and African spirituality). The originators of most African Pentecostal movements tend to be women and young men, who have fewer stakes in the old order and are thus willing to challenge social and cultural structures. Pentecostalism can provide the means for women and young people to redress the marginality experienced within established missionary churches of European origin and African patriarchal orders and post-colonial states alike. As well as appealing to the socially marginalized, Pentecostal movements worldwide evince a strong urban-poor membership, although as the churches expand, members are increasingly drawn more widely (Marshall 1995: 253).

Student revolt has always played a key role in youth politics, and is relevant to the rapid spread of African charismania (Ojo, 1988: 141-8). Although student groups (e.g. Scripture Union and Campus Crusade) have been vital as a catalyst for charismatic explosion (Atiemo, 1993: 30), students are only a minority of African youths. It is the mass of poorly-educated youths with limited ability to gain independence who form the bulk of these new movements, which they see as offering practical and emotional alternatives to their despair. In addition, young people found and join these new churches because of the vigour of the proclamation of a relevant message and what is seen as an authentic indigenous interpretation of the Bible relevant to their religious and political aspirations (Anderson, 2001: 33ff., Daneel, 1987: 101). Young Africans are the active creators of a culture-in-the-making.

Attractions of Pentecostal Movements

Although Pentecostal movements have been criticised for ignoring external socio-political realities, in fact many urban youths are attracted by opportunities for wealth, employment, solidarity and hope. The Pentecostal message is not surprisingly popular among Africa's urban educated, English speaking, upwardly-mobile youth, for whom these churches provide the support and encouragement needed to rise above their circumstances. Those aspiring to succeed are given support, and the focus on achievement serves to increase ambition and determination. More immediate and tangible benefits also come from the job opportunities (e.g. pastors, administrator, technicians etc.) arising within these growing churches (Gifford, 1998: 91). The Pentecostal focus on 'personal reformation' is particularly relevant to those who feel frustrated and directionless. The intensity of the movement provides a route to break out of this despair. Charismatic phrases such as 'breaking through' and 'victorious' are themselves an encouragement to youth to raise their ambitions (Gifford, 1998: 169-70).

The Pentecostal style of worship is exuberant and youth-orientated with emphasis on singing, dancing, and the use of popular music. This participatory and exhilarating style provides an alternative not only to the staid and traditional hymns of mainline churches, but also a free version of nightclubs, where young people can interact despite financial constraints. Some churches in Ghana even run their own music-label, and Zambian inter-Church conferences could be easily mistaken for rock-music festivals. Indeed, given the 'dearth of other entertainment and ... exciting television, the element of show time increases in importance' (Gifford, 1998: 234). Instead of spending scarce money on discos and nightclubs, teenagers now go to church to dance, entertain themselves and meet other youths.

The extreme intensity of the churches, in which high commitment is demanded, appeals to youthful passion and provides a network of support at a time when extended family support has been fractured by mobility and change. Pentecostalism creates both global and local communities. With respect to the former, each 'saved' member identifies with an international community of 'born agains', whereas the latter operates as a local support network, vital in the context of weakening family ties and the resulting anxiety and uncertainty (Marshall-Fratani, 1998: 283; Maxwell, 1998: 256-7). The Pentecostal structure provides a 'new world' for members, as a community of brothers and sisters. It offers a 'social space' where members find 'shelter, psychological security, solidarity' away from the harsh realities of their troubled nations. They exist as equal and free individuals in a mutual support mechanism enabling the individual to take charge of their own life (Gifford, 1995: 5-6). The common 'born again' identity catapults young people into a 'security circle and safe environment' in the midst of an urban society where decreasing education, unemployment, and overcrowding dominate daily life (Van Dijk, 1995: 180).

The charismatic emphasis on personal inspiration (e.g. speaking in tongues) as the source of true power and authority (rather than institutional hierarchies) provides the means for young people and women to challenge traditional African gerontocratic social structures. In societies traditionally dominated by elders, Pentecostal Churches give young people leadership and responsibility. This junior-elder frustration is not new, but the increasing worldliness of westernised African youths has decreased their willingness to submit to the perceived ignorance of elders, and Pentecostalism provides a platform to exercise this frustration. By indirectly opposing the authority of elders, a new social order is created in which youths can legitimately reject gerontocratic authority (Van Dijk, 1995: 181-2).

Whilst mainline Churches and traditional African cultures preserve leadership positions for the elderly, in the Pentecostal Churches youth are able to exercise more responsibility. Leadership training is a priority in the newer Churches, and youth is no barrier (Gifford, 1988: 171). Spiritual gifts can give their possessor a socio-political status, and the means to claim moral superiority over their elders, who may not be considered 'real' Christians, and are thus refused access to the born-again identity.

The rejection of gerontocratic authority is played out is by means of the AICs' rejection of traditional African rites, such as the worship of spirits, divination, possession, polygyny, the use of charms, or the drinking of traditionally brewed beer (Anderson 2001: 194-5). In other situations, the AIC's have appropriated certain aspects of traditional culture, transforming them in the light of a Christian interpretation (Anderson 2001: 199; Daneel 1987: 26; 1974: 309-347). These appropriations, though less radical than the outright rejection of the culture of one's elders, should also be seen as a negotiation of power by means of which young people have managed to ameliorate their status in society. At the other end of the spectrum from outright confrontation with elders, some AIC's have adopted a very subtle incorporation of the entire cosmology underpinning traditional religions. In such cases, young Pentecostal neophytes openly renounce their traditional religious practices, while their world-view and cosmology remain structured around their earlier belief systems. In such situations, the Pentecostal church must meet two challenges. On one hand it must be relevant to the local world-view its philosophical tenets (that usually remain implicit). On on the other hand, it must simultaneously address the social problems young people experience as a result of rapid social change, poverty, and political oppression. In such situations, Pentecostalism does not represent a revolutionary rejection of traditional culture and religion so much as the transformation of Christian doctrine in line with the spiritual, social and political needs of contemporary Africans (Anderson 2001: 206-210; Cox 1996: 219, 228; Pretorius and Jafta 1997: 217).

The newer Churches also address needs relevant to marginalised young people. Some Pentecostal Churches, for example, provide a marriage service, and this 'match-making function is openly admitted' (Gifford, 1998). In polygamous societies, the elite can afford to marry many wives. This situation can result in fierce competition for wives among poorer young men, many of whom cannot afford to marry, and so stay entrapped as 'youth'. In such cases, the church offers young people an opportunity to meet partners, and young women are often encouraged to dress themselves up to this end. This is not to say, however, that the AIC's are all against polygamy. One reason for their popularity follows from their resentment at Western missionary prejudice against African culture and family structures, and many of them therefore embrace polygamy as a practice that is in fact accepted in many passages of the Old Testament (Anderson 2001: 32).

The cultural appeal of Pentecostalism is also relevant for African youths who aspire to American consumerist culture and want Nikes, Levis and NY Giant baseball caps. These churches appear to have links to America, the 'land of opportunity'. Ambitious young Africans see the external links of the Pentecostal churches as a ticket to fulfil their dreams of an American education (Gifford, 1998: 317-8).

In the midst of individual and national crises, the Pentecostal movement offers young people a sense of personal and community-based identity and dignity. Anxious youths may believe they have a powerful ally in God, and thus be able to find self-worth in playing a role in their local, national and global environment (Cox, 1996).

Aspects of Youth Emphasis

An obvious criticism of the tendency of these movements to target young adults is the notion that they are preying upon a vulnerable age-group, and astute Church leaders can take advantage of weaker followers to create deceptive cults based on manipulation (Osayimwense 1995: 53-6). Cults tend to have a high youth involvement and African examples comparable to Waco and Jonestown exist. However, in many African Pentecostal movements, the leaders themselves are as young as their followers. Other concerns of youth prominence in Pentecostalism have arisen in response to the rise of schoolboy prophets and preachers, particularly in Malawi (Van Dijk, 1992, 1996; Pauw, 1996: 30-31).

Some African charismatic Churches have accentuated tensions

between elders and youths, by putting the claims of young people to the fore in societies in which elders assume all positions of responsibility. The claims of the new churches on behalf of the young challenge traditional age-based societal structures, and charismatics have been criticised for trying to 're-order society for the benefit of youth' (Gifford, 1998: 437). The extreme commitment required by Pentecostalism may lead young adherents to feel a stronger obligation to their church than to their family. Youthful frustration with marginalisation is not new, but the born-again identity legitimises the actions of those youths who break from the old order and defend their independence against their elders (Van Dijk, 1992: 76). Pentecostalism's wider networks provide both rationale and means for breaking family bonds (Marshall-Fratani, 1998: 284). Its strict moral code, including abstention from alcohol and tobacco, can be perceived as a rejection of traditional culture. Traditional spiritual cults have been a casualty of this (Maxwell, 1995: 319, 325). Pentecostalism can therefore encourage and legitimise young people's rejection of traditional social structures, with implications for family bonds, cultural continuity and social stability.

The cultural attributes of charismania, and specifically 'prosperity' teaching, have often been criticised for symbolising the American manipulation and re-colonisation of African minds (Garner, 2000: 314). There is clear evidence that in some specific cases African Pentecostalism has been U.S. 'controlled, financed and orchestrated' (e.g. in Doe's Liberia), and has subsequently created new areas of cultural expression and social tensions not necessarily suited to the African context (Gifford, 1993, 1998: 348).

However, these cases are increasingly the exceptions. New African churches have strong local roots and there are many examples of the African appropriation, or 'indigenisation' of the Pentecostal movement. While styles of music, preaching and organisational structures may have clear Western borrowings, international ties may be 'largely symbolic' (Marshall-Fratani, 1998: 284). They may, for example, be a helpful mechanism for obtaining funds and scholarships. In fact, much of the Pentecostal emphasis on spirituality has clearer roots in African healing, dreams and visions than in Western culture. Many of the charismatic movements are 'unique' in their 'visions, creativity, [and] patterns of thought' (Hexham and Poewe, 1994: 66), and it is safe to say that young Africans have appropriated Christianity to their own ends making western involvement essentially irrelevant. Africanised indigenous churches are more in tune with African cultural traits and temperaments (i.e. free and emotional rather than disciplinarian, cold and frigid western churches), and have assimilated indigenous religious practices into the fabric of Pentecostal prayer and praise (Cox, 1996). While African Pentecostal leaders draw on U.S. methods, such as prosperity teaching, the dominant message is shaped by local concerns as Africans fuse their own traditions with charismatic Christianity to create new forms of religious and social experience (Poewe, 1994: 17).

The advantages of the Pentecostal movement for young people are self-evident: increased assertiveness, detachment from structures favouring elders and socio-economic opportunities. The vast numbers of young people involved are testimony to the strength of these benefits to mitigate against the disadvantages. In fact, the ability of charismatic movements to challenge patriarchal religious and social structures and to create a new system of social relationships highlights their long-term 'potential beyond other Christian movements' to contribute positively to Africa's future (Maxwell, 1995: 334). Pentecostalism's focus on individualism and personal choice has enabled new bonds of solidarity to develop among young people. The egalitarian structures of these new churches has created opportunities for young people to take on leadership positions. In some cases 'born again' shared identity has transcended ethnic divides, enabling problems such as ethnic tensions to be addressed. The churches can reconciliation and support for the oppressed at a personal level. African Pentecostalism serves as a coping mechanism helping ordinary young Africans to face painful social and economic transitions in the midst of troubled nations. The churches are thus said to offer a 'framework with which to respond to the pressures of modernisation' rather than a full 'liberation' from pain (Maxwell, 1998: 369).

In the era of HIV/AIDS, the Pentecostal emphasis on behavioural change and strict moral code of abstention has obvious relevance. Religious groups such as 'True Love Waits' and 'Youth Alive' (both of U.S. origin) are prominent in Uganda and Zambia in stressing individual behavioural change as part of their sex and HIV/AIDS schools educational programme (Werbner and Ranger 1996; Gifford 1998: 226). Successful HIV/AIDS prevention strategies in Uganda, Zambia and Senegal have focused on strengthening social and religious attitudes and values to decrease the social acceptability of casual and extra-marital sex. Harnessing the positive influence of Pentecostal communities over their youthful members promises to be an effective component in HIV/AIDS prevention strategies. However, the fundamentalist focus on abstinence and fidelity as the *only* solutions provides relief exclusively for 'born agains.' This kind of moralising can have wider negative effects, for example by stigmatising people living with HIV and AIDS, creating problems for sex education in schools, or opposing programmes to promote condoms.

Therefore, Pentecostalism provides not just a new conceptualisation of the world-order, but also the tools for young people to tackle the restrictions of existing systems. The logic of transformation begins with the individual. The personal empowerment of spiritual re-birth cannot be detached from the subsequent 'practical power to transform [one's] social world' (Marshall, 1993: 242). The churches create their own microcosms of an alternative, transformed moral and social order—what one writer has called 'autonomous spaces of practise which defy the oppressive logic of current power monopolies' (Marshall, 1993, 1995). This implies that Pentecostal Christianity has potential for achieving the kinds of individual, social and national change that has eluded official policies for so long.

African Pentecostalism: Panacea or Pain-killer?

Young people have played key roles in the initial stages of charismatic renewals and revivals, not just in Africa but also in Europe and America. But, as these movements grow in size and influence, the numbers and prominence of young people tend to decline (Quedendeaux, 1983: 130). This 're-marginalisation' of the young has also occurred in Latin American Pentecostalism.[2] So far, African charismatic churches are not yet sufficiently established for us to ascertain if the pattern will apply wholesale.

Christian trends have a cyclical nature, in which radical movements easily lose their Pentecostal vigour because of internal bureaucratisation. As youthful initiators grow older and more conservative, however, a new sequence of increasingly vigorous fundamental movements emerge, headed by new generations of youths, to challenge 'old' Pentecostalism (Maxwell 1995: 316-7). This pattern is familiar from missionary work. For example in the fifty years after 1924, a missionary in the Congo described how 'the full circle [of Christian mission work] turned twice' (Womersley 1974: 160). This generational cycle is also familiar from movements for Islamic renewal (Last 1992).

In contemporary Africa, the 'category of "born-again" ... constitutes a powerful social and economic operator', in which the common association uniting believers is a self-conscious desire to change society and to make history for God (Marshall 1993: 242). However, the potential for this social reconstruction to be effective and/or sustainable is, as yet, unknown. How might this happen? One school of thought contends that ultimate economic and political success depends on the politicisation of the movement (Marshall, 1993: 242-3). If not seeking state power, Pentecostalists should at least help determine state policy. However, the experience of politicised Christianity has not been positive. In Liberia, for example, politicised Pentecostal Christianity has contributed only to the 'oppression, impoverishment and destruction of an entire country' (Gifford, 1993: 3). This implies that Pentecostalism is incapable of empowering young

Africans in the long-term, and that transformation in political and economic structures is a pre-requisite for achieving real change.

Pentecostalists themselves may advocate their movement as the solution to Africa's range of problems. Detractors of various shades may try to wish away the religious revival. We must see Pentecostalism as a vigorous reality that is helping to change the face of Africa. In its successes and shortcomings it again underlines the need for solid structures to empower young Africans and enable them to participate in the political life of their countries.

1. A doctrine spoken by Jesus: 'Do not store up for yourselves treasures on earth' (Matthew 6:19).

2. The Latin American example is important, not only in having witnessed unprecedented growth in charismatic Christianity at least a decade prior to the African explosion, but also because it is extremely well documented (unlike African experiences), and thus provides a potential parallel and forerunner of trends for African Pentecostalism. For further reading see particularly Freston (1997), in addition to Cox (1996), Hastings (ed., 1999), Hunt et al. (eds., 1997), and Poewe (1994).

10

Implementing the Convention on the Rights of the Child in Africa

KOMBE TEMBA AND ALEX DE WAAL

'Horrified, angry, disillusioned, and saddened...'

—OPENING WORDS OF THE YOUTH STATEMENT TO THE AFRICA DEVELOPMENT FORUM 2000

Africa's young people and children are adamant that the world's collective efforts to implement the Convention on the Rights of the Child in the last ten years leave much still to do. Theirs is the verdict we must heed. This chapter examines the extent to which Africa and the international community have succeeded in meeting the basic demands of African children and young people in the twelve years since the adoption of the Convention on the Rights of the Child.

The adoption of the CRC should have fundamentally altered the ways in which states and the international community approach the rights and welfare of children. States' obligations to children have never before been so clearly defined in international law.

The adoption of the CRC roughly coincided with the World Summit for Children and its adoption of a Declaration and Plan of Action. There are some similarities and overlaps between the two processes, which are complementary to one another. For example it is clear that the WSC encouraged many states to sign and ratify the CRC. However, the status of the CRC and the WSC Declaration and Plan of Action are markedly different. The CRC represents a legal obligation undertaken by states, while the WSC Declaration and Plan of Action are merely promises by heads of state and government. Moreover the WSC promises are focused on the more easily-achievable and measurable goals, such as certain levels of child vaccination. The most positive aspect of the WSC is that it signed an unprecedented number of heads of state and government up to a plan of action. A negative aspect is that this plan is that it was a minimum plan, focussing on what could be achieved quickly, cheaply and with minimum controversy. Important gains were made in the years immediately following the WSC but many of these were not subsequently sustained, reflecting this weakness.

This chapter is concerned with how the CRC should be implemented. This is a challenge not just for governments but for national and international civil society. The provisions of the CRC—and also the African Charter—reflect this. Implementing the CRC requires citizens' action.

The Rights Framework

'Together, our nations have the means and the knowledge to protect the lives and to diminish enormously the suffering of children, to promote the full development of their human potential and to make them aware of their needs, rights and opportunities.'

—WORLD DECLARATION ON THE SURVIVAL, PROTECTION AND DEVELOPMENT OF CHILDREN, 30 SEPTEMBER 1990, PARAGRAPH 8

At the September 1990 World Summit for Children (WSC), world leaders committed themselves to achieving a set of goals for children over the coming years ('World Declaration on the Survival, Protection and Development of Children in the 1990s' and Plan of Action for implementing the World Declaration). Seventy-one Heads of State and Government from around the world were present. Among them were seventeen African Heads of State or Government while a further 31 were represented by senior officials. Although the WSC gained a high level of prominence and publicity, in fact its main significance was that it symbolic of something more profound: shortly afterwards the Convention on the Rights of the Child (CRC) came into force, expedited by ratifications by African countries. The CRC is a far more important document than the World Declaration. This chapter will repeatedly stress that the CRC is a fundamental legal commitment by states, while the WSC and its Declaration and Plan of Action were merely tools adopted by governments relevant to a particular situation as it existed in 1990.

Subsequently the Convention has been ratified by every state in the world save Somalia and the USA. Somalia has the excuse that it has not had a recognised government for the last decade. This makes the CRC the most widely ratified international convention. The U.S. position is rooted in a philosophical stance on the nature of human rights, which it sees in the liberal tradition as legal obligations on a state to preserve the liberties of its citizens.

The African Charter on the Rights and Welfare of the Child (ACRWC) was adopted by the Organisation of African Unity (OAU) in July 1990, and contains similar provisions to the CRC on child welfare, concentrating on both rights and duties for children and parents. Drafted by the OAU and the African Network for the Protection and Prevention of Child Abuse and Neglect (ANPPCAN) with the assistance of UNICEF, the Charter is designed to 'retain the spirit as well as the substance of the letter' of the CRC while making 'special provisions guided by the ground situation in Africa'. After receiving the requisite fifteen ratifications, this came into force in December 2000.

As the African Charter is now in force, this is an appropriate moment to underline its importance, stress its complementarity with the CRC, and request more African states to sign and ratify it.

The rights in the CRC and ACRWC can be categorized in several ways: to *respect* the rights of children—that is, to act in a manner that is respectful of human rights—to *protect* children from the potentially harmful actions of third parties, to *facilitate* actions that can promote the realisation of children's rights, and to *fulfil* obligations to provide for child rights (UNICEF 2001b). Increasingly, with the 'human rights approach to programming,' UNICEF is shifting away from a basic needs approach to a human rights approach, stressing that its programmes are intended to realize the rights of children.

Throughout this book, we have asked, more than a decade after its adoption, what progress has been made in meeting the key obligations enshrined in the CRC? And have the World Declaration promises been fulfilled? And what stands in the way of full and adequate implementation? The chapters on child survival, poverty, education and conflict all indicate that a great deal more needs to be done. This chapter is concerned with strategies to implement the commitments, by national governments, civil society and the international community. Those wishing to find a more detailed review of the numerous national level policies, programmes and initiatives relevant to the achievement of the 1990 goals are referred to the reports of UNICEF's Africa Regional Offices (UNICEF-ESARO 2000, UNICEF-WCARO 2000).

Assessing the CRC and the World Declaration

The Convention on the Rights of the Child is an international treaty to which states are party. It places a legal obligation on state parties to fulfill the requirements laid down in the Convention. The World Summit for Children Declaration is a weaker commitment, by national leaders, to a programme of action. The obligation is less.

While the CRC entails legal obligations, the WSC Declaration contains only promises.

If a state ratifies an international convention outlawing (say) torture or the use of the death penalty, then it is straightforward to monitor that state's adherence to its commitments, and any lapse can be directly and unquestionably attributable to a culpable failure by the state in question. Assessing the fulfillment of the obligations contained in the 1989 Convention on the Rights of the Child is somewhat more complex and challenging. This is for several reasons.

To begin with, certain Articles in the CRC are 'first generation' rights that can and should be immediately enforced. 'First generation' rights are fundamental civil and political rights, to freedom of conscience and assembly, and to protection from abuse. These include the protection and representation rights. (However it is notable that while they included in the CRC, they are absent or very weak in the World Declaration and Plan of Action.) Other Articles are concerned with 'second generation' social, economic and cultural rights—including the right to survival. These are rights that require resources and institutional capacities for their implementation. The 'Maastricht principles' adopted by the UN Committee on Economic, Social and Cultural Rights in 1994 clarified the 'minimum core obligations' of governments constrained by poverty, which consisted in achieving a minimum immediately, making satisfactory efforts to realise the rights as rapidly as possible, and ensuring no retrogression. Still others are 'third generation' rights providing for international solidarity and cooperation.

In addition, while there is a clear state obligation to realise all the rights in the CRC, there is also a need for a plan of action to achieve the economic and social goals. In principle, the WSC Declaration and Plan of Action could be seen as a mechanism for enabling realisation of the CRC. In fact it is a weaker commitment, both in terms of the narrower substantive focus and also because of the nature of the commitment made—a promise only. Nonetheless, the WSC Declaration and Plan of Action deserve critical attention twelve years on. Some of the goals adopted are 'stretch goals' that are difficult to meet without the provision of additional resources beyond what is immediately available to poor governments. Fulfilling even one of the most straightforward rights, the right to primary education, which is an unconditional obligation on governments and not subject to progressive realisation, still requires resources not immediately available to budget-constrained African governments. Other WSC goals can be seen as short-term low-cost goals—for example the focus on vaccination against major childhood diseases—that may have been pursued at the cost of neglecting equally important longer term goals of building up sustainable health systems.

UNICEF's East and Southern Africa Regional Office review (UNICEF-ESARO 2000) notes that 'one can observe that broadly, ESAR has achieved progress in all of the major goals of the World Summit with the single exception of child nutrition. Yet it is clear from the sparse distribution of smiley faces [representing goal achieved] on the chart that most of the goals set at the World Summit have not been met' (p. 12). The review notes that the goals were ambitious and some countries revised their targets downwards during the decade (while the review still retained the original targets). For West and Central Africa the picture is much the same (UNICEF-WCARO 2000). Implicit in the WCARO review is the conclusion that a few countries and organisations score well for effort, but there is little reason for congratulation. In some areas there has been progress, in others no progress or even regression, while few countries have succeeded in achieving the stated goals.

Is it enough to mark 'progress' towards the goals? Reviewing the reviews of the 1990-2000 period, there is a distinct impression that the reviews are anxiously searching for some evidence—in some areas, *any* evidence—of 'progress'. The basic question should be, on current efforts, when (if ever) will the goals be achieved? And the answer to this is not likely to be encouraging.

Provision Rights

While all rights are 'provision rights'—requiring some actions to ensure they are realised, there is a set of rights conventionally subsumed under this title, including survival, health, nutrition and basic development as a human being (the latter best measured by education). In 1990, these rights were not realised for across Africa. In 2001, the situation is somewhat better—but the improvement is uneven and marginal. The achievement of child survival goals is outlined in chapter 2. The conclusion is sobering. African children still face the highest risks of early death, malnutrition and disease of any children across the world. In addition, they have failed to register marked progress in the last ten years. The implication is that the current trajectories for child survival and development are not such that Africa can realise the child's right to survival contained in the CRC.

The second major area of provision rights concerns education (chapter 4). Again, the trends are not encouraging. In most countries, enrollment rates for primary education are not improving at a rate that means that the continent is likely to deliver on the fundamental right to a primary education (CRC Article 28). On the contrary it is quite likely that educational provision will deteriorate, particularly in view of the impact of the HIV/AIDS pandemic on schools.

Africa's recent and ongoing economic performance also gives no serious reason to believe that the continent will meet the International Development Goals for 2015 (chapter 3). All the major indicators show that the continent as a whole is simply failing to make the necessary economic progress required to reduce poverty. In fact, the number of Africans living in absolute poverty is likely to increase over the coming decade. The depth and intractability of Africa's economic crisis is such that we need to examine the qualification clause in Article 6 of the CRC in some detail. Article 6 reads,

> States Parties recognize that every child has the inherent right to life.
>
> States Parties shall ensure to the maximum extent possible the survival and development of the child.

In the context of Africa's crisis, what do we mean by 'to the maximum extent possible'? According to the prevailing neo-liberal economic orthodoxies, governments are obliged to practice fiscal austerity. As a result they can only provide rather modest social services, and many poor governments simply do not have the resources to provide for basic health and education. Even if governments provide about five per cent of GNP to these services, the overall amounts will remain so small that they cannot provide what is needed for essential health and education (Commission on Macroeconomics and Health, 2001). In 1994, the UN Committee for Economic, Social and Cultural Rights defined the obligation to 'achieve progressively' these rights, laying down minimum conditions. However, both the CESCR's resource-constrained 'progressive realisation' and the CRC's 'maximum extent possible' are simply not enough, and Africa's children will remain deprived for the foreseeable future.

The current uneven standards of governance and economic management across Africa also mean that in many cases, Africa is not utilising its modest resources efficiently, and in turn the continent is not attracting international partnership and investment. There is no alternative but a major improvement in standards of governance and economic management.

If we disaggregate the overall picture, however, we can identify the component parts of the constraints on realising the rights contained in the CRC.

HIV/AIDS. Some unforeseen factors have made it far more difficult to realise the right to life. Prominent among these is the HIV/AIDS pandemic. In 1990, there were some good epidemiological predictions for the extent of the HIV/AIDS pandemic, but these were not taken sufficiently seriously by policymakers. In addition, in Southern Africa, the pandemic developed faster than even the worst-case scenarios had foreseen. Overcoming HIV/AIDS is an absolute prerequisite for realising the child's rights to survival, development and education. Other major communicable diseases including malaria have also been an important obstacle. In setting its specific goals, the WSC was unaware of the extent of the coming HIV/AIDS pandemic, but well aware of the threats of malaria and other infectious diseases.

Natural disasters such as floods, cyclones, and droughts have contributed to further deterioration of the situation of children in affected countries. However, this factor should not be over-estimated: Africa has generally been able to foresee and prepare itself to face these disasters effectively; this is one of the areas in which substantial progress has in fact been made in the last fifteen years. Overall, nature can plead 'not guilty.' But measures to overcome these natural adversities need to be maintained and expanded.

Economic weakness. Some external factors outside the control of African governments, but within the control of the international community, have made it impossible to realise important provision rights. These factors include declining aid levels, unsustainable levels of debt, obstacles on access to world markets for African products, and the requirement of African governments to meet stringent austerity conditions in order to qualify for debt relief. A major increase in international resource flows to Africa is required if African children are to have acceptable life chances. African governments cannot be held accountable for failures that follow from their lack of economic options, in the context of structural adjustment policies imposed from outside. However it should also be noted that important components of Africa's economic weakness lie squarely within the area of responsibility for African governments themselves, namely poor governance and economic management.

Continuing conflicts and civil strife have put child rights and actions for ensuring achievement of the time-bound goals in jeopardy. Conflict has immense adverse consequences for all aspects of social and economic development and the possibility of realising the rights of the child (chapter 5). Resolving existing conflicts, preventing the outbreak of new wars and reducing the continent's demilitarisation are all essential components of establishing the foundations for realising the rights of the child.

Political will in Africa—a term that encompasses lack of determination and deliberate political choices. African governments themselves have not been sufficiently determined in realising the CRC. In some cases, corruption and poor governance have stood in the way of progress. In others, governments have pursued other priorities, making the political choice that the CRC is less important than (say) defence expenditure. It is questionable just how much some African leaders were sincerely committed to realising the provisions of the CRC when they acceded to it. Similarly, it is questionable how genuine they were when they committed themselves to the WSC Plan of Action. Improving governance, reducing corruption, enhancing economic management, and respecting human rights, are the essential requirements if African governments are to make the necessary progress towards realising the rights of the child.

To realise the rights of the child, a decade or more later than demanded, what is required is far more than a restatement of aims. What is needed is a strategy for overcoming the five constraints outlined above. This requires a plan of action that has concrete responsibilities for all parties. It needs measurable commitments, to policies and more importantly, outcomes. It requires timetables and strategies for the achievement of these commitments. These must be realistic, as unachievable goals in tight time frames can generate cynicism. (On the other hand, adopting ambitious goals can be an effective mechanism for generating enthusiasm.) Lastly it needs mechanisms for monitoring commitments, including sanctions for failures, incentives for success (especially so in the case of aid dependent countries)

Future international conferences on children should therefore focus on the imperative of realising the CRC. Now that the CRC is in force, WSC-style restatement of goals and targets is redundant. However, a concrete plan of action is still required as a focus for mobilisation and enthusiasm, aimed at addressing the major constraints identified. Many of these constraints are specific to Africa—or are more onerous in Africa than elsewhere—which demands a particular focus on African challenges. These constraints vary between African countries. It follows that targets and goals can be set at a *national* level, in accordance with the obligations of the CRC, and involving domestic processes of mobilising coalitions in favour of children. What is required is a clear restatement that all State Parties to the CRC have undertaken clear and specific obligations, and need to indicate how they will fulfil them.

Children in Government Policy

The CRC places a number of obligations on African governments to incorporate specific requirements into national planning and constitutions. The WSC Declaration and Plan of Action provides additional detail, and the Consensus document from the 1992 Dakar conference on assistance to African children required countries to produce National Plans of Action (NPAs) for children. There are also reporting requirements.

All African countries save four (Angola, Liberia, Somalia and Togo) produced NPAs within a few years of the WSC. Several took further steps, for example Burkina Faso which incorporated its NPA into its national development strategy, and Nigeria, Uganda and Mauritania which took the initiative to decentralise their NPAs.

Numerous initiatives on a small scale have been launched, aimed at awareness raising, and targeted assistance in particular areas. These include strategies to combat child labour, such as the Sierra Leone work code restricting child labour. At a more ambitious level, several countries have incorporated child rights provisions into their national constitutions. An example is South Africa, which took a giant step when it incorporated these requirements in the new Constitution enacted in 1996. The Constitution provides protection for the right to participate in one's culture and purports to guarantee the rights to gender equality. The recognition of personal and family law systems under any culture and religion is permitted, and the application of African customary law where appropriate is required (Fishbayn 1999: 147-8). It is important in this context that culture is not seen as an unchanging archive sanctified by antiquity, but a body of changing and changeable practice, that all can participate in. African judges are encouraged to appeal to State commitments to international law, and integrate them with cultural norms (Fishbayn 1999: 147-9, 166-7). (Issues concerning customary law and legal pluralism will be discussed below.)

Concerning adherence to reporting, an impact study of the CRC reporting procedure of governments to the UN Committee on the Rights of the Child found that 'the reporting process was generally not used as a catalyst for domestic review, debate, and policy change. The study made a number of recommendations for redressing this—recommendations that are notable in that they include civil society as key actors (Woll 1999). In the area of institutional reform, democratic governance and the realisation of all human rights are identified as a conducive precondition for realising child rights. Governments should also provide information and engage in the reporting and follow-up processes, and should promote legal and judicial reform to promote child rights. A specific measure is the nomination of a Children's Rights Commissioner/Representative with political authority, who can liaise with government and civil society. Concerning reporting itself, the study recommended finer focussing of assessments, more systematic incorporation of children and youth participation in the reporting process and the facilitation of intermediary organisations for reporting abuses such as specialised bureaus.

Participation

There is a basic ambiguity surrounding children's participation rights (Gooneskere, 1998: 310-338). This is based on the fear that giving children civil and (still more so) political rights may lead to adversarial relations with adults who have duties to care for children. In countries where young people have strong traditions of political militancy, governments are unwilling to cede them greater participation rights. It is notable that although the CRC provides for participation rights, the WSC goals for children and development in the 1990s made no reference at all to these rights.

In the context of child rights, 'participation' must be interpreted with a nuance that is absent concerning adults. For an adult citizen, civil and political rights are to be enjoyed in their entirety without qualification. But for children, these are relative terms: relative both to their age and capacities, and to those who have responsibilities for them. Participation refers to personal autonomy and the exercise of freedoms of association, expression, and conscience, to express views, be heard and be involved in decisions affecting one's life. But in Africa—as in other parts of the world—the concept of children's personal autonomy is often seen as antipathetic to the fundamental values of family and community. The CRC is cognisant of this, and allows for parental direction in the context of the evolving capacity of the child. However, it grants more autonomy to the child than most traditional cultures.

The CRC's participation rights are focussed on the child's right to be heard in any decision (in a court of law or otherwise) concerning him or her. The CRC does not grant *political* rights to children but fosters the idea of freedom of speech and expression. It doesn't address the minimum voting age. These omissions are significant.

Hence, the various attempts to create National Councils of Children and Children's Parliaments in a number of countries, have been deliberately as non-political as possible. Although led by 'youth' simply because of the incapacity of younger children to take on leadership roles, these focus on children's rights rather than on youth's demands.

In all other public policy contexts, it is accepted that there is a link between the design of an intervention and the participation of those likely to be affected by it, to ensure that the outcomes are relevant. This reasoning should be accepted in relation to children. A failure to assess children's lives necessitates the incorporation of children and youth as partners in research. Children's information can be factual, unbiased, fresh, original, creative and practical. Descriptions of their daily lives are frank and revealing. In order to understand the real needs of children from a context specific perspective, systematic efforts need to be made by governments to assist children to take part in and influence policy.

The Children's Summit in South Africa is an example of such an initiative, which took place in 1992, four years before the enactment of the new constitution. The Summit was held over six days and heard the voices of more than 200 children from 20 different regions expressing their concerns and demands to be put on the political agenda. This event led to the children developing the Children's Charter of South Africa, with one of the participants, a 15-year-old girl commenting, 'We want a part of that Constitution to belong to the future leaders of South Africa, which is us'. Children and youth require supportive procedures to make their points of view heard and taken seriously (Save the Children 1995: 3-39, 56). These should be socially inclusive too, with as broad a representation as possible, from schools, sports societies, street children, youth shelters, orphanages, etc. A key area in which participation can begin is schools. Democracy is learned by those who practice it, and democratic participation can start at secondary school.

The participation of children and youth in such processes requires an enabling environment in society. This requires fostering debate within communities and at local and national levels to encourage a better understanding of children's rights and the duties of State Parties to the CRC. This in turn requires education about the CRC (rights training) to raise awareness within society; among children and youth through schools, in civil society and the private sector, and in the judiciary and all state insitutions. It is important that the education penetrates into the family and household: participation rights need to start in the family itself. This may turn out to be the most significant challenge of all.

It is easy for these participation mechanisms to lapse into symbolic sideshows, merely means for co-opting some children and giving them a profile in the national media. Effective participation requires political leverage. Sadly, when young people are denied the prospect of effective participation, they often turn to criminality or militarism. Real change will occur when political leaders have no option but to listen to young people's concerns—because they need young people's votes. A single step that would enhance young people's participation in democratic decision-making would be to lower the age of voting, to sixteen or perhaps even lower.

Protection

There are two main components to child protection requirements in Africa. One is protection under the law. This is premised on having the legislation on the books, having the institutions functioning effectively, children having access to them in a fair and reasonable manner, and children knowing what are their rights. The second component is children in special need, and particularly protection in conflict (see chapter 5).

In many African countries there is a problem of legal pluralism. Children's rights may be much less respected in customary laws than in national codes or in the CRC. Local courts are likely to be the first call for enforcing child's rights, in which customary laws are likely to be enforced. Adherence to the CRC implies a reassessment of national and personal laws that conflict with it. This applies particularly to some interpretations of Islamic laws and some customary laws. But this is rarely carried out in practice, largely because customary codes tend to be enforced in rural areas where people are poorly educated about their rights and have little or no access to higher courts for appeal. Reforming customary laws to make them more consonant with the rights of the child is more than a legal challenge: it requires education and thorough-going social change in traditional communities. Governmental and non-governmental organizations can collaborate with religious groups, churches, other local groups and community leaders to help articulate and clarify traditional norms and values.

Legal reform is possible and can be effective. A fine example is provided by Zimbabwe. The efforts of the Zimbabwe government to reform the courts began shortly after Liberation, in an attempt to redress the racist and elitist character of the judicial system under the former regime. In the mid-1990s, this culminated when the Ministry of Justice, Legal and Parliamentary Affairs established the first victim-friendly courts. The principle was, to reduce physical and mental stress on the victim, especially in cases of rape and child abuse. The programme was implemented in a collaborative manner involving the government, NGOs (Legal Resources Foundation, Catholic Commission for Justice and Peace, various women's groups) and donors (principally NORAD). The Chairman of the committee running the project, High Court judge, Luke Malaba points out that

> The committee is aware that such victims of crime have particular problems in dealing with the machinery of justice and that such difficulties may be eased by reconsidering the way in which the system approaches vulnerable witnesses...The truth must be told but with the minimum physical and mental stress to the victim.

The aim of the project is to create a relaxed atmosphere in the court room. Instead of sitting on a chair in front of an authority figure in the formal interview set up, the victim sits in an armchair with a probation officer and other relevant people (supportive people are also allowed to sit with the victim). There is a corridor system ensuring the victim and the accused never meet. The decoration is bright to minimise reminders of being in an insitution. Children are to give evidence in camera and adult rape victims can be given that option. Closed circuit television systems are also to be provided for witnesses (African Rights 1996: 95-6).

Other initiatives, for example South African projects to end the secondary victimization suffered by rape survivors, have followed similar models, and have relevance to the functioning of court systems for child victims of abuse (Human Rights Watch/Africa 1995: 118-123). One of the major challenges they face is ensuring that abuses are actually reported to the authorities. Reformed reporting processes in particular may encourage increased reporting of children's rights abuses, while legitimating a country's system of social justice and strengthen the impact of protective measures that are in place (Human Rights Watch/Africa 1995: 119).

A system conducive to crime reporting has to go hand in hand with the confidence of children and youths. A Child Service Bureau that receives complaints and acts on behalf of children for example, needs to function with a strong understanding of its socio-cultural surroundings (Mensa-Bonsu and Hammond 1994; Rwezaura 2000), and of the interplay between the social relations which mediate children's relationships with legal regimes. Local community participation is essential to this.

In an urban context, the needs of street children are often left out of formal processes. A specialist organisation such as Childhope, which works to improve the rights of children living and working on the streets plays an important role in creating a socially inclusive environment in which the experiences of children who have deviated from conventional models of 'normal childhoods' are recognized. Working with street children is a good starting point in the area of children's rights, particularly with regards to disease, conflict, poverty and social deprivation (Childhope 2000; Save the Children 1995: 39).

A Movement for Children

'Apathy can only be overcome by enthusiasm, and e nthusiasm can only be aroused by two things: an ideal which takes the imagination by storm, and an intelligible plan for carrying that ideal into practice.'
—Arnold Toynbee

Emancipatory, progressive social change rarely comes about through governmental action by itself, let alone solely by legislation. Adopting a human rights convention or setting up an international institution can be an important contributor to change, but real progress tends to be propelled by social movements. In recent years UNICEF has recognised this and advocated a 'global movement for children'. But at present it is surely too optimistic to claim that such a movement actually exists.

What would it take to create a global, or an African 'movement for children'? Based on comparative analysis of social movements (de Waal 2000, 2002) we can outline various sets of requirements.

First, it is important that the issue is defined in a way that enables it to be come the focus of a movement. The issue must be *visible.* The welfare of children always has a certain visibility, but there are different issues that become conspicuous at different times, such as educational failure, child soldiers, or child sex abuse. At ptesent, the wider issue of the CRC is relatively invisible.

Next, the issue must have *moral and political salience.* Children's issues have a head start when it comes to moral salience: children are innocent victims par excellence and always manage to elicit a sympathetic response. The challenge is to turn this moral salience into political momentum. The ill-being of children must in some way become a political scandal rather than a call to charity.

A key element is that there must be a *clear threat* to the established social or political order. Successful social movements impel change by raising the possibility of a threat to those in power. When analysed objectively, the failure to provide for children is the most fundamental threat to the wellbeing of any social and political order. However this threat is not an immediate one: other issues are invariably more urgent, especially in an unstable political climate. It is likely that the downgrading of existing urgent threats, such as national security dangers and economic crisis, will be an integral part of making the issue of young people into an incisive political issue.

The issue must be *separable* from the wider array of social ills, and it must be seen as an issue that can be *surmounted*. No challenge that is unmanageable can be treated seriously. This underlines the importance of a clear plan of action.

Lastly there must be a clear *focus of responsibility*. If the moral and political salience is to be translated into action, there must be an institution that has clear responsibility and is impelled to act. A government or corporation is the ideal focus; an abstraction such as 'the international community' is not.

The above considerations highlight the importance of disaggregating the issue of children's rights, and focussing on a set of components within it. Campaigning against child soldiers is one possible focus, which has been taken up by a coalition of organisations. In this line, southern African experience with implementing the CRC led to the identification of six key action points (Diop and Ennew 1996). These include mapping social exclusions to identify vulnerable groups; making an inventory of ongoing local actions to facilitate better coordination; setting 'do-able' local goals based on the WSC; monitoring and acting on local-level disparities; preparing local annual child development reports; and establishing local level child policy coordination team charged with following up the overall results for children.

An effective campaign maintains a clear overall goal with tactical flexibility. It identifies the constituent issues and tackles each one, advancing wherever progress is possible. In all cases it is important to master the language and skills of the adversary—for example, those seeking to promote children's right to survival and health must fully master the complexities of public finance and theories of the economic returns to a longer life, as well as understanding the medical and epidemiological aspects of child health.

A second set of requirements relates to the social forces that pursue the issue. Any campaign requires a coalition of forces; the question is, how is this coalition put together and how the constituent parts operate together? The key to any campaign is *mass mobilisation.* This consists of the mobilisation of individuals, with multiple grassroots organisations and constituencies in pursuit of what they see to be their own interests, or a wider moral cause. Their intimate and ongoing involvement is the key to the maintaining the relevance, moral determination, sensitivity and sense of accountability of such a campaign. In the case of children, there are evident possibilities for mobilisation by young people. The participation element of rights provided by the CRC can be considered as a learning process that includes teaching about democracy and human rights in the school curriculum, and practising 'classroom democracy.'

Campaigns also require *professional advocacy.* Advocacy organisations represent the 'second generation' of human rights activism. Advocacy in this sense has policy-oriented and adversarial components. Policy-oriented advocacy is the activism of professionals in the area who can bring the issue to the public eye, provide legal and policy expertise, and advise governments and international organisations. Research is an important component of this. In the case of children, studies on structural adjustment and social development played a key role in providing the intellectual ammunition for new approaches to health and education (Cornia et al. 1987, Mehrotra and Jolly 1997). Adversarial advocacy is the investigation and documentation of cases of abuse, and the extent of abuse, in different countries; and the exposure ('naming and shaming') of governments that have turned a blind eye or worse to the practice. This includes bringing cases to court and providing legal aid to victims. Journalism and law are key professions in this kind of work. Both kinds of activism are required in any ambitious campaign. Professional groups and specialist organisations, such as legal firms engaged in pro bono work or public interest or social action litigation, and human rights documentation and advocacy organisations, are important partners. Their experience, analytical capacity and leadership skills will be important to the success of the campaign in different countries. There is experience of using this kind of advocacy to great effect in Europe, America and South Asia.

In the context of South Asia, the concept of social action litigation (developed by the Indian Supreme Court) creates opportunities for action through the courts to promote the CRC, and enforce group rights and interests. Laws are required to permit third parties such as concerned NGOs to bring cases of children's rights abuse before the courts. Social action litigation can be employed as a strategy promoting community monitoring and involvement in the realisation of child survival and development rights, in the context of social and economic rights (Gooneskere 1998: 71-2, 233).

International NGO strategies for advocating the CRC and ending children's rights abuses have focused on documentation and research, supporting local NGOs, using the media to publicise findings and embarrass governments, enlisting the help of donor governments to bring pressure by withholding assistance (Whitman 1998).

Material assistance can play an important role. Assistance agencies, ranging from local NGOs and community-based advice centres, to international NGOs, UN organisations and governmental donors, all will have a role here. Aid provision can be vital, but it also has its dangers, because assistance organisations tend to play down the political and adversarial components of any campaign, in favour of promoting uncontroversial and 'charitable' images that are invariably better for fundraising. This is particularly probable where children are involved. A balance must be struck between assistance and human rights advocacy: each must support the other.

Lastly, a campaign can develop *coalitions with concerned policymakers.* Sympathetic individuals in governments (legislature, executive and judiciary), and also in business, the UN, foundations, etc., can be key allies in any campaign. These 'policymakers with a conscience' will be strategic allies in terms of enacting legislation and policy changes. The judicial activism of some judges and advocates has been extremely important in South Asia, where there is an attempt to make judicial activism 'the last resort for the oppressed and bewildered.' (Gooneskere 1998: 70-2, 234). Child rights commissioners can also be an effective tool. But it is important that policymakers do not take the leadership of the campaign: this is for the grass-roots. There is a standing danger of cooption of a campaign by the powerful.

We must now turn to the facilitating conditions for a social movement to become active. These constraints have been analysed with regard to the possibility of pro-poor policies or respect for human rights emerging in different political environments (Moore and Putzel 1999, Risse and Sikkink 1999). Similar considerations apply for children. In countries beset by civil conflict, the basic precondition for any effective action on behalf of children is peace and the establishment of functioning authorities. Almost the only opportunity for promoting the rights of children is through putting pressure on the belligerent parties through outside organisations and governments. Hence the international linkages of individuals and organisations in the country concerned will be crucial to the success of any measures. These linkages have to be carefully handled, however, to avoid jeopardising those who are active inside the country.

In countries under personalised rule, there are very limited opportunities for mobilising any coalition on behalf of children, or implementing pro-child policies. If the leader so wishes, such policies may be decreed and perhaps implemented, but progress is likely to be extremely precarious. Again, international linkages with governments and NGOs may be the crucial factor in making any progress in favour of children. Engagement with the international reporting and monitoring procedures for the CRC may be one important modality for pursuing this (Woll 1999).

In authoritarian countries it may simply be difficult for any independent civil society to function. But there may be possibilities for more enlightened governments to pursue welfare policies that improve the wellbeing of children, or their legal rights. In these cases, the challenge will be to institutionalise these policies so as to make them effective and durable. Where the government is uninterested in child rights, it may be possible to move it in the right direction through international pressure. The government may make tactical concessions to its adversaries, but then over time the lip service it pays to child rights may become 'domesticated', and it may actually come to live up to its commitments (Risse and Sikkink 1999).

In countries with a more plural political system and a developed civil society, the opportunities for putting together the kinds of coalitions outlined are considerable. Here, the full range of strategies can be utilised and the chances of serious improvements in children's rights and welfare are considerable. Civil society groups can pursue their agendas most freely, the judiciary can develop a tradition of activism, the media can explore and expose issues, and elected parliamentarians can raise key concerns and push for progressive legislation. Institutions function most effectively and are most accountable under such conditions (Brett 1998). Moreover the downgrading of issues of national security and increases the scope for raising wider social agendas.

This analysis underlines the indivisibility of rights. One of the important means for promoting children's rights is the creation of an enabling environment with political stability, democratic government and strong civil society.

Leadership and a Plan of Action

A Movement for Children demands a flexible, participatory, democratic and non-hierarchical mode of operation. It demands a coalition a range of movements, associations and institutions, each of which can play their own role. A movement cannot operate according to a set programmatic agenda. It must be based on a moral vision and a participatory, associational mode of action. It should have a strategic plan, but it cannot have an institutional blueprint. There is a role for professional, bureaucratic institutions. But leadership must come from consensus and participation.

Some institutions—such as UNICEF, the OAU and other African multilateral organisations—can provide an enabling environment, helping the movement to flourish. Others provide technical and organisational expertise. They can facilitate engagement with the African and UN committees to monitor countries' compliance with the provisions of the CRC, a mechanism which could prove to be a key means for international mobilisation.

The core of a movement must be the mass participation of the affected people themselves—that is, African youth and children. The mobilisation of this constituency must be done primarily through local civil society organisations. UNICEF can facilitate, advise and support. If a movement is to flourish, it must deliver tangible material benefits to its members. The Movement for Children in Africa must fix its sights on certain specific, visible, deliverable material gains for children and youth.

African institutions, notably the OAU, have been among the most enthusiastic and supportive of international initiatives for children. This leadership should be encouraged. However, the capacity for the OAU and subregional organisations to deliver on the promise of progress for children is open to question. They can provide political leadership at a symbolic level, and can provide a supportive environment for pro-child initiatives, helping to establish a continent-wide political consensus on the importance of the Movement for Children. Given the importance of economic and social issues for children, the Economic Commission for Africa (ECA) can also play a leading role in identifying best practices, enabling governments to develop their capacities for policymaking and implementation, and advocating for the widest range of children's rights.

UNICEF can be a pivotal member of the movement for Children in Africa. But it should not seek to monopolise leadership, or to act without participation and consensus among a wide coalition of other organisations, associations and mass movements. It can develop a media strategy, global, continental, national and local, in partnership with other members of the Movement. The strategy must be constantly re-assessed through ongoing consultation with and feedback from national and local partners—the most important members of the Movement.

Bilateral and multilateral agencies should internalise the provisions of the CRC in their own lending and technical assistance programmes. Sweden, Norway and the Netherlands have already reviewed their development cooperation programmes in light of the CRC. More widely, only a minority of development agencies are committed to integrating human rights into development practice. Along with the UK, only Canada and Australia have so far adopted a rights-based approach to development.

The ILO has an important role to play in reducing child labour. The organisation needs to strengthen its poverty and gender focus and to collaborate with UNICEF and other agencies to obtain a maximum impact.

The World Bank's support for the development of nationally-owned poverty reduction strategies as a basis for debt relief and loans provides a potential mechanism for governments to identify ways of fulfilling their human rights obligations without the imposition of external conditions. Reducing poverty and realising the CRC are intimately linked, the two can be emphasised together in Poverty Reduction Strategies and national Comprehensive Development Frameworks. This leads to a future agenda of linking the fulfilment of the rights of the child with emerging modalities for international assistance to Africa under the auspices of the New Partnership for Africa's Development initiated by South Africa, Nigeria, Senegal and Algeria, and the Compact for African Recovery of the ECA.

Civil society must help to define clear performance standards. Civil society action and political mechanisms are central to holding the state accountable to its obligations to promote all human rights. The new meaning of participation (to be adopted in a rights based approach to development) has moved from beneficiary to holding the state accountable. The new way of strengthening this approach includes participatory policy research, participatory budgeting and citizen monitoring and evaluation. One of the main challenges facing child-focused organisations in the coming years is to integrate the participation of youth and children into such an approach to development. This may yet prove to be the most critical action taken to promote the rights of the child in Africa.

Conclusion

More than ten years after the CRC came into force, the challenges of fulfilling the rights and meeting the needs of Africa's children is still evident. In many respects, progress has been disappointing. But, much has been learned about the obstacles to creating an Africa fit for children, and what can be done to overcome these obstacles. If these lessons can be learned and applied, if a broad-based movement can be mobilised; and if the necessary resources can be found; and if youth and children themselves can be given the role they demand and require, then Africa finally faces the prospect of fulfilling its promises to its children.

Information About Authors

Ali Abdel Gadir Ali is a Sudanese national holding a PhD in Economics from the University of Essex in England. He taught economics at universities in Sudan and Kuwait and has served as a consultant to, among others, the Government of Sudan, the ILO, the World Bank, and the Arab Organization for Agricultural Development. He worked as Senior Economist for the Arab Bank for Economic Development in Africa, Director of Research for the Inter-Arab Guarantee Corporation (Kuwait) and Director of the Economic and Social Policy Division of the UN Economic Commission for Africa. Currently, he is an Economic Advisor at the Arab Planning Institute (Kuwait) and is a member of the Steering Committee of the Multilateral Evaluation of the Comprehensive Development Framework of the World Bank. His research interests are in development economics with emphasis on policy analysis, economic growth, poverty and income distribution, and the economics of civil conflicts.

Nicolas Argenti carried out doctoral research in the North West Province of Cameroon from 1992 to 1994, receiving his doctorate from University College London in 1996. Following a further period of post-doctoral research in Southern Sri Lanka from 1996 to 1998, he is now a research fellow at the Centre for the Anthropology of Children and Child Development, Brunel University, London.

Anne Bakilana obtained her PhD in demography from the London School of Economics and is currently a lecturer at the University of Cape Town, South Africa.

Jessica Bridges-Palmer lives and works in London. Since completing a Masters in International Development Management at the LSE she has been working with the New Economics Foundation, an independent think tank.

Alex de Waal is a director of Justice Africa. After completing a DPhil in social anthropology at Oxford University he worked with Human Rights Watch, African Rights and the International African Institute before setting up Justice Africa in 1999. He served as chair of Mines Advisory Group and has acted as consultant to the Economic Commission for Africa and UNICEF. He has written or edited ten books, most recently 'Demilitarising the Mind: African Agendas for Peace and Security' (Africa World Press 2002) and 'When Peace Comes: Civil Society and Development in Sudan' (with Yoanes Ajawin, Red Sea Press 2002).

Alexandra Galperin holds a MA in Slavonic Literature and Languages from the Free University, Berlin and a MSc in Development Management from the LSE, London. She has worked for 10 years with the Red Cross moving from emergency work to longer term support to the creation of disaster preparedness capacities at national and local levels. Currently she is a programme manager of a disaster management program with the Albanian government for UNDP in Tirana.

Okwir Rabwoni obtained his primary and secondary school education in western Uganda and in Kampala. He joined the National Resistance Army that overthrew the Obote and Okello regimes in 1985 at the age of 15, staying in the army as it fought its way north to the Sudan border. Between 1986 and 1990 he attended military courses in Libya, Cuba, North Korea and Tanzania, with a break in 1988 in southern Sudan assisting the SPLA. In 1990 he was admitted to Makerere University in Uganda to study law but cut it short to take part in the RPF invasion of Rwanda. Subsequently, he took part in the 1996-97 war that overthrew President Mobutu. He returned home at the end of 1997 to work as Director of Political Affairs in the Global Pan African Movement Secretariat in Kampala, and joined the Ugandan parliament in May 1998 representing the youth of western Uganda. He supported the main opposition candidate, Col. Dr. Kizza Besigye in the 2001 Presidential elections, but was arrested, detained and forced into exile shortly before the elections too place. He now lives in Glasgow, Scotland.

Charlotte Spinks is a Research and Teaching Assistant in the Development Planning Unit at University College London. She completed her MSc in Development Management at the London School of Economics, and prior to that worked as a social development practitioner amongst disadvantaged youths in urban South Africa. Her research interests focus on social and community development in post-apartheid urban South Africa.

Kombe Temba recently completed a MSc in Development Management, and is seeking to pursue her passion for gender and development by working in her native Malawi.

Bibliography

Adam, Bernard, 1997, 'Les Transferts des Armes' in: *Conflits en Afrique. Analyse des Crises et Pistes pour une Prevention*, Bruxelles, Fondation Roi Boudoin/Medecins Sans Frontieres.

Adetunji, J., 1994. 'Infant Mortality in Nigeria.' *Journal of Biosocial Science* 26: 469-477.

African Rights, 1993, 'The Nightmare Continues… Human Rights Abuses Against Somali Refugees in Kenya,' London.

African Rights, 1994a, *Rwanda: Death, Despair and Defiance*, London.

African Rights, 1994b, 'Crimes Without Punishment: Sexual Harassment and Violence against Female Students in Schools and Universities in Africa,' London.

African Rights, 1996, *Justice in Zimbabwe*, London.

African Rights, 1997, *Food and Power in Sudan: A Critique of Humanitarianism*, London.

Aigbe, S.A., 1993, *Theory of Social Involvement: A Case Study in the Anthropology of Religion, State, and Society*, University Press of America.

Ali, A.A.G. and I. Elbadawi, 1999, 'Inequality and the Dynamics of Poverty and Growth in Developing Countries', AERC, Nairobi.

Ali, A.A.G., 1999, 'The Challenge of Poverty Reduction in Africa', *Eastern Africa Social Science Research Review.*

Ali, A.A.G., 2000, 'The Economics of Conflict in Africa: An Overview,' *Journal of African Economies*, 9.3.

Anderson, Allan. 2001. *African Reformation: African Initiated Christianity in the 20th Century.* Trenton, New Jersey and Asmara, Eritrea: Africa World Press.

Andersson, Efraim, 1958, *Messianic Popular Movements in the Lower Congo*, Uppsala: Studia Ethnographica Upsaliensia 16.

Ankrah, M., 1993. 'The Impact of HIV/AIDS on the Family and Other Significant Relationships: the African Clan Revisited.' *AIDS Care* 5: 5-22.

Annan, K., 1998, 'The Causes of Conflict and the Promotion of Durable and Sustainable Peace in Africa', Report of the UN Secretary General to the Security Council, UN, New York.

Appadurai, Arjun. 1990. 'Disjuncture and difference in the global cultural economy'. Theory, Culture and Society 7: 295-310.

Argenti, Nicolas, 2001. '*Kesum-body* and the places of the gods: the politics of children's masking and second-world realities in Oku, (Cameroon).' *Journal of the Royal Anthropological Institute*, 7(1): 67-94.

Argenti, Nicolas, 2001a. '*Kesum-body* and the places of the gods: the politics of children's masking and second-world realities in Oku (Cameroon).' *Journal of the Royal Anthropological Institute* (N.S.), 7(1): 67-94.

Argenti, Nicolas, 2002a. 'Dancing in the borderlands: the forbidden masquerades of Oku youth and women'. Forthcoming in F. De Boeck and A. Honwana (eds), *Children and Youth as Emerging Categories in Postcolonial Africa.* Chicago: University of Chicago Press.

Argenti, Nicolas, 2002b. 'People of the chisel: apprenticeship, youth and elites in Oku (Cameroon)'. *American Ethnologist* 29(3).

Aryee, A. F., 1997, 'The African family and changing nuptiality patterns,' in Aderanti Adepoju (ed.) *Family, Population and Development in Africa*, London, Zed Press.

Asike, I. J., 1995. 'Cultural Identity and Modernity in Africa: A Case for a New Philosophy.' *Cultural Heritage and Contemporary Change Series II.* Africa, 3.

Atiemo, A., *The rise of the charismatic movement in the mainline Churches in Ghana*, Accra, Asempa Publishers, 1993

Ayegboyin, Deji and Ishola, S. Ademola. 1997. *African Indigenous Churches: An Historical Perspective*, Lagos: Greater Heights Publications.

Ayieko, M.A., 1997. 'From Single Parents to Child-headed Households: The Case of Children Orphaned by AIDS in Kisumu and Siaya Districts'. *UNDP HIV and Development Programme Issue Paper* No. 32. http://www.undp.org/hiv/study/SP/htm 06/05/99

Balandier, G. 1974. *Anthropo-logiques.* Paris: Presses Universitaires de France.

Balsvik, Randi Ronning, 1985 *Haile Selassie's Students: The Intellectual and Social Background to Revolution 1952-1977,* E. Lansing, Michigan.

Bangura, Yusuf. 1997. 'Understanding the political and cultural dynamics of the Sierra Leone war: a critique of Paul Richards's *Fighting For the Rain Forest.* Africa Development 22(3/4): 117-148.

Banya, K., and Juliet Elu, 1997, 'Implementing Basic Education: An African Experience.' *International Review of Education*, 43, 481-496.

Barro, R., 1997, 'Determinants of Economic Growth: A Cross-Country Empirical Study', MIT Press, Cambridge, Ma.

Bayart, Jean-Francois et al. (eds.) 1992. *Le Politique Par Le Bas en Afrique Noire*. Paris: Karthala.

Bayart, Jean-Francois, 1985 [1979]. *L'Etat au Cameroun*. Paris: Presses de la Fondation Nationale des Sciences Politiques.

Bayart, Jean-Francois, 1989. *L'Etat en Afrique: La Politique du Ventre*. Paris: Fayard.

Bayart, Jean-Francois, 1999. 'The Social Capital of the Felonious State, or the Ruses of Political Intelligence', in J-F. Bayart, S. Ellis and B. Hibou, *The Criminalization of the State in Africa*, Oxford: James Currey: 32-48.

Bayart, Jean-Francois, Peter Geschiere and Francis Nyamnjoh, 2001. 'Autochtonie, démocracie et citoyenneté en Afrique'. *Critique Internationale* 10: 177- 194.

Baylies, C., 1999, 'International Partnership in the Fight Against AIDS: Addressing Need and Redressing Injustice?', *Review of African Political Economy*, vol. 32, no.81

Bazenguissa-Ganga, Rémy, 1996. 'Milices politiques et bandes armées à Brazzaville: Enquête sur la violence politique et sociale des jeunes déclassés.' *Les Etudes du CERI* 13 (April).

Best, Geoffrey, 1994, *War and Law since 1945*, Oxford, Clarendon Press.

Bledsoe, C. 1990. 'The Policies of Children: Fosterage and the social management of fertility among the Mende of Sierra Leone,' in W. P. Handwerker (ed.), *Births and Power: Social Change and the Politics of Reproduction*, Boulder: Westview Press.

Bloch, Carole, 1999, 'The Potential Of Early Childhood For Developing And Sustaining Literacy in Africa.' *Social Dynamics*, 25, 101.

Bloom, David and Jeffrey Sachs, 1998, 'Geography, Demography and Economic Growth in Africa', Brookings Papers in Economic Activity, no. 2.

Bloom, David, David Canning and Japee Sevilla, 2001 'Health, human capital and economic growth,' Commission on Macroeconomics and Health Working Paper, WG1:8, April. (http://www.cmhealth.org/cmh_papersandreports.htm)

Bourdillon, M.F.C., 1993. *Where Are the Ancestors? Changing Culture in Zimbabwe.* Mount Pleasant, Harare: University of Zimbabwe Publications.

Boyden, Jo and Gibbs, Sara, 1997, *Children of War. Responses to psychosocial distress in Cambodia*, Geneva, UNRISD.

Brass, W. and Jolly, R, 1995. *Population Dynamics of Kenya*, National Academy Press. Washington DC.

Brenner, L. 1994. 'Youth as political actors in Mali', paper presented to the SSRC workshop, Political Transitions in Africa. Chapel Hill: University of North Carolina, 10-12 March.

Brett, Rachel. 1999. 'Armed and dangerous: child soldiers'. In: *In the Firing Line: War and Children's Rights.* London: Amnesty International. Pp. 55-68.

Brett, Teddy, 1998, *Autonomy, Diversity and Interdependence in Inter-organisational Relationships*, Development Studies Institute, London School of Economics and Political Science.

Brock-Utne, B., 2000, *Whose Education for All: The Recolonisation of the African Mind.* Falmer Press: New York and London.

Brokerhoff, M., 1995. 'Child Mortality in East Africa: The Impact of Preventative Health Care.' Research Division Working Paper no 76. New York: The Population Council.

Burnett, N., 1999, 'I went for the well for water and I left in peace,' *Financial Times*, 14, March.

Caldwell, J. *et al.*, 1992, 'Underreaction to AIDS in Sub-Saharan Africa', *Social Science and Medicine*, vol.34, no.11

Caldwell, J.C., 1981. 'Maternal Education as a Factor in Child Mortality.' *World Health Forum* 2(1): 75-78.

Campbell, Catherine and Brian Williams, 2001, 'Riding the Tiger: Conceptualizing HIV Prevention in South Africa,' *African Affairs*, 100, no 398.

Childhope, 2000, *Annual Review 2000*, London.

Christie, F. and Hanlon, J., 2001, *Mozambique and the Great Flood of 2000*, Oxford, James Currey.

Clayton, Anthony, 1999, *Frontiersmen: Warfare in Africa since 1950,* London, UCL Press.

Cleland, J., 1991. 'Maternal Education and Child Survival: Further Evidence and Explanations.' *What We Know about Health Transitions: The Cultural, Social and Behavioural Determinants of Health.* Canberra.

Cleland, J., Bicego, G and G. Fegan., 1992. 'Socio-economic Inequalities in Childhood Mortality: the 1970s to the 1980s.' *Health Transition Review* 2(2):1-18.

Colclough, C., and Samer Al –Samarrai, 2000, 'Achieving Schooling for All: Budgetary Expenditures On Education In Sub-Saharan Africa And South Asia'. *World Development*, 28. 1927-44.

Collier, P. and A. Hoeffler, 1998, 'On the Economic Causes of Civil Wars', Oxford Economic Papers.

Collier, P. and W. Gunning, 1999a, 'Explaining African Economic Performance', *Journal of Economic Literature*, 37.1.

Collier, P. and W. Gunning, 1999b, 'Why Has African Grown Slowly?' *Journal of Economic Perspective*, vol. 13. 3: 3-22.

Collier, P., 1998, 'The Economics of Civil War', University of Birmingham.

Collier, P., 1999, 'On the Economic Consequences of Civil War', Oxford Economic Papers.

Collins, J. and B. Rau, 1999, 'AIDS in the Context of Development', Geneva, UNRISD.

Collins, S. and B. Bosworth, 1996, 'Economic Growth in East Asia: Accumulation versus Assimilation', Brookings Papers on Economic Activity, no. 2.

Comaroff, Jean. 1985, *Body of Power, Spirit of Resistance: The Culture and History of a South African People*, Chicago and London: University of Chicago Press.

Commission on Macroeconomics and Health, 2001, *Macroeconomics and Health: Investing in Health for Economic Development*, WHO, 2001.

Coovadia, H., 2000. 'For the sake of the six billionth child.' *Children*

First, June/July 2000 (4) No. 31.

Cornia, G., Jolly, R., and F. Stewart, 1986, *Adjustment with a Human Face: vol. 1: Protecting the Vulnerable and Enhancing Growth*, Clarendon Press, Oxford.

Cox, Harvey, 1987, *Quest For Belonging*, Gweru, Zimbabwe: Mambo Press.

Cox, Harvey, 1996. 'Healers and Ecologists: Primal Spirituality in Black Africa', in his, *Fire from heaven: the rise of Pentecostal Spirituality in the Twenty-first century*, (Cassell): 243-262

Cox, Harvey, 1997, *Fire From Heaven: The Rise of Pentecostal Spirituality and the Reshaping of Religion in the Twenty-First Century*. London: Cassell.

Cruise O'Brien, Donal 1996. 'A lost generation? Youth identity and state decay in West Africa'. In Richard Werbner and Terence Ranger (eds.) *Postcolonial Identities in Africa*. London and New Jersey: Zed Books. Pp. 55-74.

Daily Mail and Guardian newspaper, 1999, 'Rocking to the call of Islam', 17 December.

Daneel, M., 1974, *Old and New in Southern Shona Independent Churches. Vol. 2*. The Hague: Mouton.

Dawson, S., L. Manderson, and V.L. Tallo., 1992. 'The Focus Group Manual for Social and Economic Research in Tropical Diseases' No. 1. Geneva, Switzerland: World Health Organisation.

De Berry, Jo, and Boyden, Jo, 2000, 'Children in adversity' in: *Forced Migration Review*, December.

De Sardan, Olivier, 1984. *Les Sociétés Songhay-Zarma (Niger-Mali)*.

Chefs, Guerriers, Esclaves, Paysants... Paris: Karthala.

De Sardan, Olivier, 1993. La surinterprétation politique: les cultes de possèssion *hawka* du Niger. In J.-F. Bayart (ed.) *Religion et Modernité Politique en Afrique Noire. Dieu Pour Tous et Chacun Pour Soi*. Paris: Karthala. pp. 163-213.

De Villiers, A. P., 1999, 'South African Education: A Principal Agent Problem.' *South African Journal of Economics*, 67, 381-403.

de Waal, Alex (ed.), 2000, *Who Fights? Who Cares? War And Humanitarian Action In Africa*, Trenton N.J., Africa World Press.

de Waal, Alex, 1989, 'Famine mortality: A case study of Darfur, Sudan, 1984-1985,' *Population Studies*, 43:1-35.

de Waal, Alex, 1997a, *Famine Crimes: Politics and the disaster relief industry in Africa*, London, James Currey, 1997.

de Waal, Alex, 1997b, 'Contemporary warfare in Africa' in: Kaldor, Mary and Basker Vashee, *Restructuring the Global Military Sector. Vol. 1, New Wars*, London, Pinter.

de Waal, Alex, 2000, 'AIDS: Africa's Greatest Leadership Challenge: Roles for an Effective Response,' UNICEF/ECA, African Development Forum.

de Waal, Alex (ed.), 2002, *Demilitarising the Mind: African Agendas for Peace and Security,* Trenton N.J., Africa World Press.

DeBoeck, Filip, 1996. 'Postcolonialism, power and identity: local and global perspectives from Zaire.' In Richard Werbner and Terence Ranger (eds.) *Postcolonial Identities in Africa*. London and New Jersey: Zed Books. Pp. 75-106.

DeBoeck, Filip, 1999. 'Domesticating diamonds and dollars: identity, expenditure and sharing in Southwestern Zaire.' In *Globalization and Identity: Dialectics of Flow and Closure*. Birgit Meyer and Peter Geschiere (eds.) Oxford: Blackwell. Pp. 177-210.

DeBoeck, Filip, 2000. '"Le deuxième monde" et les "enfants-sorciers" en République Démocratique du Congo'. *Politique Africaine*, 80, December: 32-57.

DeBoeck, Filip, 2001. Paper forthcoming in F. De Boeck and A. Honwana (eds), *Children and Youth as Emerging Categories in Postcolonial Africa*. Chicago: University of Chicago Press.

Delgado, C., 1995, 'Africa's Changing Agricultural Development Strategies: Past and Present Paradigms and a Guide to the Future', FAE discussion paper no. 3, IFPRI, Washington DC.

Demery, L. and L. Squire, 1996, 'Macroeconomic Adjustment and Poverty in Africa: An Emerging Picture', World Bank Research Observer, vol. 11, no.1.

Department for International Development, 2000, *Realising Human Rights for Poor People: Strategies for Achieving the International Development Targets*, London, DFID.

Devisch, René. 1995. 'Frenzy, violence and ethical renewal in Kinshasa'. In *Public Culture* 7 (3): 593-629.

Dewey, William. 1994. 'AK-47s for the ancestors'. *Journal of Religion in Africa*, 24(4): 358-374.

Diamond, J., 1997, *Guns, Germs, and Steel: The Fates of Human Societies*, Norton, New York.

Diop, Ngoné, and Judith Ennew, 1996, Seminar Report on *The African Contexts of Children's* Rights, Harare, Zimbabwe.

Djiena Wembou, Michel-Cyr, 2000, 'Le Droit Humanitaire Africain:

Sources, Contenu et Portee' in: *African Journal of International and Comparative Law*, 12 (1), 1-22

Dodge, Cole and Raundalen, Magne, 1991, ' War experiences and psychological impact on children' in: Dodge, C. and Raundalen, M., *Reaching Children in War. Sudan, Uganda and Mozambique,* Bergen, Sigma Forlag.

Dodge, Cole, 1991, 'National And Societal Implications Of War On Children' in: Dodge, C. and Raundalen, M., *Reaching Children In War. Sudan, Uganda And Mozambique,* Bergen, Sigma Forlag.

Drewal, Henry John. 1988. 'Performing the other: Mammi Watta worship in West Africa'. *The Drama Review* 32(2): 160-185.

Drèze, Jean, 1990, 'Famine Prevention in India,' in J. Drèze and A. Sen (eds.) *The Political Economy of Hunger: Vol. II: Famine Prevention*, Oxford, Clarendon Press.

Durham, Deborah, 2000. 'Youth and the social imagination in Africa.' Anthropological Quarterly: 73 (3): 113-120.

Easterly, W. and R. Levine, 1997, 'Africa's Growth Tragedy: Politics and Ethnic Divisions', Quarterly Journal of Economics, vol. 112, no. 4.

Easterly, W. and R. Levine, 1998, 'Troubles with the Neighbours: Africa's Problem, Africa's Opportunity', *Journal of African Economies*, vol. 7, no. 1.

Economic Commission for Africa, 1999, *Economic Report on Africa 1999: The Challenge of Poverty Reduction and Sustainability*, Addis Ababa, Ethiopia.

Economic Commission for Africa, 2000, *The Economic Report on Africa 2000: The Initial Conditions for Africa's Development in the 21st Century*, draft, Addis Ababa, Ethiopia.

Economic Commission for Africa, 2001 'Compact for African Recovery', Document presented at the joint meeting of African Ministers of Finance and Economic Planning, Algiers, May 2001.

Economist, 2000, 'The Hopeless Continent', 13-19 May, pp. 17 and 23-25.

Edwards, Michael and John Gaventa (eds.), 2001, *Global Citizen Action*, Boulder Co., Lynne Reiner.

El-Affendi, Abdelwahab, 1991, *Turabi's Revolution: Islam and Power in Sudan*, London, Grey Seal.

Elbadawi, I., and Sanbanis, N. 2000a, 'Why Are There So Many Civil Wars in Africa? Understanding and Preventing Violence and Conflict', *Journal of African Economies.*

Elbadawi, I., and Sanbanis, N. 2000b 'How Much War Will We See? Estimating the Incidence of Civil War in 161 Countries', DERG, World Bank, Washington DC.

Elley, W.B., 2000, 'The Potential of Book Floods Form Raising Literacy Levels.' *International Review of Education*, 46, 233-256.

Ellis, Stephen, 1999, *The Mask of Anarchy: the Role of Religion in Liberia's Civil War*, London, Hurst.

Evans, Judith, 1997, 'Children as Zones of Peace. Working with Young Children Affected by Armed Violence' in: *The Coordinator's Note-Book On-Line*, 19, (Early Childhood Care and Development Web-Site; http://www.ecdgroup.com/cn)

Ewbank, DC. and J.M. Gribble., 1993, *Effects of Health Programs on Child Mortality in Sub-Saharan Africa.* National Academy Press, Washington DC.

Fantu Cheru, 2001, 'Africa's Human Rights and Debt Relief Conditions,' UN Human Commission on Human Rights, January.

Ferguson, J. 1999. *Expectations of Modernity: Myths and Meanings of Urban Life in the Zambian Copper Belt*. Berkeley: University of California Press.

Fishbayn, L., 1999, 'Litigating the right to culture: family law in the new South Africa,' *International Journal of Law, Policy and the Family*, 13.12.

Foster, G. and C. Makufa, 1997. 'Children Rearing Children: A Study of Child-headed Households.' IUSSP, Durban.

Foundation For Democracy in Africa, 2000, 'HIV-AIDS Epidemic in Africa.' Lagos, Nigeria. (http://www.democracy-africa.org/hivaids.htm)

Fredland, R. 1996, 'A Decade of the AIDS Pandemic in Africa: Politics and Policy', *Scandinavian Journal of Development Alternatives*, vol. 15, no.2

Fredland, R. 1998, 'AIDS and Development: An Inverse Correlation?', *Journal of Modern African Studies*, vol. 36, no.4

Freedom House, 1999-a, Freedom in the World: The Annual Survey of Political Rights and Civil Liberties 1998-1999, at http//www.freedomhouse.org/survey99.

Freedom House, 1999-b, Country Ratings, at http//freedom-house.org/ratings.

Freston, P., 1997, 'Charismatic Evangelicals in Latin America: Mission and Politics on the Frontiers of Protestant Growth', in Hunt S., Hamilton M., and Walter T., (eds), *Charismatic Christianity: soci-*

ological perspectives, London, Macmillan.

Friedman, J. 1990. Being in the world: Globalization and localization. In *Theory, Culture and Society* 7: 311-328.

Gallup, John Luke, and Jeffrey D. Sachs, 2001, 'The Economic Burden of Malaria,' *Suppl. Am. J. Trop. Med. Hyg. 64.1.* 85-96.

Gandoulou, J-D. 1989 [1984]. *Au Coeur de la Sape. Moeurs et Aventures de Congolais à Paris.* Paris: L'Harmattan.

Gantzel, K.-J., 1997, 'War in the Post World War II World: Some Empirical Trends and a Theoretical Approach' in: Turton, D. (ed.), *War and Ethnicity: Global Connections and Local Violence*, New York, University of Rochester.

Garbarino et al., 1992, *Children in Danger. Coping with Consequences of Community Violence*, San Francisco, Jossey-Bass.

Garner, R.C., 2000, 'Religion as a source of social change in the new South Africa', *Journal of Religion in Africa*, 30 (2), 310-43.

Geschiere, Peter. 1997. *The Modernity of Witchcraft: Politics and the Occult in Postcolonial Africa.* Charlottesville and London: University Press of Virginia.

Gifford, P., 1987, 'Africa shall be saved': an appraisal of Reinhard Bonnke's pan-African crusade', *Journal of Religion in Africa*, 17 (1) 63-92.

Gifford, P., 1988, *The New Crusaders: Christianity and the New Right in Southern Africa*, London, Pluto.

Gifford, P., 1990, 'Prosperity: a new and foreign element in African Christianity', *Religion*, 20 (4) 373-88.

Gifford, P., 1993, *Christianity and Politics in Doe's Liberia*,

Cambridge University Press.

Gifford, P., 1994, 'Ghana's Charismatic Churches', *Journal of Religion in Africa*, 24 (3), 241-65.

Gifford, P., 1995, 'Democratisation and the Churches', in Gifford, P., *The Christian Churches and the Democratisation of Africa*, Leiden.

Gifford, P., 1998, *African Christianity: Its Public Role*, London, Hurst.

Ginsberg, M., et al. 2000, 'The Politics of Linking Educational Research, Policy And Practice: The Case Of Improving Educational Quality In Ghana, Guatemala And Mali.' USAID.

Goheen, Miriam. 1996. *Men Own the Fields, Women Own the Crops: Gender and Power in the Cameroon Grassfields.* Madison, Wisconsin: The University of Wisconsin Press.

Gooneskere, Savitri, 1998, *Children, Law and Justice: A South Asian Perspective*, New Delhi, Sage.

Government of South Africa, 2001, 'The New Partnership for Africa's Development (NEPAD),' October. (http://www.gov.za/issues/nepad.htm)

Gregson, S., Zhuwau T., Anderson, R.M., and S. Chandiwana, 1996, 'The Early Socio-demographic Impact of the HIV/AIDS Epidemic in Rural Zimbabwe.' Oxford University: Department of Zoology and Harare, Zimbabwe: Blair Research Institute.

Greitens, Eric, 2001, 'The Treatment of Children during Conflict' in: Stewart, Frances and Fitzgerald, Valpy, *War and Underdevelopment. Volume 1: The Economic and Social Consequences of Conflict*, Oxford, Oxford University Press.

Guest, Emma, 2001, *Children of AIDS: Africa's Orphan Crisis*, London, Pluto.

Gupta, M., 1990, 'Death Clustering, Mother's Education and the Determinants of Child Mortality in Rural Punjab, India.' *Population Studies*, 44: 489-505.

Hamilton, C. and Abu El-Haj, T., 1997, 'Armed conflict: The protection of children under international law' in: *The International Journal of Children's Rights*, 5 (1), 1-47

Hastings, Adrian. 1994, *The Church in Africa, 1450-1930*, Oxford: Clarendon Press.

Cox, H., 1996, *Fire from heaven: the rise of Pentecostal Spirituality in the Twenty-first century*, London, Cassell.

Hastings, Adrian (ed.), 1999, *A World History of Christianity*, London, Cassell.

Hunt, S., Hamilton, M., and Walker, T., (eds)., 1997, *Charismatic Christianity: Sociological Perspectives*, London, Macmillan.

Helle, Daniel, 2000, 'Optional Protocol on he involvement of children in armed conflict to the Convention on the Rights of the Child', in: *International Review of the Red Cross*, 839, 797-809

Helleiner, Gerry, 2000, 'Towards Balance in Aid Relationships: Donor performance monitoring in low-income countries,' *Cooperation South, 2.*

Hexham, I., and Poewe, K., 1994, 'Charismatic Churches in South Africa: a critique of criticisms and problems of bias', in Poewe, K., (ed), *Charismatic Christianity as a Global Culture*, University of South Carolina.

Hill, A., 1991, 'Infant and Child Mortality: Levels, Trends and Data

Deficiency' in *Disease and Mortality in Sub-Saharan Africa*, in R. Feachem and D. Jamison (eds.), New York, Oxford University Press for the World Bank.

Hodges, R. K. 1992. 'A view of psychological problems resulting from the Liberian civil conflict and recommendations for counselling and other corrective activities'. Appendix V, in *A Report of the Round Table Conference on Strategies and Direction for the Reconstruction and Development of Liberia*. Monrovia: The New African Research and Development Agency.

Hooper, Ed, 2000, *The River: A Journey Back to the Source of HIV and AIDS*, Harmondsworth, Penguin.

Human Rights Watch. 1999. *Aucun témoin ne doit survivre: Le genocide au Rwanda*. Paris: Karthala.

Human Rights Watch/Africa, 1995a, *Children of Sudan; Slaves, Street Children and Child Soldiers*, New York.

Human Rights Watch/Africa, 1995b, *Violence against women in South Africa: the state response to domestic violence and rape*, New York, Human Rights Watch.

Human Rights Watch/Africa, 1997, *The Scars of Death; Children Abducted by the Lord's Resistance Army in Uganda*.

Hunt S., Hamilton M., and Walter T., 1997, 'Tongues, Toronto and the Millennium', in Hunt S., Hamilton, M., and Walter, T., (eds), *Charismatic Christianity: sociological perspectives*, London, MacMillan.

Hunt, S., 1997, 'Doing the Stuff: the Vineyard Connection', in Hunt S., Hamilton, M., and Walter, T., (eds), *Charismatic Christianity: sociological perspectives*, London, MacMillan.

Husain, I. and R. Faruqee, (eds.), 1994, 'Adjustment in Africa:

Lessons from Country Case Studies', Oxford University Press, Oxford.

ICRC, 2001, *Legal protection of children in armed conflict*, Geneva, Leaflet.

Joset, P.E. 1955. *Les Sociétés Secrètes des Hommes-léopards en Afrique Noire*. Paris: Payot.

Kallaway, P., 1996, 'Policy Challenges for Education in the New South Africa: The Case For School Feeding in the Context of Social and Economic Reconstruction.' *Transformation*, 31.

Kaplan, R. 1994. 'The coming anarchy: how scarcity, crime, overpopulation and disease are rapidly destroying the social fabric of our planet.' *Atlantic Monthly*, February.

Kaspin, Deborah. 1993. 'Chewa visions and revisions of power: Transformations of the Nyau dance in Central Malawi.' In J. and J. Comaroff (eds.), *Modernity and its Malcontents: Ritual and Power in Postcolonial Africa*. Chicago: University of Chicago Press.

Kaul, Inge, Isabelle Grunberg and Marc Stern (eds.), 1999, *Global Public Goods: International Cooperation in the 21st Century*, New York, Oxford University Press for UNDP.

Kaul, Inge, Isabelle Grunberg and Marc Stern, 1999, 'Defining global public goods,' in Kaul, Inge, Isabelle Grunberg and Marc A. Stern (eds.) *Global Public Goods: International Cooperation in the 21st Century*, Oxford University Press for UNDP.

Keen, David, 2000, 'Incentives and Disincentives for Violence' in: Berdal, M., Malone D. (eds), *Greed and Grievance. Economic Agendas in Civil Wars,* Boulder, Colorado and London, Lynne Riehmer Publishers.

Kgobe, M., 1997, 'The National Qualifications Framework in South

Africa and 'Out-of-School' Youth: Problems and Possibilities.' *International Review of Education*, 43, 317-330.

Kilson, M. 1966. *Political Change in a West African State: A study of the Modernization Process in Sierra Leone*. Harvard: Harvard University Press.

King, Edward, 1993, *Safety in Numbers*, London, Cassell.

Konadu Agyemang, K., 1998, 'Structural Adjustment Programmes and the Perpetuating of Poverty and Underdevelopment in Africa: Ghana's Experience.' *Scandinavian Journal of Development Alternatives and Area Studies*, 17,127-44.

Kramer, F. 1993 [1987]. *The Red Fez: Art and Spirit Possession in Africa*. London: Verso.

Krill, Francoise, 1992, 'The Protection of Children in Armed Conflicts' in: Freeman, M. and Veerman (eds.), *The Ideologies of Children's Rights,* Netherlands, Kluwer.

Kuper, Jenny, 2000a, 'Children in Armed Conflicts: The law and its uses' in: *Development: Journal of the Society for International Development,* 43 (1), 32-39.

Kuper, Jenny, 2000b, 'Children and Armed Conflict – Some Problems in Law and Policy' in: Fottrell, D. (ed.), *Revisiting Children's Rights: A Decade on from the Children's Convention*, Kluwer.

Landes, D., 1998, *The Wealth and Poverty of Nations: Why Some Are So Rich and Some Are So Poor*, Abacus, London.

Last, Murray, 1992, 'The Power of Youth, Youth of Power: Notes on the religions of the young in northern Nigeria,' in Helene d'Almeida-Topor, Catherine Coquery-Vidrovitch, Odile Goer and Francoise

Guitart (eds.) *Les Jeunes en Afrique: La Politique et al ville*, Paris, Editions L'Harmattan.

Lemon, A., 1999, 'Shifting Inequalitues in South Africa's Schools: Some Evidences from the Western Cape.' *South African Geographical Journal*, 81,96-105.

Lent, Tom, and Roy Trivedy, 2001, 'National coalitions and global campaigns: The international children's rights movement,' in Edwards, Michael and John Gaventa (eds.), *Global Citizen Action*, Boulder Co., Lynne Reiner.

MacGaffey, J. and Bazanguissa, R. 2000, *Congo-Paris: Transnational traders on the margins of the law*, Oxford, James Currey.

Machel, Graca, 2000, *The Impact of Armed Conflict on Children. A critical review of progress made and obstacles encountered in increasing protection for war-affected children,* presented at the Winnipeg International Conference on War-Affected Children, September.

Machel, Graca, 2001. *The Impact of War on Children: A review of Progress Since the 1996 United Nations Report on the Impact of Armed Conflict on Children.* London: Hurst.

Magadi, M., 1997, 'Status of Women and Infant and Child Health in Kenya: Nyanza Province.' Union of African Population Scientists. Dakar Senegal.

Mahjoub el Tijani, 2002, 'The rights of children: A challenge for the transition,' in Yoanes Ajawin and Alex de Waal (eds.) *When Peace Comes: Civil Society and Development in Sudan*, Trenton N.J., Red Sea Press.

Malaquais, Dominique. 2001. 'Anatomie d'une arnaque: feymen et feymania au Cameroun.' *Etudes du CERI*, 77.

Manjante, R.M. *et. al.* 2000, 'Lovers, Hookers, and Wives: Unbraiding the Social Contradictions of Urban Mozambican Women's Sexual and Economic Lives'. In: Turshen, M. (ed.), *African Women's Health.* Trenton, NJ and Asmara, Africa World Press.

Mannathoko, C., 1999, 'Theoretical Perspectives on Gender in Education: The Case of Eastern and Southern Africa.' *International Review of Education*, 45,445-60.

Marchal, Roland, 1993. 'Les Mooryan de Mogadiscio. Formes de la violence dans un espace urbain en guerre.' *Cahiers d'Etudes Africaines* 130 (XXXIII-2): 295-320.

Marchal, Roland, 2000. 'Atomisation des fins et radicalism des moyens: de quelques conflits Africains.' *Critique Internationale* 6: 158-175.

Marcus, T., 1999a, 'Children in Distress, Communities and Care-giving—A Qualitative Case Study.' Unpublished Paper Presented at the Development Society of Southern Africa Conference, RAU, South Africa.

Marcus, T., 1999b, Wo! Zaphela Izingane. 'Living and Dying with AIDS.' CINDI Network, South Africa.

Marie, A. 1976, 'Rapports de parenté et rapports de production dans les sociétés lignagères'. In F. Pouillon et. al. *L'Anthropologie Economique Courants et Problèmes.* Paris, Maspero.

Marshall, R., 1992, 'Pentecostalism in Southern Nigeria', in Gifford, P., (ed), *New Dimensions in African Christianity*, Act Prent.

Marshall, R., 1993, 'Power in the Name of Jesus: Social Transformation and Pentecostalism in Western Nigeria Revisited', in Ranger, T., and Vaughan, O., (eds), *Legitimacy and the State in*

Twentieth-Century Africa, London, Macmillan.

Marshall, R., 1995, 'God is Not a Democrat'; Pentecostalism and Democratisation in Nigeria', in Gifford, P. (ed), *The Christian Churches and the Democratisation of Africa*, Leiden.

Marshall-Fratani, R., 1998, 'Mediating the global and local in Nigerian Pentecostalism', *Journal of Religion in Africa*, 28 (3), 278-315.

Martin, Lisa, 1999, 'The Political Economy of International Cooperation,' in Kaul, Inge, Isabelle Grunberg and Marc Stern (eds.), 1999, *Global Public Goods: International Cooperation in the 21st Century*, New York, Oxford University Press for UNDP.

Masquelier, Adeline. 1992. 'Encounter with a road siren: machines bodies and commodities in the imagination of a Mawri healer'. *Visual Anthropology Review* 8(1): 56-69.

Maxwell, David, 1995, 'Witches, Prophets and Avenging Spirits: the second Christian movement in north-east Zimbabwe', *Journal of Religion in Africa*, 25 (3), 309-39.

Maxwell, David, 1998a, 'Delivered from the spirit of poverty?: Pentecostalism, Prosperity and Modernity in Zimbabwe', *Journal of Religion in Africa*, 28 (3), 350-73.

Maxwell, David, 1998b, 'Editorial', *Journal of Religion in Africa*, 28 (3), 255-7.

Maxwell, David. 1997. 'The spirit and the scapular: Pentecostal and Catholic interactions in Northern Nyanga District, Zimbabwe in the 1950's and early 1960's.' *Journal of Southern African Studies* 23 (2): 283-300.

Mbembe, Achille, and Janet Roitman. 1995. 'Figures of the subject in times of crisis.' *Public Culture* 7: 323-352.

Mbembe, Achille. 1985. *Les Jeunes et L'Ordre Politique en Afrique Noire*. Paris: L'Harmattan.

Mehotra, Santosh and Richard Jolly (eds.) 1997, *Development with a Human Face: Experiences in social achievement and economic growth*, Oxford, Clarendon Press.

Mehrotra, Santosh, and Jan Vandemoortele, 1997, 'Cost and Financing of Primary Education,' UNICEF Staff Working Papers, EVL-97-006.

Meillasoux, Claude. 1975. Femmes, Greniers et Capitaux. Paris: Maspero.

Mensa-Bonsu, H. J. A. N., and C. Dowuona-Hammond, 1994, *The Rights of the Child in Ghana – Perspectives*, Ghana, Woeli Publishing Services.

Meyer, B., 1992. '"If you are a devil, you are a witch and, if you are a witch, you are a devil." The integration of "pagan" ideas into the conceptual universe of Ewe Christians in Southeastern Ghana.' *Journal of Religion in Africa* 22(2): 98-132.

Meyer, B., 1998. 'Make a complete break with the past: memory and post-colonial modernity in Ghanaian Pentecostal discourse', in *Journal of Religion in Africa*, 28 (3): 317-349. Also in Richard Werbner (ed.), *Memory and the Postcolony: African Anthropology and the Critique of Power*. London: Zed Books.

Miller, R. and D. Murray, 1999, 'The Impact of HIV Illness on Parents and Children, With Particular Reference to African Families.' *Journal of Family Therapy* 21:284-302.

Mkandawire, T. and C. Soludo, 1999, *Our Continent, Our Future: African Perspectives on Structural Adjustment*, Trenton NJ, Africa World Press.

Monga, Yvette. '"Au Village!": Space, culture, and politics in Cameroon'. *Cahiers d'Etudes Africaines* 160 XL-4: 723-749.

Moodley, K., 2000, 'African Renaissance and Language Policies in Comparative Perspective.' *Politikon* 27, 103-15.

Moore, Mick and James Putzel, 1999, 'Thinking Strategically about Politics and Poverty,' Sussex, IDS Working Paper no. 101, October.

Moorehead, Caroline, 1998, *Dunant's Dream: War, Switzerland and the History of the Red Cross*, London, Harper Collins.

Mosley, H., 1991, 'The Challenge of World Health.' *Population Bulletin* 46. Population Reference Bureau, Washington.

Mottin-Sylla, Marie-Hélène, 1993, 'Violences contres les femmes au Sénégal,' Dakar, ENDA-SYNFEV.

Mukasa, Dorothy, 1997, 'African Communities Living with HIV in Britain: Inequality and injustice,' in Joshua Oppenheimer and Helena Reckitt (eds.) *Acting on AIDS: Sex, Drugs and Politics*, London, Serpent's Tail.

Nakamura, Y. et al., 1999, 'Basic Education In Sub-Saharan Africa and the Possibilities for Japanese Assistance: Based on Social Changes in the 1990s.' *Technology and Development*, 12, 33-8.

Nduati, Ruth and Wambui Kiai, 1997, 'Communicating with Adolescents about AIDS, Experience from Eastern and Southern Africa.' International Development Research Centre.

Ndulu, B. and S. O' Connell, 1999, 'Governance and Growth in Sub-Saharan Africa', *Journal of Economic Perspectives*, 13,3.

Nordstrom, Carolyn, 1997, 'Girls and Warzones; Troubling Questions', Life and Peace Institute, Uppsala.

Nunga Kuzwe, C., 1998, 'The Role of NGOs in Democratisation and Education in Peace Time (Rwanda).' *Journal of Social Development in Africa*, 13, 37-40.

Nunley, J. 1987. *Moving With the Face of the Devil: Art and Politics in Urban West Africa*. Urbana: University of Illinois Press.

Nylund, Bo, 1998, 'International Law and the child victim of armed conflict – Is the 'First Call' for children?' in: *The International Journal of Children's Rights,* 6 (1), 23–53

O'Connel, S.A. and B. Ndulu, 2000, 'Africa's Growth Experience: A Focus on Sources of Growth; AERC, Nairobi.

OAU, 1990, *African Charter on the Rights and Welfare of the Child*, (OAU doc. CAB/LEG/24.9/49 (1990), entered into force 29 November 1999.

Odets, Walt, 1997, 'Why We do not do Primary Prevention for Gay Men,' in Joshua Oppenheimer and Helena Reckitt (eds.) *Acting on AIDS: Sex, Drugs and Politics*, London, Serpent's Tail.

Ojo, M.A., 1988, 'Deeper Christian Life Ministry: a case study of the charismatic movements in Western Nigeria', *Journal of Religion in Africa*, 18 (2), 141-62.

Olawale, A., 1997, 'Kano: Religious fundamentalism and violence', in Herault, G., and Adesanmi, P., (eds), *Youth, street culture and urban violence in Africa*, IFRA).

Oppong C., 1981, *Middle-class African Marriage: A family Study of Ghanaian Senior Civil Servants.* London: Allen and Unwin.

Osayimwense, O., 1995, *African Children's and Youth Literature*, Twayne Publishers.

Pakenham, T., 1991, *The Scramble for Africa*, Abacus, London

Pauw, C. M., 1996, 'African Independent Churches in Malawi: Background and Historical Development', in Kitshoff, M. C., (ed), *African Independent Churches Today: Kaleidoscope of Afro-Christianity*, Edwin Mellen Press.

Pisani, Elizabeth, 2000, 'HIV/AIDS and Children,' Report for UNICEF ESARO, Nairobi.

Poewe, K., 1994, 'The Nature, Globality, and History of Charismatic Christianity', in Poewe, K., (ed), *Charismatic Christianity as a Global Culture*, University of South Carolina.

Pretorius, Hennie and Jafta, Lizo, 1997, '"A branch springs out": African initiated churches'. In Elphic and Davenport, eds., *Christianity in South Africa*, Oxford and Cape Town.

Pritchett, L., 2000, 'Patterns of Economic Growth: Hills, Plateaus, Mountains and Plains', World Bank Economic Review.

Qaoud, Ala, 2000, *Towards Reform of Religious Sciences: The Model of Azharic Education*, Cairo Institute for Human Rights Studies, Human Rights Studies Series No 7 (in Arabic).

Quaranta, Ivo. 2001. 'A few notes on AIDS in Nso'. Unpublished manuscript.

Quebendeaux, R., 1983, *The New Charismatics II*, 2nd edn, Harper and Row.

Ranger, Terence. 1975. *Dance and Society in Eastern Africa. 1890-1970: The Beni Ngoma*. London: Heineman.

Rashid, Ishmail. 1997. 'Subaltern reactions: lumpen, students and the left.' *Africa Development* 22(3/4): 19-44.

Rasool, N., 1999, 'Literacy and Social Development in ihe Information Age: Redefining Possibilities in Sub-Saharan Africa.' *Social Dynamics*, 25, 130.

Reno, W. 1995. *Corruption and State Politics in Sierra Leone*. Cambridge: Cambridge University Press.

Reno, W., 2000, 'Shadow States and the Political Economy of Civil Wars' in: Berdal, M., Malone D. (eds.), *Greed and Grievance. Economic Agendas in Civil Wars*, Boulder, Colorado and London, Lynne Riehmer Publishers.

Ressler, Everett et al., 1998, *Unaccompanied Children. Care and Protection in Wars, Natural Disasters and Refugee Movements,* New York/ Oxford, Oxford University Press.

Rey, P.P. 1971. Colonialisme, Néocolonialisme et Transition au Capitalisme. Paris: Maspero.

Reychler, Luc, 1997. 'Les conflits en Afrique: comment les gerer ou les prevenir' in: Rapport de la commission 'Regions africaines en crise', *Conflits en Afrique. Analyse Des Crises Et Pistes Pour Une Prevention,* Bruxelles, Fondation Roi Boudoin/Medecins Sans Frontieres.

Richards, Paul, 1996, *Fighting for the Rainforest: War, Youth and Resources in Sierra Leone*, Oxford, James Currey.

Richards, Paul, 1999, 'Hurry, We are All Dying of AIDS: Linking cultural and agro-technological responses to the challenge of living with AIDS in Africa,' Unpublished paper, University of Wageningen.

Risse, Thomas, and Kathryn Sikkink, 1999, 'The socialization of international human rights norms into domestic practices: introduction,' in Thomas Risse, Stephen Ropp and Kathryn Sikkink (eds.) *The Power of Human Rights: International Norms and Domestic Change*, Cambridge University Press.

Rodrik, D., 1999a, The New Global Economy and Developing: Making Openness Work, Policy Essay No. 24, ODC, John Hopkins University Press, Washington, DC.

Rodrik, D., 1999b, 'Institutions for High-Quality Growth: What they Are and How to Acquire Them', Harvard University.

Rodrik, D., 2000, 'Development Strategies for the Next Century', Institute for Developing Economies, Japan.

Rothchild, D., 1997, *Managing Ethnic Conflict in Africa. Pressures and Incentives for Cooperation*, Washington, The Brookings Association.

Rouch, Jean. 1955. *Les Maitres Fous.* Film Documentary.

Rowlands, Michael and Jean-Pierre Warnier. 1988. 'Sorcery, power and the modern state in Cameroon.' *Man* (N.S.) 23: 118-132.

Rwezaura, Bart, 2000, 'The Value of a Child: Marginal children and the law in contemporary Tanzania,' *International Journal of Law, Policy and the Family*, 14.3.

Sachs, Jeffrey, 2001, 'Helping the Poorest: A New Agenda for the G-8,' unpublished paper for OECD.

Sachs, Jeffrey, and A. Warner, 1997, 'Sources of Slow Growth in African Economies', *Journal of African Economies*, 6.3.

Sala-i-Martin, X., 1997, 'I Just Ran Two Million Regressions', *American Economic Review*, 87.

Sambanis, N., 2000, 'Partition as a Solution to Ethnic War: An Empirical Critique of the Theoretical Literature', *World Politics*, 52.

Sandler, Todd, 'Intergenerational Public Goods: Strategies, Efficiency and Institutions,' in, Kaul, Inge, Isabelle Grunberg and Marc Stern, *Global Public Goods: International Cooperation in the 21st Century*, New York, Oxford University Press, 1999.

Sarel, M., 1997, 'How Macroeconomic Factors Affect Income Distribution: The Cross-Country Evidence', IMF Working Papers no. WP/97/152, IMF, Washington DC.

Sarro, Ramon. 1996. 'Youth vs. elders: football and revitalisation among the Baga of Guinea.' Paper presented at the 39th conference of the American Anthropological Association, San Francisco.

Save the Children Fund, 2000, *Children's Rights: Reality or Rhetoric? The UN Convention on the Rights of the Child: The First ten Years*, London, The International Save the Children Alliance.

Save the Children, 1995, *Towards a Children's Agenda: New challenges for social development*, London, Save the Children.

Schietinger, H. 1998 'Psychosocial Support for People Living with AIDS.' Discussion Paper No. 5. Washington: The Synergy Project/USAID.

Schindler, Dietrich, 1999, 'Significance of the Geneva Conventions for the temporary world', *International Revue of the Red Cross,* 81 (836), 715-31

Seekings, Jeremy, 1993, *Heroes or Villains? Youth Politics in the 1980s*, Johannesburg, Raven Press.

Seekings, Jeremy, 1993. *Heroes or Villains? Youth Politics in the 1980s'* Johannesburg: Raven Press.

Semali, L., 1999, 'Community as Classroom: Dilemmas of Valuing African Indigenous Literacy in Education.' *International Review of Education*, 45,305-20.

Sen, Amartya K., 1990, 'Individual freedom as a social commitment,' *New York Review of Books*, 14 June.

Sen, Amartya K., 1999, *Development as Freedom*, Oxford University Press, Oxford.

Silin, Jonathan G., 1997, 'AIDS Education for a Democratic Citizenship', in J. Oppenheimer and H. Reckitt (eds.) *Acting on AIDS: Sex, Drugs and Politics*, London, Serpent's Tail.

Simms, Chris, John T. Milimo and Gerald Bloom, 1998, 'The Reasons for the Rise in Childhood Mortality during the 1980s in Zambia,' Sussex, IDS Working Paper No. 76.

Starrett, Gregory, 1998, *Putting Islam to Work: Education, Politics and Religious Transformation in Egypt*, Berkeley, University of California Press.

Stavraki, Emmanuelle, 1996, 'La Protection Internationale des Enfants en Situation de Conflict Arme' in: *Revue Hellenique de Droit International*, 49 (1), 127-59.

Stein, J.A., Riedel, M., and M.J. Rotheram-Borus, 1999, 'Parentification and Its Impact on Adolescent Children of Parents with AIDS.' *Family Process* 38 No. 2.

Steiner, Christopher. 1997. 'The invisible face: masks, ethnicity and the state in Cote d'Ivoire.' In R. Grinker and C. Steiner (eds.) *Perspectives on Africa*. Oxford: Blackwell, pp. 671-677.

Stewart, Frances, 1995, *Adjustment and Poverty: Options and Choices*, London, Routledge.

Stoller, Paul. 1989. *Fusion of the Worlds: An Ethnography of Possession Among the Songhay of Niger.* Chicago and London: University of Chicago Press.

Summers, R. and A. Heston, 1991, 'The Penn World Table (Mark 5): An Expanded Set of International Comparisons, 1950-1988', *Quarterly Journal of Economics.*

Taussig, M. 1993. *Mimesis and Alterity: A particular History of the Senses.* New York: Routledge.

Taylor, L., 1993, 'The World Bank and the Environment: The World Development Report 1992'; *World Development.*

Taylor, Lance, Santosh Mehrotra and Enrique Delamonica, 1997, 'The Links Between Economic Growth, Poverty Reduction and Social Development: Theory and Policy,' in Santosh Mehrotra and Richard Jolly (eds.) *Development with a Human Face: Experiences in Social Achievement and Economic Growth*, Oxford, Clarendon Press.

The Mail and Guardian, November 24-30, 2000.

Tinbergen, J., 1994, 'The Duration of Development', in K. Dopfer, (editor), *The Global Dimension of Economic Evolution*, Physica-Verlag, Heidelberg.

Toulabor, Comi. 1992. 'L'énonciation du pouvoir et de la richesse chez les jeunes "conjuncturés" de Lomé (Togo).' In J-F. Bayart et. al. (eds.) *Le Politique Par Le Bas en Afrique Noire.* Paris: Karthala. Pp. 131-145.

Tozy, Mohamed, 1996, 'Movements of Religious Renewal', in Stephen Ellis (ed.) *Africa Now: People, Policies, Institutions*, Oxford, James Currey.

Turner, H. W., 1978, 'Patterns of Ministry and Structure within Independent Churches', in Fashole-Luke, E., et al., (eds), *Christianity in Independent Africa*, London, Rex Collings.

Turton, David, 1997, 'Introduction: War and Ethnicity' in: Turton, D. (ed.), War and Ethnicity: Global Connections and Local Violence, New York, University of Rochester.

UN, 1996, Report of the expert of the Secretary General, Ms Graca Machel, *The Impact of Armed Conflict on Children* (UN Doc. A/51/306 (26 August 1996))

UN, 2000, Report of the Special Representative of the Secretary General for Children and Armed Conflict, *Protection of Children affected by Armed Conflict* (UN Doc. A/ 55/ 442 (03 October 2000))

UNAIDS, 1998, 'HIV/AIDS: The Global Epidemic.' Geneva, Switzerland.

UNAIDS, 1999a, 'Children Orphaned by AIDS: Frontline Responses from Eastern and Southern Africa.'

UNAIDS, 1999b, 'Sexual Behavioural Change: Where have the theories taken us?'

UNAIDS, 2000a, 'Report on the Global HIV/AIDS Epidemic.' Geneva, Switzerland.

UNAIDS, 2000b, 'Botswana Epidemiological Fact Sheet on HIV/AIDS and Sexually Transmitted Diseases, 2000 Update.'

UNDP, 2000, *Human Development Report 2000*, Oxford University Press, Oxford.

UNHCR, 2000, *The State of the World's Refugees. Fifty years of humanitarian action*, Oxford, UNHCR/Oxford University Press.

UNICEF (Botswana) 2000, in *The Mail and Guardian*, November 24-30, 2000.

UNICEF, 1993, *AIDS: The Second Decade—A Focus on Youth and Women*, New York.

UNICEF, 1995. *The State of the World's Children, 1995.* Oxford University Press.

UNICEF, 1996, *The State of the World's Children, 1996*, Oxford University Press.

UNICEF, 1999, 'Children Orphaned by AIDS: Front-line Responses from Eastern and Southern Africa.' New York.

UNICEF, 2000a, *The State of the World's Children, 2000*, Oxford University Press.

UNICEF, 2000b, *The UN Convention on the Rights of the Child*, UK Committee, London, 2000

UNICEF, 2001a, *Child Workers in the Shadow of AIDS: Listening to the Children*, New York.

UNICEF, 2001b, 'Operationalization for ESAR of UNICEF Global Guidelines for Human Rights Programming,' Nairobi, UNICEF ESARO.

UNICEF-ESARO, 2000, 'End Decade Reviews on Goals for Children,' Nairobi, ESARO.

UNICEF-WCARO, 2001, 'End Decade Review on Goals for Children,' Abidjan, UNICEF.

United Nations, 2000, 'Emerging Issues for Children in the Twenty First Century', document no. A/AC.256/3-E/ICEF/2000/13.

Ushari Mahmoud and Suleiman Baldo, 1987, 'El-Diein massacre and slavery in the Sudan,' Khartoum.

Vail, Leroy and Landeg White. 1989. 'Tribalism in the political history of Malawi.' In L. Vail (ed.), *The Creation of Tribalism in Southern Africa*. London: James Currey.

van der Vliet, Virginia, 1996, *The Politics of AIDS*, London, Bowderdean.

Van Dijk, Rik, 1992, 'Young Born-Again Preachers in Post-Independent Malawi: the significance of an extraneous identity', in Gifford, P., (ed), *New Dimensions in African Christianity*, Act Prent.

Van Dijk, Rik, 1998. 'Pentecostalism, cultural memory and the state: Contested representation of time in postcolonial Malawi.' In Richard Werbner (ed.), *Memory and the Postcolony: African Anthropology and the Critique of Power*. London: Zed Books. Pp. 155-181.

Van Dijk, Rik, and Pels, P., 1996, 'Contested authorities and the politics of perception: deconstructing the study of religion in Africa', in Werbner, R., and Ranger, T., (eds), *Postcolonial Identities in Africa*, London, Zed Books.

Vidal, Claudine. 1995. 'Les politiques de la haine: Rwanda, Burundi 1994-95.' *Les Temps Modernes* 50 (583): 6-33.

Vittachi, A., n.d. 'Joining the Dots for Children: Networking Rural Areas through Digital Opportunity Telecentres to Improve Early Childhood Care and Development.' www.dotforce.oneworld.net.

Volman, Daniel, 1998, 'The Militarization of Africa' in: Turshen, M.

and Twagiramayia, C., *What Women do in Wartime,* London/ New York, Zed Books.

Walker, A., 1997, 'Thoroughly Modern: sociological reflections on the charismatic movement from the end of the twentieth century', in Hunt S., Hamilton M., and Walter T., (eds), *Charismatic Christianity: sociological perspectives*, London, Macmillan.

Wallman, Sandra, 1996, *Kampala Women Getting By: Wellbeing in the Time of AIDS*, London, James Currey.

Ward, K., 1999, 'Africa', in Hastings, A., (ed), *A World History of Christianity*, London, Cassell.

Warnier, Jean-Pierre, 1985. *Echange, Développements et Hiérarchie Dans le Bamenda Pré-colonial (Cameroun). Studien Zur Kulturkunde* 76. Wiesbaden: Franz Steiner Verlag.

Warnier, Jean-Pierre, 1993. *L'Esprit de L'Entreprise au Cameroun.* Paris: Karthala.

Watkins, K., 2000, *The Oxfam Education Report.* Oxford, Oxfam UKI.

Webb, D., 1995. 'Orphans in Zambia: Nature and Extent of Demographic Change.' *AIDS Analysis Africa Southern Africa Edition* 6.2.

Werbner, Richard. 1997. 'The suffering body: passion and ritual allegory in Christian encounters.' *Journal of Southern African Studies* 23 (2): 311-324.

Whitman, Lois, 1998, 'The Torture of Children: assessing torture and devising methods to prevent it' in Geraldine Van Bueren eds., *Childhood Abused: protecting children against torture, cruel, inhuman and degrading treatment and punishment*, Ashgate, Dartmouth.

Wigram, S. 1994. *Elites, Vanguards and Vandals: The Political Role of Students in Senegal and Mali (1968-1993)*. MSc. thesis. London: School of Oriental and African Studies.

Winnipeg International Conference on War-Affected Children, Experts final report, 2000, *Caught in the Crossfire No More: A Framework for Commitment to War-Affected Children,* September.

Woll, Lisa, 1999, 'Reporting to the UN Committee on the Rights of the Child: A catalyst for domestic debate and policy change?' *Journal of Children's Rights,* 8.

Womersley, H., 1974, *Congo Miracle: Fifty Years of God's Working in Congo (Zaire)*, Victory Press.

World Bank, 1990, *World Development Report 1990*, Oxford University Press, Oxford.

World Bank, 1993, *World Development Report 1993*, Oxford University Press, Oxford.

World Bank, 1994, *Adjustment in Africa: Reforms, Results and the Road Ahead*, Oxford University Press, Oxford.

World Bank, 1995, *Taking Action for Poverty Reduction in Sub-Saharan Africa*, World Bank, Washington DC.

World Bank, 1999a, 'African Development Indicators', Washington DC.

World Bank, 1999b, *Confronting AIDS: Public Priorities in a Global Epidemic*, Washington DC.

World Bank, 2000a, *World Development Report 2000/2001: Attacking Poverty*, Oxford University Press, Oxford.

World Bank, 2000b, *Can Africa Claim the 21st Century*? collaborative report with ADB, AERC, GCA and ECA, Washington DC.

Young, C. and Kanté, B. 1992. 'Governance, democracy and the 1988 elections (Senegal).' In G. Hyden and M. Bratten (eds.) Governance and Politics in Africa. Boulder, Co: Lynne Rienner.

Yousif Kuwa, 2001, 'Things Were No Longer the Same,' in Suleiman Rahhal (ed.) *The Right to be Nuba: The Story of a Sudanese People's Struggle for Survival*, Trenton N.J., Red Sea Press.

A

B

C

D

D

E

F

G

N

O

P

R

R

W

Y

Z